SO-BJR-891

THE CONSCIOUSNESS
OF D. H. LAWRENCE

THE CONSCIOUSNESS
OF D. H. LAWRENCE

AN INTELLECTUAL BIOGRAPHY

DANIEL J. SCHNEIDER

UNIVERSITY PRESS OF KANSAS

Published by the University Press of Kansas
(Lawrence, Kansas 66045), which was organized
by the Kansas Board of Regents and is operated
and funded by Emporia State University, Fort
Hays State University, Kansas State University,
Pittsburg State University, the University of
Kansas, and Wichita State University

Library of Congress Cataloging in Publication Data

Schneider, Daniel J., 1927–
  The consciousness of D. H. Lawrence.
  Bibliography: p.
  Includes index.
  1. Lawrence, D. H. (David Herbert), 1885–1930—
Criticism and interpretation. I. Title.
PR 6023.A93Z8658 1986   823'.912   85-29415
ISBN 0-7006-0285-2

Printed in the United States of America

FOR JAMES,
GEOF, AND SANDY

CONTENTS

Preface   ix

Abbreviations Used in Citing Works by D. H. Lawrence   xiii

1 The Religious Sense of Life   1

2 The Oedipal Problem and the Young Bachelor   17

3 Lawrence's Early Beliefs and Novels (1901–12)   47

4 Love and Rebirth: *Sons and Lovers* and *The Rainbow*   69

5 Construction and Destruction: World War I
   and Rananim   88

6 The Going Apart: *Women in Love* and
   "The Reality of Peace"   109

7 The Search for Wholeness   129

8 Blood Consciousness   152

9 Phallic Consciousness   176

Selected Bibliography   195

Index   203

PREFACE

This book was written chiefly for general readers who, on this centennial of the birth of D. H. Lawrence, wish to deepen their understanding of the development of Lawrence's thought and feeling over the course of his lifetime. The events of Lawrence's life are well known to specialists; but insight into Lawrence's inner life of thought and emotion alters our grasp of these facts (for there *are* no facts, as Nietzsche observed, but only interpretations); and in several instances, because of the focus of this study, I have stressed influences on and emphases in Lawrence's thought that have necessarily received less attention in the broader biographies by Harry T. Moore, Richard Aldington, Emile Delavenay, and others.

The title of my book echoes Richard Ellmann's *The Consciousness of Joyce*; and the word *consciousness* here, as in Ellmann's fine study, denotes "the movement of the mind both in recognizing its own shape and in maintaining that shape in the face of attack or change." I have sought to lay bare Lawrence's incessant, all-absorbing, and passionate effort over a lifetime to develop a religious alternative to contemporary skepticism or outworn belief. For readers unfamiliar with the major biographies of Lawrence, I have included at the beginning of each chapter a chronology of some important events in Lawrence's life. In the text I assume a general familiarity with these events so that I may focus on the preoccupations of Lawrence's consciousness at various stages in his development. Chapter 1, for example, examines his early sense of life—his intuitive response to nature, his "resonance to the All" (which Pierre Teilhard de Chardin calls "the keynote of pure poetry and pure religion"), and his strong feminine or maternal sympathies, together with his unusual sense of responsibility. Chapter 2 stresses the conflict between his adolescent and postadolescent loves and his growing sense of a mission in life and his fear of not being able to carry out his mission. Chapter 3 traces the incubation of his beliefs—the chief influences on his thought from 1900 to 1912—and the early syntheses of his imagination. In Chapter 4, his marriage and his "coming through" are examined in relation to his newly clarified understanding of his "philosophy" and of his religious mission. Chapters 5 and 6 deal with the severe threats to his beliefs during World War I and with his struggle to remain positive as he lost the support of his friends and became increasingly isolated. Chapter 7 reviews his postwar efforts to define a positive alternative to the dead beliefs of a dying civilization and his continuing affirmation that "I am I." Chapters 8 and 9 trace his efforts during the last seven years of his life to define the nature and operation of consciousnesses that were fundamentally different from Western "ideal" or "mental" consciousness—the blood consciousness and the phallic consciousness, which he believed can bring men together again despite their living in an age of fragmentation and egoistic individualism. Events in Lawrence's life are subordinated to the tracing of these vital movements of his consciousness—the creative excitements, the surges of joy and confidence, the disillusionments and humiliations—all of these being reflected in his unremitting meditations on his "philosophy," that ever-expanding body of insights that has so often seemed inconsistent or illogical to critics who have not grasped his thought in its wholeness.

Biographical and critical studies of Lawrence, though usually recognizing his religious nature, frequently ignore that nature as a shaping force in his life. For example, his relationship with his mother is explained, *tout simplement,* as oedipal, without much thought about the unique roles that mother and father assume for the religious person. Lawrence's early loves and the whole ordeal of his "coming through" from a painful adolescence to an uneasy marriage are not referred to the deep fear that Erik H. Erikson has noted in the religious man—the fear that women, the mother included, constitute a threat to his inviolacy and to the accomplishment of his mission. Lawrence's quarrels with his friends are too seldom referred to the religious man's fear and distrust of those who would seduce him away from his life "in the infinite." Again, Lawrence's reading needs to be related to his religious quest—his effort to ground his religious philosophy on solid scientific information as well as on the critical revaluation of all values made necessary by the new ideas in anthropology, in comparative religion, and in psychology.

The failure to appreciate Lawrence's religious nature at all stages of his life has led to subtle but significant distortions not only of his psychology but also of the emphases of his work. Although Emile Delavenay's massively and expertly researched biography and critical study evinces a limited sympathy with Lawrence's religious nature, Delavenay concludes, "Flight, not revolt, is the keynote of [Lawrence's] work: flight into the anonymously divine creative instinct, into the song of eternal rebirth; flight from social responsibility; from painstaking construction of a world of stable relationships: flight into art . . . " (522). But "flight" may well be the religious man's effort to remain inviolate in

an impure world, and "flight from social responsibility" a refusal to
cooperate with an evil system which Lawrence saw as based on egoistic
rivalry, selfishness, and the profit motive. All Lawrence scholars must
be grateful to Delavenay for his immense labors; his achievement is
unparalleled; yet subsequent scholars, having a deeper sympathy with
Lawrence's purposes and with the means Lawrence took to achieve
those purposes, must inevitably reassess every influence on his life and
work. For instance, in Delavenay's account of the influences on Lawrence, there are some forty references to Houston Stewart Chamberlain
and some twenty to Otto Weininger; Delavenay refers only twice to
Herbert Spencer and only four times to William James; yet the latter
two's influences were at least as strong as Chamberlain's or
Weininger's.

In recreating Lawrence' consciousness, the biographer is given a
mighty assist by Lawrence himself: few writers have laid bare the
movements of their minds as precisely and as honestly as did Lawrence,
for whom it was an article of faith that one must not suppress one's
deepest thoughts and feelings. But inevitably there is much of his inner
life about which he does not speak, and a technique of inference is
needed to assess his response to experiences and reading that he does
not discuss. That technique is exhibited strikingly in Delavenay's *D. H.
Lawrence and Edward Carpenter.* There is no direct evidence that Lawrence
either read Carpenter or was influenced by him, but when one considers
not only the intellectual climate of Lawrence's maturation but also the
ideas that most spurred his enthusiasm in his youth—the rebellion
against Victorian morality, capitalism, and middle-class conformity; the
embrace of a new naturalism; the idea of regeneration through new love
relationships—the possibility of a Carpenter influence is suggested.
When one finds, moreover, that a cluster of ideas in Carpenter's books
is also found in Lawrence—the idea of the *égoisme à deux* of married
couples, of the interchange of vital elements in love, of woman as
providing the center and balance for the adventuring male, of a
sympathetic system of nerves as the seat of the emotions—possibility
becomes probability. To be sure, one can find many of the same ideas in
Bernard Shaw (whose *Man and Superman* Lawrence considerd to be
"very good"), but Delavenay's claim for Carpenter's influence seems to
be justified by the coalescence of internal evidence, even though no
direct evidence proves that Lawrence read Carpenter or spoke of
Carpenter's ideas.

Sometimes the biographer needs a sixth sense, but there is nothing
mysterious about the process of inference. A sixth sense is at bottom a
sense of probability, the intuition that such a man, with such a
temperament and such interests, at such a period of his life, and in such

an intellectual climate, would be likely to see and respond strongly to such-and-such elements in his experience. To appreciate Lawrence's response, biographers of the Inner Life must try to learn his habits of thought; his sense of importance; the principle of selection that operates characteristically in his experiences. And the biographer must cultivate his own "negative capability"—his ability to imagine life as Lawrence imagined it, to understand it and respond to it as Lawrence understood and responded to it.

In this centennial year of Lawrence's birth, a new biography of his consciousness may deepen understanding of his importance for a world that more than ever needs to counter the threat of its ideal will-to-power and its consequent deep *ressentiments*.

I am especially indebted to Lawrence's biographers and to the many critics who have studied his thought with care. Harry T. Moore's *The Priest of Love* is invaluable, as is Emile Delavenay's *D. H. Lawrence: The Man and His Work*. I have profited too from Richard Aldington's *Portrait of a Genius, But—*, Edward Nehls's *D. H. Lawrence: A Composite Biography*, Norman Page's *D. H. Lawrence: Interviews and Recollections*, and from the work of such scholars as Paul Delany, George A. Panichas, James C. Cowan, H. M. Daleski, Colin Clarke, F. R. Leavis, and many others—so many that I cannot hope to indicate my debt to all of them.

To James C. Cowan I am especially indebted for a wise, thorough, and invariably helpful reading of the manuscript; and to Richard Ellmann, my old mentor, I am once again indebted for support and for a splendid example.

The John C. Hodges Better English Fund, managed by the English Department of the University of Tennessee, provided travel money for me to do research at the Humanities Research Center of the University of Texas at Austin. I am grateful to the fund's administrators and to the Humanities Research Center for their kind assistance.

The Office of Graduate Studies and Research of the University of Tennessee provided a stipend that made it possible for me to devote an entire summer to the study of Lawrence.

The University of Tennessee's Lindsay Young Award enabled me to appreciate the significance of Lawrence's experience in the Southwest and to examine the Lawrence collection at the Zimmerman Library of the University of New Mexico. To Joseph Trahern, chairman of the English Department; Robert Landen, dean of the Humanities; and Ralph Norman, vice-chancellor of the University of Tennessee, I am indebted for thoughtfulness and kindness that much facilitated my work.

ABBREVIATIONS USED
IN CITING WORKS BY D. H. LAWRENCE

A   *Apocalypse.* Introduction by Richard Aldington. New York: Viking Press, Compass Books, 1966.

AR   *Aaron's Rod.* Harmondsworth, Eng.: Penguin Books Ltd., 1950.

BB   *The Boy in the Bush,* with Mollie L. Skinner. Harmondsworth, Eng.: Penguin Books Ltd., 1972.

CL   *The Collected Letters of D. H. Lawrence,* edited by Harry T. Moore. 2 vols. New York: Viking Press, 1962.

CP   *The Complete Poems of D. H. Lawrence,* edited by Vivan de Sola Pinto and Warren Roberts. 2 vols. New York: Viking Press, 1964.

CSS   *The Complete Short Stories.* 3 vols. Harmondsworth, Eng.: Penguin Books Ltd., 1980.

EP   *Etruscan Places.* In *"Mornings in Mexico" and "Etruscan Places."* London: William Heinemann Ltd., 1956.

FU   *Fantasia of the Unconscious.* In *"Fantasia of the Unconscious" and "Psychoanalysis and the Unconscious."* Harmondsworth, Eng.: Penguin Books Ltd., 1977.

Huxley   *The Letters of D. H. Lawrence,* edited by Aldous Huxley. New York: Viking Press, 1932.

K   *Kangaroo.* New York: Viking Compass, 1976.

L   *The Letters of D. H. Lawrence,* edited by James T. Boulton. 3 vols. Cambridge: Cambridge University Press, 1979, 1981, 1984.

LCL   *Lady Chatterley's Lover.* New York: Grove Press, Inc., 1957.

LG   *The Lost Girl.* Harmondsworth, Eng.: Penguin Books Ltd., 1950.

MEH   *Movements in European History.* Oxford: Oxford University Press, 1925.

MM   *Mornings in Mexico.* In *"Mornings in Mexico" and "Etruscan Places."* London: William Heinemann Ltd., 1956.

Plays   *The Complete Plays of D. H. Lawrence.* New York: Viking Press, 1966.

PS   *The Plumed Serpent.* New York: Vintage Books, Inc., 1951.

PU   *Psychoanalysis and the Unconscious.* In *"Fantasia of the Unconscious" and "Psychoanalysis and the Unconscious."* Harmondsworth, Eng.: Penguin Books Ltd., 1977.

R   *The Rainbow.* Harmondsworth, Eng.: Penguin Books Ltd., 1976.

SCAL   *Studies in Classic American Literature.* Harmondsworth, Eng.: Penguin Books Ltd., 1977.

SL   *Sons and Lovers.* Harmondsworth, Eng.: Penguin Books Ltd., 1979.

SM   *"St. Mawr" and "The Man Who Died."* New York: Random House, Vintage, 1959.

SS   *Sea and Sardinia.* In *D. H. Lawrence and Italy: "Twilight in Italy," "Sea and Sardinia," "Etruscan Places."* New York: Viking Press, 1972.

T   *The Trespasser.* London: William Heinemann Ltd., 1955.

TI   *Twilight in Italy.* In *D. H. Lawrence and Italy: "Twilight in Italy," "Sea and Sardinia," "Etruscan Places."* New York: Viking Press, 1972.

WL   *Women in Love.* New York: Random House, Modern Library, 1950.

WP   *The White Peacock.* London: William Heinemann Ltd., 1955.

THOUGHT

Thought, I love thought.
But not the jiggling and twisting of already existent ideas
I despise that self-important game.
Thought is the welling up of unknown life into consciousness,
Thought is the testing of statements on the touchstone of the con-
     science,
Thought is gazing on to the face of life, and reading what can be read,
Thought is pondering over experience, and coming to a conclusion.
Thought is not a trick, or an exercise, or a set of dodges,
Thought is a man in his wholeness wholly attending.

                                              —D. H. Lawrence

1

THE RELIGIOUS SENSE OF LIFE

1885: Born 11 September at Eastwood, Nottinghamshire; 1891–98: attends Beauvale Board School, Eastwood; early sense of wonder; influence of "the old England of the forest and agricultural past"; early manifestations of maternal sympathy; early associations, chiefly with girls; tendency to withdraw from male competition—the "only boy with paints"; influence of Congregational Chapel; 1893: friendship with George Neville begins; 1898: wins County Council Scholarship to Nottingham High School; 1898–1901: attends Nottingham High School; 1901: stricken with pneumonia; 1901: at Haggs Farm, with the Chambers family, he experiences "a new life" (a model for his Utopian Rananim?); friendship with Alan Chambers.

Flame is the image his friends often used to describe the man whose emblem was the phoenix. "The spirit of flame," said Lady Ottoline Morrel. "His swift and flamelike quality," said Catherine Carswell. "A flame burning on," said Aldous Huxley. That the flame was "genius" and that there was something almost preternatural about D. H. Lawrence's aliveness, sensitivity, awareness, and responsiveness—these conclusions have become commonplaces. But how explain the "genius" of D. H. Lawrence? Explanations collapse before the mystery of heredity—his inheritance from his parents not only of extraordinary intelligence and imagination but also of a stubborn vitality that spurned lethargic compromise with an irreverent world. Whatever his temperamental heritage, however, a unique concatenation of circumstances shaped his nature and, to a degree, accounts for his conduct.

Perhaps the most important of these circumstances was that Lawrence's extremely delicate health, as a small child, precluded all possibility of his entering into rough-and-tumble boyish rivalry. Five years younger than his brother Ernest, seven years younger than George, his oldest brother, Lawrence was not thrust into an intense rivalry with his male siblings. Pale, thin, the youngest boy, he was, in a sense, in a privileged position: "We all petted and spoiled him from the time he was born," said George; "my mother poured her very soul into him" (Nehls, 1:17). Nor was the father insensitive to the boy's frailty: as Lawrence noted in his autobiographical *Sons and Lovers*, the father was "always very gentle if anyone were ill" and "particularly lavish of endearments" to his thin, pale child.

The child responded warmly to this outpouring of warmth. Norman Douglas said that Lawrence had a "naturally blithe disposition" (Nehls, 2:14), and many, like May Chambers or Catherine Carswell, found him "merry" or "gay" (Nehls, 3:555; Carswell, xxiii). Treated with sympathy and tenderness, he responded "in full measure," as his friend William E. Hopkin observed (Nehls, 1:23). It would also be true to say that he responded in kind. Early in life he showed a sensitivity to the feelings of others, a tenderness and feminine responsiveness and sympathy, that set him apart from other boys. It was a sympathy that extended beyond his immediate family and, indeed, beyond the human world—a sympathy manifested not only in his artist's ability to feel the being of other forms of life but also in his highly developed maternal impulse to take responsibility for others, particularly for the weak or the burdened or handicapped.

His uncanny attention and responsiveness to nature has been stressed by almost all who knew him. His sister Ada's comment is typical: "Not a flower, tree or bird escaped Bert's notice, and he found wonderful adventure in seeing the first celandine or early violet" (Nehls, 1:14). His older sister, Emily, added: "He was so quick, he could notice things that you would just walk past and never see. He always noticed it" (Nehls, 1:14). William Hopkin noted that "even as a youth he seemed to see things differently from other folk, and his descriptions were often unusual but illuminating" (Nehls, 1:24). Later in Lawrence's life, Aldous Huxley and Lady Cynthia Asquith called attention to the same remarkable awareness and responsiveness. Lady Cynthia Asquith said:

> I don't believe anyone could have been in Lawrence's presence for two minutes without being struck by his difference from other people. It was not a difference of degree; it was a difference of kind. Some electric, elemental quality gave him a flickering radiance. Apart from this strange otherness, one could see at once that he was preternaturally alive. . . .
>
> You couldn't possibly be out of doors with Lawrence without becoming aware of the astonishing acuteness of his senses, and realising that he belonged to an intenser existence. Yet to some degree—and this was your great debt to him—he enabled you temporarily to share that intensified existence; for his faculty for communicating to others something of his own perceptiveness made a walk with him a wonderfully enhanced experience. In fact it made me feel that hitherto I had to all intents and purposes walked the earth with my eyes blindfolded and my ears plugged.

> So receptive, so alert was he to every outdoor sight and sound, that I had the impression that he must know what it was like to be a bird or a wild animal—could feel himself inside the skin of anything living. (Nehls, 1:207–8)

Aldoux Huxley's comment is similar:

> To be with Lawrence was a kind of adventure, a voyage of discovery into newness and otherness. . . . He looked at things with the eyes, so it seemed, of a man who had been at the brink of death and to whom, as he emerges from the darkness, the world reveals itself as unfathomably beautiful and mysterious. . . . He seemed to know, by personal experience, what it was like to be a tree or a daisy or a breaking wave or even the mysterious moon itself. He could get inside the skin of an animal and tell you in the most convincing detail how it felt and how, dimly, inhumanly, it thought. (Nehls, 3:172–73)

This astonishing ability to respond to, and to feel, the inner life of other living things, which is reflected in his extraordinary gift for mimicry, is what Keats had in mind when he spoke of the poet's "negative capability"—a capacity (which is opposite to self-assertion or "positive" capability) to enter empathically into other human beings or other forms of being, indeed to *become* those other forms. Keats does not explain this gift any more than calling it "empathy" explains it. It seems to be connected with a sense of the sheer miracle of being—the sense of wonder that Lawrence defined as "the religious element inherent in all life." All things are precious because they are manifestations of a divine energy, a sacred mystery. Nothing exists that does not manifest this immanent power and glory. All derives from the great source; all is accordingly deserving of respect or reverence. Nothing is intrinsically despicable or ignoble, and one's own life is not intrinsically superior to the life of other forms of being. Keats defined the poet as "that man who with another man is equal"; perhaps he could have added that the poet is that man who with all other forms of being is equal—equal in sharing the divine spark. Was it that sense of the oneness and affinity of all things that Lawrence had in mind when he referred to himself as a "mystical" child with a "fervent private religion"? One cannot be sure. His early reverence for life is certainly suggested by a report by May Chambers, who asked him if he had seen the violets in the woods near the farm; Lawrence replied, "'Am I blind? Why, we were ever so careful not to tread on any'" (Nehls, 3:562). Something similar is suggested in the anecdote told by Mabel Thurlby Collishaw, who played with Lawrence as a child: "Bertie talked to the flowers, and I told him, 'You *are* potty.' He would look at me, and then I'd say quickly, 'No, you are *not* potty,' because I thought he would cry" (Nehls, 1:29). The anecdote calls attention not only to Lawrence's sense of a connection with other forms of life but also to his extreme sensitivity to the sort of jeering criticism that he was subjected to by other children in the rough mining village. His heightened sensitivity to the feelings of others was in part an imaginative identification with those who suffered *as he did* from persecution.

Branded as babyish and effeminate—"mardy"—by other boys, Lawrence suffered acutely from their contempt. He was "easily hurt," Mabel Thurlby Collishaw recalled (Nehls, 1:31), and according to William Hopkin, "Never in his life could he bear anything like severe criticism" (Nehls, 1:23). The pain he suffered from the jeering of the other boys caused him to withdraw. According to a schoolmate, J. E. Hobbs, Lawrence "never played with boys, never joined in their games, and at playtime always shunned other boys, standing leaning against the playground wall" (Nehls, 1:33). According to Albert Limb, who, like so many of Lawrence's classmates, left school at twelve to go into the pit, Lawrence was "the most effeminate boy I ever knew" and "the most cowardly boy I ever knew. Any little boy could go and punch him, and he would not retaliate" (Nehls, 1:32). It is hardly surprising that later in life Lawrence would single out the bullying democratic mob as a chief object of his hatred. He grew up subjected to gratuitous cruelty; and in his own home he witnessed what he called the "horror" of his father's cruelty to his mother. So acutely did he feel the brutality and injustice of such persecutions that all of his native sympathy was intensified for those subjected to similar suffering.

His strong feminine or maternal impulses were manifested early in life. Most striking, to be sure, is his concern for his mother's suffering. It is difficult to say how early in life he became aware of her situation. His very early consciousness of the parental conflict is perhaps suggested in Ada's recollection that he "became morbid frequently" and "sometimes . . . would burst into tears and irritate mother, who would say 'Bless the child—whatever is he crying for now?' Bert invariably sobbed, 'I don't know,' and continued to cry" (Nehls, 1:17). Lawrence himself said that he always hated his father and that he shivered whenever his father touched him. Very early, he was so keenly aware of his mother's bitterness and of the disappointment and suffering in her life that he could not help turning against the father, who, she made clear, was the cause of her misery. And Lawrence began early in life to help her with her work, "sharing her burden in order to lighten it," as he says in *Sons and Lovers*. He did this without complaint—indeed, with a positive zest in his effort to cheer her up and to restore happiness to the tormented household.

But his sensitivity to the sufferings of others extended far beyond his relationship to his mother—far beyond the oedipal conflict. A child's love for small animals is not unusual, but there is a suggestion of Lawrence's empathy in the story that Ada tells about the black-and-white terrier that, brought from Nottingham to be raised for one of their uncles, was forced to stay downstairs while the family went upstairs to sleep:

> No sooner was the rascal left alone than he set up piteous howls, and we shed tears in sympathy. At last Bert could stand it no longer, and whispering, "I'm going to fetch him up here," he crept downstairs and quietly brought the wretched little fellow to bed, where he cuddled close to him and slept soundly until morning, when he hurried down and put him back on the sofa before mother was up. (Nehls, 1:15)

More revealing is Lawrence's depiction, in *Sons and Lovers*, of the incident in which Paul Morel damages his sister's doll and makes his sister weep. "Helpless with misery," the boy must atone for his thoughtlessness: he does it by making "an altar of bricks" and by setting the doll afire as a "sacrifice": "He seemed to hate the doll intensely because he had broken it" (*SL*, 58). Equally revealing is Mabel Thurlby Collishaw's memory of the occasion when, aged eleven, she was forced by her father to bake bread and was not sure of how to do it. As she knelt down to knead the bread, her tears falling, Lawrence appeared to ask her father to help Lawrence's father, who had encountered a roof fall in the pit. Having delivered his message,

> Bertie knelt down on the other side of panchion and said, "Don't cry! Your tears are *salty*!"
> I could not dry my tears because my hands were covered with dough. So he took a red handkerchief from his pocket to wipe my face.
> I looked up to say thank you, and saw that he was crying too. Our tears mingled in that two stone of bread. (Nehls, 1:31)

George Neville, Lawrence's very close friend from 1901 to 1912, said in his *Memoir* that "the slightest hint of pain or cruelty to the very meanest of creatures upon earth was suffering" to Lawrence (*A Memoir*, 115). While that testimony sounds exaggerated, the quick response that Lawrence showed to Mabel Thurlby Collishaw was duplicated in Lawrence's assistance to Jessie Chamber's little brother, J. D. Chambers, when Lawrence was eighteen:

> I remember him helping me with this [fetching coal inside] one day when I stood petrified in the pouring rain and the hurly-burly of a summer thunderstorm. He darted out to help me, picked up the coal and hurried me in along with it while my brothers watched shamefaced at the window where they had sat jeering at me as brothers do. Such incalculable acts of kindness endeared him to us. (Nehls, 1:49)

Yet the acts were not "incalculable" if one grasps the strength of the sympathetic impulse that impelled Lawrence to mother others. His concern for his own mother was matched by a similar concern for Mrs. Chambers, Jessie's mother. As Jessie said,

> He was most considerate towards mother, with her big, unruly family, so hard to manage. . . . Several times when he came in and found her with more to do than she could get through he fetched water for the boiler, tidied up the hearth, and made a fire in the parlour. . . . And I well remember a basket of tiny pickling onions that stood on the stone slab outside the back door for weeks, waiting to be peeled. They suddenly disappeared, and mother said that Bert had peeled them; he just sat down and did them without saying a word to anyone. (Nehls, 1:40)

Again, May Chambers reports a number of incidents in which Lawrence automatically assumed a maternal responsibility for others. On one occasion he was walking with "a troop of girls—his sister and cousin and two others." May Chambers invited Lawrence and his sister to visit May's family the next afternoon, and Lawrence hesitated. "'And can we bring these, too?' begged Bert, indicating his companions. 'They've never been, you know. We couldn't leave them. They would so like to come'" (Nehls, 3:580). On another occasion, Lawrence and May were talking about fairy tales, and May said that the sense of all that has been "means much more than fairy tales" (Nehls, 3:586). "'To you it does, but what about these?' Bert asked, indicating the mean street and playing children. 'Fairy tales may teach them to look for what's behind. Anyway they need the fun of fairy tales. You do,' he sighed, 'when you live among bricks and mortar. I know'" (Nehls, 3:586). Yet again, May recounts:

> Bert's sympathy with people's misfortunes was quick and active. When an aunt was struck with cancer, he brought a party of girls up to our fields to pick violet leaves which were considered very soothing. He pressed us into service.
> "We shall need pounds and pounds, you know. You will help, won't you? You could pick some every time you go out, and I could take them home on Saturdays."
> It was the same when an orphan cousin was opening a business in our town. He solicited custom[ers] for her among all acquaintances.
> "You will have a blouse made just to give her a start, won't you? You see, she's in expenses, heavy expenses, too. Having no home, she has to pay rent and lodgings and everything." (Nehls, 3:597–98)

Lawrence also, after getting home from college, "went to read to a girl ill with consumption," even though his day, May observed, "was a long one" (Nehls, 3:606).

What is striking in this is that Lawrence spontaneously took on himself the responsibility of lightening the burden of others. The same concern was exhibited when he saw how unhappy Jessie Chambers was because she was "the family drudge." Again, Lawrence, as Paul Morel in *Sons and Lovers*, tried to help Fanny, the "long-legged hunchback" who appears in *Sons and Lovers* at the factory where Paul is a clerk. Paul "was made the recipient of all her woes, and he had to plead her cause with Polly."

Yet again, Lawrence's strong maternal inclinations were manifested in his love of his "boys" when he became a teacher and in his mothering of his landlady's baby in Croydon. Forced into the paternal role of disciplinarian, Lawrence hated the school system based on power and bullying—as he made vividly clear in *The Rainbow*. "I should love to laugh with my boys," he wrote in November of 1908,

> to play with them, and be a bit naturally riotous with them. They recognise this; when I am giving them a history lesson they are enforcing it by pretending to shoot arrows at me, drawing back the bow with vigour, and looking at me with bright brown eyes. I rebuke them sternly, but my heart is laughing. Oh my discipline!—My old boys liked me nearly as much as I loved them. (*L*, 1:89)

His "love" for Hilda Mary Jones, his landlady's baby, was equally strong. In his poem "Ten Months Old," written on 20 January 1909, Lawrence calls the weeping child "my wee squirrel" and "my white bird" and "my own baby." The child's tears, her "hot red cheek," cause "a smart, / Stinging down to my heart" (*L*, 1:108–9). Having cared for Ada when she was a baby, Lawrence found it easy to mother Hilda Mary—and to give the Joneses some freedom from their burdens. And he obviously enjoyed caring for others. Later in life he would nurse not only his mother but also Middleton Murry and Witter Bynner; he would care for Monica Meynell when the girl suffered a nervous breakdown and "[took] refuge in me" (*L*, 2:345). Someone, he said, had to do it. Again, H. D. (Hilda Doolittle), in her autobiographical novel *Bid Me to Live*, indicates that after she had given birth to a stillborn child, Lawrence "was the only one who seemed remotely to understand what I felt" (*Bid Me to Live*, 65).

Contemplating all those instances of Lawrence's maternal impulse, one is struck inevitably by two important conclusions. The first, as I have indicated, is that Lawrence's assumption of responsibility for others was spontaneous: it is as if he took for granted that he was appointed to this maternal, protective role. The second is that he assumed early in life "a peculiar authority," as J. D. Chambers called it. He appeared to be prematurely "old," one of those rare individuals who, as Erik Erikson observes of Gandhi, "painfully early, reverse positions" with their parents and become "the giving and judging and, in fact, the *parental agens*" (101). It is this precocious maturity and mature acceptance of responsibility that J. D. Chambers had in mind, I suspect, when he observed:

> He was Bert, as much one of the household as any of us, and vested with a peculiar authority. What he said went with our rather unruly and outspoken family. I remember it was his especial duty to see that the rare delicacies, such as a tin of fruit or salmon, were fairly distributed at Sunday tea-time. . . . And needless to say, his opinions were vested with similar authority. (Nehls, 1:49)

When May Chambers complained that Lawrence was "always grumbling at us and finding fault," Lawrence replied: " 'No, I'm not. I'm setting you right. That shows I like you. You don't think I should take the trouble to bother with you if I didn't like you, do you? I'm going to teach you to dance now' "! (Nehls, 3:572). Later in life he would often show a similar zeal, as when he lectured Bertrand Russell on his faults or, appalled by Duncan Grant's paintings, found it necessary, as David Garnett remarked, "to open Duncan's eyes and tell him the truth" (Page, 1:111). Lawrence was born to "set people right," and even as a boy—considered "an exceedingly 'nice' little lad"—he was treated, said George Neville, "as being a little 'superior', which . . . he most certainly was" (*A Memoir*, 48).

What the Chambers children and others sensed in young Lawrence might be interpreted as the uniqueness of an "artistic," bookish, and possibly neurotic adolescent; but as I hope to establish, they were also aware of the sort of authority that Erik Erikson has observed in *homo religiosus*—in a man who "is early and painfully conscious of a special mission, a direction which must lead to all or to nothing" (100). Such a man, according to Erikson, maintains throughout childhood and adolescence "a certain inviolacy of spirit" (100). The overweening emotional necessity of such a man is to "remain unblemished," and all threats to his "higher loyalties" must be fought off and overcome. The peculiar authority of such a man arises from a consciousness of a reality and truthfulness unknown to the irreligious. As Erikson writes:

> An overweening conscience can find peace only by always believing that the budding "I" harbors a truthfulness superior to that of all authorities because this truth is the convenant of the "I" with God, the "I" being even more central and more pervasive than all parent images and moralities. This I would consider to be the core of a *homo religiosus*. (117–18)

In these comments, I anticipate much that will be revealed later. For the present, it is perhaps enough to point out that Lawrence, deeply influenced by his intolerant, puritanical, and aspiring mother, had early in life a sense of his own dignity and authority, "his inviolacy of spirit," as one who has a special obligation in life.

The shaping influence of his mother was obviously paramount. According to Ada, Mrs. Lawrence was "deeply religious and a stickler for truth, having great contempt for anything petty, vain or frivolous" (Nehls, 1:9). She was also fiercely proud and, as a daughter of middle-class parents, felt herself to be superior to the working-class people among whom she found herself after her marriage. Later in life, Lawrence condemned her as a "superior soul" and repudiated altogether her middle-class ambitions; indeed, as I shall point out, there is evidence that he was, very early, critical of his undeviatingly middle-class mother. Yet he did feel that she was "superior" in her intelligence and in her refusal to bear fools gladly. It was from her that he acquired the intellectual confidence to challenge received ideas, including the idea that one should turn the other cheek—a doctrine that Ursula in *The Rainbow* finds unsupportable. Lawrence, although he showed an almost medical detachment and sympathy in his analysis of psychic wounds, was deeply influenced by his mother's intolerance of all forms of weakness, wickedness, or stupidity. Mrs. Lawrence, said George Neville, "had that strain of stubbornness which she transmitted, in a marked degree, to each of her sons, and to David Herbert in particular, and her little toss of the head and irritating 'sniff' that I remember so well, were answers to all objections" (Nehls, 1:26).

He also acquired her tough-minded realism—the sort of stern objectivity that she exhibits as Mrs. Morel in *Sons and Lovers*. "She could turn that sharp little tongue of hers to cynicism," said George Neville, recalling an occasion when, "at the time of Arthur Lawrence's second accident," he, Neville, tried to "introduce a ray of cheery light by quoting the line, 'Man never is but always to be blest.'" Mrs. Lawrence sharply asked him what he thought that line *meant*, and after he had fatuously stammered some words about clouds and silver linings, she corrected him:

> "It means that you are being deceived just like so many, many thousands more besides. It is the delusive promise that keeps people going, because they deceive themselves . . . it really expresses one of the greatest truths of life: Man never is blessed but he always buoys himself up with the false hope that he's going to be. And he generally finds it out too late. . . ." (*A Memoir*, 98)

If Lawrence was temperamentally inclined to be optimistic or romantic, his mother's hard-boiled realism checked him. And like his mother, he did not seek to cover up unpleasant realities. When May Chambers told him that it was "awful" to work at a concern that made surgical bandages, he said "with a grimace: 'Their brass is as good as the next one's, and we've got to have money—so I've got to put up with it' " (Nehls, 3:573). He also showed a rare objectivity and candor when he defended himself against May's accusation that "you're with girls so much, it's silly." " 'It isn't silly,' " Lawrence replied. " 'I like girls. I like boys as well. Why can't you be with both? I think it's silly to stay just with boys all the time, especially when you can't play rough games like football' " (Nehls, 3:565–66).

Lawrence's father was, of course, a different influence altogether. A warm-hearted man, he did not judge his wife, although she spent much of her married life judging *him*. After her death, when asked why he did not marry again, the coal miner said, " 'I've had one good woman—the finest woman in the world, and I don't want another' " (Nehls, 1:11). Though there may be some ambiguity in the statement "I don't want another," the fact remains that generosity seems to have been marked in the Lawrence family: it is seen in the grandfather, whom Ada described as a generous-hearted man, and also in the father's sister, Aunt Emma, "whose generosity was as unstinted as her sister's [Aunt Sally] was confined." That same generosity would be marked also in David Herbert.

Yet Lawrence's father, like his mother, was stubborn and independent. He refused to kowtow to his superiors in the mine, even though his defiance resulted in his being assigned the poorest "stalls." His trouble, according to George Neville, was that "if he thought he would like to say a certain thing, he would say it, entirely regardless of the place he was in, or the members of the company present" (*A Memoir*, 52). His tirades were matched by those of the son who would tell his American *padrona*, Mabel Dodge Luhan: "As for reviling you, when I am angry, I say what I feel. I hope you do the same" (*CL* 2:756, 17 Oct. 1923). Lawrence, in his rages, was, according to George Neville, "most truly his father's son" (*A Memoir*, 52). Neville's vivid illustration of Lawrence's angry response "to even the slightest suggestion of injustice or exploitation" is an account of Lawrence's prolonged denunciation of the railway that charged nearly double the usual fare during Regatta Week at Cowes: "He turned in a fury on the poor booking-clerk, 'Ar'n't you ashamed of yourself? You certainly ought to be. . . .' But Lawrence's expressions of anger and disgust then were as nothing compared with the anathema he called down upon the heads of the management" (106). The father's defiance became the model for the noble defiance of the gamekeeper in *Lady Chatterley's Lover*, in which, by the alchemy of anagrams, the coal miner Morel became the gamekeeper Mellors.

The uncompromising independence of his parents helps to explain the ferocity of Lawrence's own righteous indignation—and his intense anger whenever he was criticized. His mother's pride, in particular, explains his intense hatred of any circumstances that threatened his dignity and his independence. As Ada remarked, "It was the terrible indignity of such poverty that embittered my brother so much" (Nehls, 1:17). He seems to have felt that any interference with his free development was a potentially catastrophic violation of his soul. He would argue later in life, in *Fantasia of the Unconscious*, that the great crime of parents and of society is to interfere with a child's free development— the effort to bully the child into submission to the false ideals of the middle class. Even as a child, he was acutely conscious of the threat of coercion—the threat to his soul's development.

There was school, for example. Like many artists and men of genius, Lawrence was made miserable by the narrowness and coercion of the school system. "I shall never forget," he wrote, "the anguish with which I wept, the first day. I was captured. I was roped in. The other boys felt the same. They hated schools because they felt captives there. They hated the masters because they felt them as jailers" (Nehls, 1:28). His happiest moments were those when he could tramp about the countryside and feel in touch with the real world. Confinement of any sort stirred his hatred. His sister Emily observed: "He hated housing— houses in rows, all clustered up together. . . . He didn't like a lot of people all around about him, you know" (Nehls, 1:14). Emily's comment may refer to an older Lawrence—the Lawrence who raged against the miners' being unnecessarily condemned to ugliness and to the "barracks like enclosure" that "shut in" the children—but his lifelong dislike of people "all around about him" is vividly dramatized in *Sons and Lovers*, where Paul Morel, forced to collect his father's wages at the mine office, protests to his mother that the miners stand so close "I can't breathe"—and then vows that he will never again go to fetch the wages. The accuracy of this scene is confirmed by Mabel Thurlby Collishaw, who recalled:

> The most unhappy day of Bertie Lawrence's week was Friday when . . . he had to go to the offices on Nether Green to draw his father's wages. . . . I always got a beating when I reached home, because my pinafore was so dirty from pushing Bertie between the miners to reach the counter when his father's name was called. Mother would say, "You have been with Mardy Lawrence again, *I* can see." (Nehls, 1:29)

His happiest days, as he grew older, were those spent at Haggs Farm with the Chambers family. The openness of the country and the warmth of the Chamberses became the unstated model of the joyous life that Lawrence later envisioned in his utopian Rananim. "Whatever I forget," he wrote to David Chambers in 1928, "I shall never forget the

Haggs—I loved it so. I loved to come to you all, it really was a new life began in me there. . . . *Son' tempi passati, cari miei! quanto cari, non saprete mai!* [Those times are gone, my dear ones! how dear, you will never know!]—I could never tell you in English how much it all meant to me, how I still feel about it" (*CL*, 2:1100).

In his pride and independence, he was acutely sensitive to any circumstances that seemed demeaning. "He was easily hurt," as Mabel Thurlby Collishaw said, and in this connection she recalled Boxing Day, when the miners' children were invited to Lamb Close House, the home of the colliery owner, "and were given one new penny and one large orange each." Lawrence's shyness and, I suspect, his pride prevented him from going forward like the others for the handout:

> On one occasion Bertie dared not go forward, so I took my presents, gave them to him, and then went back for his. The butler looked at me very hard, and I was afraid he would not give me another penny and orange. My words tumbled out:
> "Please, I am not taking two pennies for myself. One was for Bertie Lawrence."
> As we walked home and crossed the brook by the alder trees, we polished our new coins on our sleeves, and changed our minds so often as to how we would spend them. Bertie decided he would give his to his mother, and with mine we would buy sweets and divide them. (Nehls, 1:31)

His dignity, his inviolacy, must be maintained at all costs. The jeering bullies who taunted him for being "mardy" (effeminate), the coarse miners who were amused by his shyness, the girl who told him he was "potty" to talk to flowers, the schoolmasters who forced him into submission—all combined to demean him. His solution, as I said earlier, was to remove himself from contact with them. As Lawrence grew older, William E. Hopkin observed, he "developed a habit I disliked. If any person he took a dislike to was in the room he would not speak but sat silent and sullen. When the person had gone he asked angrily what the devil we had asked him for" (Nehls, 1:24). George Neville said that Lawrence "would do anything to avoid" certain people whom he detested (*A Memoir*, 64). Thus one of the major patterns of his life was formed: escape or insulation from all those who would force him to endure conversation that he considered idle, frivolous, cynical, or irreverent. Like his mother, he could not bear fools gladly, and he felt that life was defiled by people who were not fundamentally serious. His most violent rages were directed against bourgeois bullies—against all who prevented the spontaneous expression of true feeling or the free development of the spirit. "And as I hate lying," he wrote in 1927, "I keep to myself as much as possible" (*CL*, 2:967).

It would be easy to conclude from this that Lawrence was, at bottom, an escapist; and this indeed is the conclusion reached by Emile Delavenay. But if Lawrence "escaped," he did his utmost to tie his dreams to life. What he sought always to protect and defend was his own inviolacy of spirit. In a sense, he sought to preserve his own unworldliness, the purity of his vision. As he said in 1927, "One has to preserve one's *central* innocence, and not get [em?]bittered" (*CL*, 2:967). It was perhaps this impulse in him that led Henry James Forman to conclude that Lawrence had "the soul of a child," Dollie Radford to describe him as "touchingly childlike," and Catherine Carswell to take note of his comic and lovable "boyishness" (Nehls, 2:109, 1:292, 2:296). It was his "sensitive innocence," Carswell says, that captivated his staunch friend S. S. Koteliansky, as it was sensitive innocence that enabled him to respond so freshly and accurately to nature.

In his youth, at any rate, he was largely removed from the rough and tumble of competition with other boys and was insulated from much of their cynicism. Encouraged to read and paint ("the only child with paints," as Mabel Thurlby Collishaw said [Nehls, 1:29]), he lived far more than other children did in his imagination. Thus he seemed to others "quite often up in the clouds," as William E. Hopkin observed (Nehls, 1:23); and Emile Delavenay speaks of his "deep need for evasion and for make-believe" (*D. H. Lawrence: The Man and His Work*, 40). In his inner world, Lawrence could always find solace and joy. In one of his last poems he said: "I know no greater delight than the sheer delight of being alone" (*CP*, 610). And he had only contempt for " 'people that have got nothing inside them, that must depend on outside amusement the whole of the time!' " (Nehls, 1:21). It was not amusement or gaiety that offended him, but rather, as Emily said, "artificial amusement; he used to like homemade amusements, you know" (Nehls, 1:20). Where there was creativity and spontaneity, he could let himself go. He loved songs, charades, walks, dancing. And it was because he gave himself so entirely, with such unstinted enthusiasm, to such activities that he became, almost invariably, the leader, the organizer. "Whatever games were played he must be the leader," said William Hopkin (Nehls, 1:23). As the leader, as the "creator" of the game, he also seems to have regarded winning as his due. "If his side failed to win he was very cross," Hopkin added. It must have upset Lawrence to see others triumphing in a game that *he* had organized. Authority is not to be challenged, and Unerring Nature had conferred on him all the rights and perquisites of the creative authority! Later in his life, Lawrence did not hesitate to state the fact:

> I feel I'm the superior of most men I meet. Not in birth, because I never had a great-grandfather. Not in money, because I've got none.

Not in education, because I'm merely scrappy. And certainly not in beauty or in manly strength.

Well, what then?

Just in myself.

When I'm challenged, I do feel myself superior to most of the men I meet. Just a natural superiority. (*SCAL*, 44)

Lawrence is often less than endearing; but his unabashed statement here simply acknowledges the "peculiar authority" that others felt in his presence.

Because his freedom to develop his inner life was so important to him, it is not surprising that, like many Victorian boys—Bernard Shaw is a notable example—he chafed under "that stiff, null 'propriety' which used to come over us, like a sort of deliberate and self-inflicted cramp, on Sundays" (*TI*, 146). Yet Lawrence, although he disliked the cramp of propriety as well as all didacticism and sentimentality in religion, responded ardently to the *poetry* of the religion that he was exposed to in the Congregational Church. In his lovely little essay "Hymns in a Man's Life," he stated:

With regard to the hymns which had such a profound influence on my childish consciousness, there has been no crystallizing out, no dwindling into actuality, no hardening into the commonplace. They are the same to my man's experience as they were to me nearly forty years ago. (*Phoenix II*, 597)

What he felt when he sang these hymns, he goes on to say, is the sense of wonder, "which we may call the religious element inherent in all life, even in a flea" (*Phoenix II*, 598–99). And he calls wonder "the most precious element in life" because the deepest emotions—love and power—are based on wonder. A word such as "Galilee" carried him to "one of those lovely, glamorous worlds, not places, that exist in the golden haze of a child's half-formed imagination" (597). Again, he loved "Canaan's pleasant land" (599). And in another essay, he speaks of his boyhood wish that Eastwood would be "a golden city, as in the hymns we sang in the Congregational Chapel" (*Phoenix*, 829).

The vision of beauty, purity, and perfection seized his imagination; he also responded to the beauty of the chapel: "I liked our chapel, which was tall and full of light, and yet still; and colour-washed pale green and blue, with a bit of lotus pattern. And over the organ-loft, 'O worship the Lord in the beauty of holiness,' in big letters." The phrase "the beauty of holiness" was "magic." And the "sense of splendor" was produced by a favorite hymn that repeated the phrase:

O worship the Lord, in the beauty of holiness
Bow down before him, His glory proclaim;

> With gold of obedience and incense of lowliness
> Kneel and adore Him, the Lord is His name.

Equally stirring were the "healthy Hymns" that called for battle against the foe: "Fight the good fight with all thy might" and that "battle-cry of a stout soul,"

> Stand up, stand up for Jesus,
> Ye soldiers of the Lord. (*Phoenix II*, 600–601)

It is not surprising that he was also fond of Browning's stirring and confident "Rabbi Ben Ezra," which he read over and over to Jessie Chambers.

It was not just the poetry of the church that affected him deeply. George A. Panichas, in his *Adventure in Consciousness: The Meaning of D. H. Lawrence's Religious Quest,* has underscored the importance of Lawrence's nonconformist upbringing to our understanding of his life and thought. As a Congregationalist, Lawrence was, as he observed, a descendant of "the Oliver Cromwell Independents"—the natural heir of that "intense sense of responsibility for one's conscience" which Professor Richard Hoggart has identified as the chief characteristic of the Puritan. Moreover, both Lawrence's own intuitions and his religious upbringing led him to accept easily the Puritan belief that (as Edward Dowden puts it) "the relation between the invisible spirit of man and the invisible God was immediate rather than mediate" (Panichas, 49, 50). And Lawrence was to exhibit all the essential characteristics of the Puritan preacher who, according to William Haller,

> proffered to a multitude in his own age what seemed enlightenment and a new freedom. He proffered the means to a more active and significant life, a means of overcoming fears, a counsel of courage, a vision of adventure for courage to undertake, a program of self-discipline for making adventure a success, a prospect of success certain to be attained sooner or later. (Panichas, 50)

In his prolonged "soul fight" against "the ghastly kisses and the poison-bites of the myriad evil ones," Lawrence showed the active temper of the Puritan rather than the contemplative spirit of the mystic. Jessie Chambers observed: "In all his reading he seemed to be groping for something that he could lay hold of as a guiding principle in his own life. There was never the least touch of the academic or the scholastic in his approach. What he read was to be applied here and now" (Chambers, 112–13). Repeatedly in his life he would stress the importance of making an active fight against evil: "What's the good being hopeless, so long as one has a hob-nailed boot to kick with? *Down with the Poor in Spirit!*" (CL, 801).

Despite his Puritan zeal, he did not ever lose his childhood sense of wonder—the religious element inherent in all life. It is closely related, as I suggested earlier, to his response to nature—his delight in the miracle of being, his sympathy with all manifestations of life. That sense of wonder, "the most precious element in life," was to become the foundation of all his later reverence and his later beliefs. In *Mornings in Mexico* the great positive "commandment" that Lawrence discovered in the ancient religion of the American Indian is *"Thou shalt acknowledge the wonder."* Although he knew that he could not "cluster round the drum," Lawrence by 1923 believed that the Indians' animistic religion is "the only live one" (Huxley, 618) and that the Indian, by seeking to "get his life into direct contact with the elemental life of the cosmos . . . *without an intermediary or mediator"* had developed a religion "greater and deeper than any god-religion" (*Phoenix*, 146–47).

Although he did not know it, the foundations of his own animistic religion had been laid in his spontaneous sense of life. And his mission, although he did not recognize it, had been defined. He must celebrate life at all costs; must fight against all enemies of life, all who in their egotism refuse to acknowledge the wonder. In one of his last poems he said: "There is no such thing as sin. / There is only life and anti-life" (*CP*, 679). As these conclusions took shape in his mind, there was the necessity, through all the bitter conflicts of his adolescence and early manhood, to preserve his soul's inviolacy against anything that threatened to destroy it.

2

THE OEDIPAL PROBLEM
AND THE YOUNG BACHELOR

1901: Clerk at J. H. Haywood, surgical appliance manufacturer in Nottingham; death of Ernest Lawrence (William of *Sons and Lovers*); serious illness; **1902:** reading of Sir Walter Scott, James Fenimore Cooper, Robert Louis Stevenson, George Eliot, Charles Lamb's essays, Henry David Thoreau, Thomas Carlyle; **1902–5:** pupil-teacher at British School, Eastwood; **1904–10:** "unofficial" engagement to Jessie Chambers; **1904:** King's Scholarship; **1905:** uncertified assistant teacher in Eastwood; writes first poems; **1906–8:** student at University College, Nottingham, where Louisa Burrows was also a student; **1908:** passes examination for Teacher's Certificate; **1908–11:** the Croydon period; teaching at Davidson Road School, Croydon; meets Helen Corke, A. W. McLeod; success as a teacher although he is forcing himself against his inclination to write; desire for intimacy with several women—Agnes Holt, Jessie Chambers, Helen Corke, his landlady; **1909:** meets Ford Madox Ford, Violet Hunt, Ezra Pound, H. G. Wells, and other literati; **1910:** completes *The White Peacock*, begun in 1908; begins *The Trespasser*, using material supplied by Helen Corke; begins *Sons and Lovers*; breaks six-year relationship with Jessie Chambers; is engaged to Louie Burrows; death of Mrs. Lawrence; **1911:** publication of *The White Peacock*; works on *Sons and Lovers*; serious illness in November forces him to quit teaching; next year resigns at Croydon; **1912:** breaks engagement with Louie Burrows; meets Frieda Weekley.

Lawrence was twenty-five when his mother died in December of 1910—a bachelor who, like the heroes of several stories that he wrote about his life from 1910 to 1912, was "quite chaste" or, ambiguously, "almost chaste." There is no doubt that his sexual experience was meager. As a schoolboy—despised by other boys—he had sought out the company of girls and had suffered in full measure for this abnormality: "Dicky Dicky Denches Plays with the Wenches," went the merciless chant of the playground pack. But the strong feminine element in his nature inclined him to girls: he enjoyed their company, he found he could talk to them easily and enjoyably. Doubtless he found them more mature than boys and more sensitive. As he said in a letter of 15 December 1908 to Blanche Jennings: "That's why I like you so much—that's why I like women—they are so suggestible—on the whole—and they respond so heartily" (*L*, 1:100). Yet his sexual awakening was long delayed. Carl Baron, likening Lawrence to Peter Pan, accurately de-

17

scribes his "tenacious and retarded adolescence" (Neville, *A Memoir*, 19). In his relationship with girls, Lawrence made no advances. According to May Chambers, when girls discussed Lawrence, they said:

> "Isn't Bert nice!"
> "Isn't he gentlemanly!"
> "He never spoons."
> "There's never any soft mushy talk where Bert is. You should have heard him rave over a note I showed him from a fellow. It started, 'My own sweetheart.' I thought it was spiffin', but Bert said it was 'drivil and piffle and utter rot.' " (Nehls, 3:584).

May Chambers also observed that "though always in the company of girls, Bert never touched or linked arms, which was the chief reason for his popularity with them. 'You can trust him anywhere' was the verdict of all" (Nehls, 3:600).

According to Albert Limb, a classmate, "Lawrence was innocent of the facts of life when he was fourteen or fifteen years old" (Nehls, 1:32–33); and George Neville confirms the impression of protracted innocence. Mrs. Lawrence's puritanism ruled out all frank discussion of sex, and like countless Victorian lads, he was deeply inhibited by feelings of shame and guilt connected with sex. He had throughout his life an almost fanatical hatred of uncleanness in any form; his insistence on cleanness and purity was to be reflected over and over in his condemnations of an unclean society that had plunged into the slime and corruption of an obscene "sensationalism" and violent "reductionism." And there is little doubt that the guilt he felt for his own impurity went deep. The frequency of his references to masturbation in his later writings suggests that the act had for him an unusual significance: it was an unforgivable sin against his dignity and inviolacy. The early and exacting "conscience development" that Erik Erikson has noted in Gandhi was no less early and exacting in Lawrence. So deep was Lawrence's disgust with lewdness and cynicism in sexual matters that, according to George Neville, Lawrence never told a story "approaching the ordinary 'smutty' club-story," and once, when forced in a train compartment to listen to a young man telling "really wicked" stories, Lawrence "sprang to his feet, his face white, horribly distorted and more passionate than I would have believed possible," and hissed to his tormentor: " 'Shut up, you filthy little beast. Who wants to hear the muck from your stables? If there is any more of it, I'll knock your head through that pane' " (*A Memoir*, 66–67). Neville, who never heard Lawrence say anything that he would not "just as readily have said . . . had his mother or my mother been present," was sure that Lawrence would have carried out his threat if necessary (103, 67).

Lawrence's innocence extended also to his relationships with other males. Was Lawrence homosexual, or a latent homosexual? The question cannot be avoided, particularly when one considers the unpublished "Prologue" of *Women in Love*, in which Birkin is shown as being indifferent to women but attracted "intoxicatingly in his blood" to men: "This was the one and only secret he kept to himself, this secret of his passionate and sudden, spasmodic affinity for men he saw. *He kept this secret even from himself*" (*Phoenix II*, 105, 107; emphasis added). Birkin's love for Gerald Crich is another version of the early love that Lawrence had felt for his old schoolmate and friend George Neville, a love depicted in *The White Peacock* in a passage that, according to Neville, is "true, all true." Lawrence writes:

> We bathed. . . . He knew how I admired the noble, white fruitfulness of his form. As I watched him, he stood in white relief against the mass of green. . . .
> He saw I had forgotten to continue my rubbing, and, laughing he took hold of me and began to rub me briskly, as if I were a child, or rather, a woman he loved and did not fear. I left myself quite limply in his hands, and, to get a better grip of me, he put his arm around me and pressed me against him, and the sweetness of the touch of our naked bodies against each other was superb. It satisfied in some measure, the vague, indecipherable yearning of my soul, and it was the same with him. When he had rubbed me all warm, he let me go, and we looked at each other with eyes of still laughter, and our love was perfect for a moment, more perfect than any love I have known since, either for man or woman. (*WP*, 245)

"All true," George Neville said, except that Lawrence had omitted the event that had led to this embrace: Neville, swimming in the very cold water of Felley Mill, had suddenly been seized by cramps in both legs, and Lawrence in his terror had imagined Neville's death—"was frozen with the horror of it" (*A Memoir*, 96). Neville, having made shore, saw a Lawrence whose eyes were "fixed and staring, . . . his body was blue with cold" (96). At that point Neville "seized him somewhat roughly, calling to him that I was quite alright" (97). And the "holding and rubbing" commenced, Neville thus assuring the terrified Lawrence that he was "enfolded in the arms of Love" (97).

The incident is remarkable for what it reveals about both young men. Neither entertains any notion of an ulterior motive. Their love was naturally expressed in the embrace, the rubbing. For a moment they were one, brothers and lovers, not with any suggestion of homosexuality but with the closeness of men who have shared their youth together and have shared each other's secrets. For a post-Freudian age, such love is inevitably tinged with homosexuality. But Elizabethan men spoke of their love for other men without any suggestion of homosexual desires, and the custom has not yet died out. In 1915, when Lawrence confronted the reality of homosexuality—when he met John Maynard Keynes and Frankie Birrell at Cambridge—he was horrified. What he had felt for men like George Neville or Alan Chambers, what he imagined to be the nature of a "further" relationship with a man, was an idealized love inseparable from commitment not only to each other but also to higher purposes. Physical love for a man, as he imagined it, would be the natural flowering of a trust and tenderness that were deeply significant. In this connection, one must remember that in the unpublished "Prologue" to *Women in Love,* Birkin turns to Gerald Crich partly because Birkin cannot find in Hermione Roddice the *warmth* that he finds in Gerald, who did not "even know that he loved Birkin" but feels "a great tenderness towards" him (*Phoenix II,* 96). The spiritual woman—Lettie of *The White Peacock,* Helena of *The Trespasser,* Miriam of *Sons and Lovers,* Hermione of *Women in Love*—gives none of the warmth that Lawrence found in simple unlettered men, and Birkin is split in two by the woman's insistence on "spiritual, sisterly love" (104). Although he does not want to be "a libertine," his desire drives him to prostitutes; but he feels degraded by his contacts with women "of purely sensual, sensational attraction" (101). His frustrated passion focuses often on the bodies of men (106). Yet "for weeks," we learn, "it would all be gone from him, this passionate admiration of the rich body of a man" (107). For he wants to love a woman—a woman who desires him and will give him more than spiritual, sisterly love (99, 100). In short, Birkin in this "Prologue" is like the Lawrence who has not yet met Frieda: a young man desiring almost desperately an "integrity of being," yearning to love "both body and soul at once," not with the split "spiritual half" or "sensual half" (103, 102). And he is deeply afraid that his self-consciousness and shyness will prevent him from loving a woman as other men can.

As the young Lawrence imagined an idealized love with a man, so his imagined love for a woman was idealized. Sexual intimacy with a girl was virtually unthinkable for the adolescent Lawrence. (When he slept with a woman for the first time, apparently in 1909, the woman, the emancipated Alice Dax, was the one who had to take the initiative.) In 1901, at sixteen, Lawrence, according to George Neville, "wouldn't have known what to do with himself had he been left alone with a girl" (*A Memoir,* 121). When Lawrence met Jessie Chambers and their "lad and girl love" commenced, friendship—the sort of friendship that Lawrence always enjoyed with girls—was the core of the relationship for several years. He could talk to Jessie about books, ideas, feelings; she was "suggestible" and responded heartily. Moreover, she elicited some of Lawrence's maternal instincts: he could help her to learn algebra and French; he could cheer her up. More important than anything else, however, she shared his interest in literature—and encouraged him to write. He profited immensely from this; his relationship with Jessie was marked by his first awareness of his powers, his first sense of his calling as an artist. He turned to her, as he turned to women repeatedly in his early manhood, for support—the sort of support that he would not be able to get from his mother, who he knew would disapprove of his frankness.

Lawrence's "unofficial" engagement to Jessie lasted for about six years—from 1904 to 1910. When Lawrence broke the engagement, he told Jessie that he could not love her because he had always loved his mother—not innocently, but "like lovers." And Jessie, dismayed and embittered by her portrait as Miriam in *Sons and Lovers*, claimed that Mrs. Lawrence had turned him against her and had poisoned his view of her. Certainly Jessie had good reason to be bitter. When Lawrence broke off the engagement, the blow was crushing. And Lawrence knew he had acted dishonorably. But was the oedipal problem as severe as Lawrence made it out to be? One must look again at Lawrence's relationship to his mother—and to all the other women he was close to.

As I have indicated, Lawrence's comments seem to support a purely Freudian view of his oedipal relationship: "It is true, we have been great lovers" and, again, "She is my first, great love" (*L*, 1:187, 195). Yet a different attitude toward his mother is suggested in his letter of 3 December 1910 to Rachel Annand Taylor:

> *Muriel* is the girl I have broken with. She loves me to madness, and demands the soul of me. . . .
> Nobody can have the soul of me. My mother has had it, and nobody can have it again. Nobody can come into my very self again, and breathe me like an atmosphere. Don't say I am hasty this time—I know. (*L*, 1:190)

There is a strong note of anger and resentment here—the resentment that was to suffuse all of Lawrence's later references to that "superior soul," his mother. And in truth, the evidence suggests that early in his youth, Lawrence's feelings toward his mother were ambivalent.

One sign of his resentment was shown when his brother Ernest brought his fiancée to Eastwood and Mrs. Lawrence became furious because the couple "lay on the sofa all one afternoon." The young Lawrence could not see why that should matter and why his mother made such a fuss about it. When she told him "There's safety in numbers," he complained to May Chambers:

> "Safety from what? Anything I ask brings, 'Wait till you're older.' I hate growing older to find things out. It's like getting lost before you

can find the proper way. . . . If there's a mystery, tell us straight out, and let us see the reason for making a fuss, instead of hiding something from us that we have to get to know. What could that be? I am a kid. I don't know. I ask why shouldn't they lie on the sofa and talk? And mother says, 'Because they shouldn't!' But I don't know why, and that's what she won't explain!"

"I give up!" I announced.

"Yes, and you're always wondering if you're doing something you shouldn't. A least I am." (Nehls, 3:569)

The resentment of the Victorian conspiracy of silence was scarcely unique in the boys of Lawrence's generation; and Lawrence was quick to resent any suppression that prevented him from growing at his own pace. At sixteen, he was acutely aware, especially after he had begun to visit Haggs Farm, where the Chambers family (even Jessie!) accepted so casually the facts of reproduction, that he had been cut off from knowledge that was the common possession of most of mankind! He blushed; he could not believe that " 'they let the children see these things!' " (George Neville, in *A Memoir,* 73). Then blushing turned to resentment. Perhaps it is not surprising that Lawrence, the Good Boy ("too good to live"), during the delirium brought on by his pneumonia, turned "against all the members of his own family" (90). Conscious of his swiftly developing powers, he resented any limitations on his freedom to develop—any form of Eastwood provincialism and pudency. When May Chambers told him that his family resented his tutoring of Jessie, he "passed it off contemptuously. 'Them! You don't think they're going to run my life!' " (Nehls, 3:590). And he invited his friends to his house despite his mother's "obvious annoyance" and "deep aversion" to the visitors (Nehls, 3:591).

There was more to resent, however, than his mother's puritanism. As Gandhi showed "some vindictiveness, especially toward woman as the temptress" (Erikson, 122), so Lawrence very early sensed the threat of the mother who would violate her son's integrity and deflect him from his mission. If his mother had destroyed his father "by trying to make him better than he was," she was also the potential destroyer of her son—not only because of her devouring love and because, as Lawrence saw later, she had set the children against the father, but also—and most importantly—because, with her middle-class ambition, she would make him "a prisoner of industrialism." The problem is dramatized in *Sons and Lovers.* Determined that her sons shall rise and become respectable members of the bourgeoisie, Mrs. Morel takes Paul to Jordan's, the manufacturer of surgical supplies, to be interviewed for the job of clerk. Lawrence's account of this encounter is suffused with resentment of the mother. Paul feels that he is "being taken into bondage." His mother's outspokenness in the railway carriage embarrasses him, and when she is obsequious toward the head of the firm, "Paul hated her for not being prouder with this common man." The interview leaves Paul with a feeling of "ignominy and rage"—the sort of rage that Lawrence invariably showed at any assault on his dignity. Moreover, Lawrence suggests that Mrs. Morel, in her determination to make her sons "work out what *she* wanted," is careless of Paul's health: "She herself had had to put up with so much that she expected her children to take the same odds. They must go through with what came. And Paul stayed at Jordan's, although all the time he was there his health suffered from the darkness and the lack of air and the long hours" (*SL*, 108–9). The proud, ambitious Mrs. Lawrence was not one to coddle her children. Her expectation that her children should "take the same odds" was observed by May Chambers, who quotes Lawrence's mother as declaring: " 'My father was exacting. He made us wait on him hand and foot, and I used to say, "I'll never have a husband like you," then I'd have to fly. But it taught me not to dance attention on a man and to let a boy learn to help himself' " (Nehls, 3:564).

Thus the mother is associated with the middle-class ambition and the submission to the way of the world that violated the integrity of the son and threatened his very life. As Gandhi saw his wife as "a threat to higher loyalties" and saw woman as "the temptress" who would seduce him away from himself, so Lawrence was to realize that his mother's insistence on respectability, "success," and conformity was the deepest threat to his personal development. The threat of such a strong-willed mother is suggested in a letter of 27 March 1912 in which Lawrence, speaking of a Mrs. Titterton, said, "She gives me to understand she would mother me: manage me, that means" (*L*, 1:377).

As for Lawrence's oedipal hatred of his father, it was unquestionably intense. "I was born hating my father," he said in December of 1910 (*L*, 1:190); "as early as ever I can remember, I shivered with horror when he touched me. He was very bad before I was born." Later in life, in response to Catherine Carswell's remark that she couldn't "get over" her early experiences, he said: "One can't. One is cut down to the quick. . . . One can't forget that. One is never the same after that" (Nehls, 3:97). Indirectly his resentment is reflected in his story "The Christening," in which the father, whose mind is weakening, prays over an illegitimate grandchild, freely acknowledging the harm he has done to his children: " 'They've been plants under a stone because of me. Lord, if it hadn't been for me, they might ha' been trees in the sunshine.' " Even in his "dissolution," the old man "compelled their being. They had never lived; his life, his will had always been upon them and contained them" (*CSS*, 2:281–82).

What Lawrence hated most deeply in his father is suggested, I think, in that sentence "They had never lived." As far as his own father was concerned, the role of his sons was to work and to "bring summat in." When his father walked in one day to find Lawrence wearing a new gray-flannel suit, the collier exploded: " 'It's my money as peed for it; an' it's a damn shame. 'Ere I ain't got a copper even ter get mesen a drink, an' 'e can 'ave owt 'e wants. What's 'e want wi' new suits? An' if 'e does why can't 'e goo out an' earn 'em? Not get you ter rob me for 'em' " (*A Memoir*, 58). Thus George Neville recounted the scene and Lawrence's rage afterwards, when the two young men talked it over and Lawrence said:

> "I didn't ask him to be my father. . . . He took the responsibility of bringing me into the world and is too mean to stand the responsibility for what he has done. What does he want? He wanted me to go to school till I was thirteen and then go out and start to 'bring summat in' no matter whether I was fit for it or not, as so many other colliers' children have to do. He's like all those others. What do they care about their children? They come by accident, and with no consideration on the part of the parents, and, so far as the parents are concerned, nothing matters so long as, at about the age of thirteen, they start to 'bring summat in.' " (*A Memoir*, 60)

The father was "just mean," George Neville said. "What sacrifices he made were forced upon him by his wife, and he found them nothing but irksome" (55).

And yet Lawrence's hatred of his father was not undiluted. A different attitude is suggested in May Chambers's report of an incident at Haggs Farm, where Lawrence picked some mushrooms and quarreled with the Chambers boys, who maintained that the mushrooms were *theirs* because the land was theirs. Later, when asked why he had made such a fuss over the mushrooms, Lawrence confessed:

> "Well, if you want to know, I want them for my father's tea. . . ."
> "Well," I [May Chambers] cried in sheer surprise, "and you hating him as you hate him! You don't hate him as you pretend you do, or you'd never make trouble with your friends to take their mushrooms for him!"
> "I have to hate him for Mother's sake," he replied. (Nehls, 3:578)

By the time he wrote *Sons and Lovers*, Lawrence was beginning to share Ada's view that there might not have been "so much misery in our childhood if mother had been just a little more tolerant" (Nehls, 1:10). (A similar view was held by William Hopkin, who said: "I'm sure that if she had shown tact and patience things might have been very different. Arthur Lawrence was not of the material to mould into his wife's idea of a gentleman. He was one naturally" [Nehls, 1:22]). Although the father seems "mean" in his automatic expectation that his sons would "bring summat in," the depth of the father's love has been suggested by George Neville, who believed that the collier "was full of a consuming love for his wife and all his children, and for Bert (D. H.) in particular." And Neville reported that the old man wept freely when his son had pneumonia (*A Memoir*, 48, 63). In *Sons and Lovers*, Paul is aware of his father's warmth and tenderness, as he is aware of his father's essential honesty. Lawrence condemns Mr. Morel because the coal miner "denied the God in him," but later in life Lawrence came to see that his father had exhibited a rare "integrity." Lawrence told Achsah Brewster that his father and Norman Douglas "were the only people he had known who always followed joy. . . . They were sun-flowers sure enough! They had their brightness too. Nothing else really existed for either of them, nothing but themselves." They were "blithe spirits, true to themselves," and "they were right in a way. They had kept themselves unbroken, while the rest of us have cared too much and let ourselves be shattered by the depths of our affections. We must let things go, one after another, finally even love—only keeping oneself true to oneself, just that integrity. Nothing else matters in life or death" (Nehls, 3:245). Lawrence also told Rhys Davies that "he had come to respect his father much more than when he wrote *Sons and Lovers*. He grieved having painted him in such a bitterly hostile way in that book. He could see now that his father had possessed a great deal of the old gay male spirit of England, pre-puritan, he was natural and unruined deep in himself" (Nehls, 3:276). Again, when Lawrence was watching a workman in Ceylon, Achsah Brewster reports that Lawrence said the worker

> resembled his father—the same clean-cut and exuberant spirit, a true pagan. He added that he had not done justice to his father in *Sons and Lovers* and felt like rewriting it. When children they had accepted the dictum of their mother that their father was a drunkard, therefore was contemptible, but . . . as Lawrence had grown older he had come to see . . . his unquenchable fire and relish for living. Now he blamed his mother for her self-righteousness, her invulnerable Christian virtue within which she was entrenched. She had brought down terrible scenes of vituperation upon their heads from which she might have protected them. She would gather the children in a row and they would sit quaking, waiting for their father to return while she would picture his shortcomings blacker and blacker to their childish horror. At last the father would come in softly, taking off his shoes, hoping to escape unnoticed to bed, but that was not allowed him. She would burst out upon him, reviling him for a drunken sot, a good-for-nothing father. She would turn to the whimpering children and ask them if they

were not disgusted with such a father. He would look at the row of frightened children, and say: "Never mind, my duckies, you needna be afraid of me. I'll do ye na harm." (Nehls, 2:126)

The gentleness and tenderness that Lawrence saw in his pagan father was to be stressed over and over in the last stories, written when Lawrence, with death hanging over him, atoned in full for his injustice to his father. The coal miner Morel became the noble Mellors of *Lady Chatterley's Lover*. But even before he had completed *Sons and Lovers*, Lawrence had begun to feel some sympathy for his father. As he wrote in December of 1910, "I look at my father—he is like a cinder. It is very terrible, mis-marriage" (*L*, 1:191).

Lawrence's ambivalent feelings for his mother thus tilted very gradually against her. And Lawrence's lifelong celebration of the stubborn, defiant man who refuses to knuckle under to bourgeois pressures, as well as his lifelong attack on the mother who seduces the son and pits him against the father, elaborately atoned for his early hatred of his father and for his oedipal appropriation of the mother. In this, Lawrence shows some of the originality that, in *homo religiosus*, seems to "point beyond competition with the personal father." Erik Erikson has observed that *homo religiosus* reenacts the oedipal curse but, feeling an intolerable guilt, seeks to transcend the hatred peculiar to the oedipal situation. Gandhi could not forgive himself for his failure to be present when his father died; and according to Erikson, Gandhi's extreme guilt feelings became the foundation for the Mahatma's lifelong effort to "save" a superior adversary "as well as those whom he oppressed" (129).

Whether or not one accepts a psychoanalytic explanation of Lawrence's "atonement" for his oedipal hatred, the mother personified for Lawrence all the women who threaten the higher loyalties of the religious man by their insistence on home, children, success, and possessive or egoistic love as the proper goal of their men. The bullying "spiritual" woman—spokeswoman for the entire society—is the destroyer. Submission to her subverts the religious man's integrity, poisons his health, and prevents the accomplishment of his mission. Lawrence, like Gandhi, viewed his illness as a punishment—the inevitable result of acquiescence to circumstances that violated his integrity. As I have mentioned, Lawrence saw Paul's mother as being indirectly responsible for the deterioration of Paul's health. And because he surrendered as a child to her influence, he nearly died at her death. Health was possible only after he had thrown off her suffocating influence and was reborn as a new man, able to do the will of God instead of the petty, human will of the woman.

Lawrence's rejection of the spiritually bullying mother presages his attitude toward all women. The strong religious bent of Lawrence's nature—his determination to "surpass and create at all costs"—inevitably caused him to fear the bondage that women might impose. But his intensity was widely misunderstood. Idella Purnell Stone, who knew Lawrence in Mexico, concluded that he was "sexually immature" and "preoccupied by a desire to understand, with his head, something he could never really understand with his body" (Nehls, 2:251). There is a grain of truth in this. In his youth and into his later life, Lawrence had very little sexual experience except with Frieda. And although he tried to free himself from all bourgeois scruples, he found it hard to "let go." His early conception of love was idealized, charged with religious attitudes of consecration, sacredness, eternality; he was puritanically horrified by philandering, sensation seeking, and unclean or "mechanical" sex, as he was horrified by the possibility of contracting syphilis—a disease that, he argued, caused "the crippling of the consciousness of man" in the Renaissance (*Phoenix*, 556). But his abhorrence of "reduction" in sexual relations cannot be understood except in relation to his sense of a mission—his fear, as a religious man, that love could destroy his integrity.

Returning to his early "love" for Jessie Chambers, one cannot avoid the conclusion that Lawrence innocently allowed himself to be paired with her before he became aware of the threat that she represented—the threat that she would confine or entrap him. His mother had already possessed his soul. As he grew older, and as his sexual desire became more and more irrepressible, he had to seek out other women; yet the woman he needed had to be one who would not entrap him—and condemn him to slavery within Eastwood and within the bourgeiosie. She had to be one who was free from all middle-class expectations and values that threatened his "higher loyalties." Jessie Chambers was not such a woman. Lawrence did not realize this at first. As he said after breaking off the engagement, "I have been cruel to her, and wronged her, *but I did not know*" (L, 1:190; emphasis added): he did not know, that is, that Jessie demanded "the soul of him."

It was only gradually that he saw his attachment to Jessie as dangerous. On 11 May 1910—six or seven months before breaking the engagement—he wrote to Helen Corke: "Muriel [Jessie] will take me. She will do me great, infinite good—for a time. But what is awake in me shivers with terror at the issue. Whatever happens, in the near present, I can't help it—I cannot" (L, 1:160). The "issue" that made him shiver with terror could have been his mother's opposition. Lawrence was acutely aware of that opposition in January 1910, when he told Blanche Jennings that "Muriel" would visit him for a weekend, and added:

"What would my people and hers say?—but what do I care—not a damn!—they will not know. '*I* am the master of my fate / *I* am the captain of my soul'" (*L*, 1:154). But Lawrence knew that Jessie would do him good only "for a time"; and apparently what frightened him most deeply was being trapped. (When he learned that George Neville had "'got a girl into trouble'" and would have to face the consequences, Lawrence burst out "vehemently: 'Thank God . . . I've been saved from that . . . so far'"—thus Jessie Chambers reported in *D. H. Lawrence: A Personal Record*, 125–26.) What Lawrence feared was not commitment, however; it was commitment to a woman like Jessie. As he confided to Willie Hopkin when the latter asked why Lawrence did not marry Jessie: "'It would have been a fatal step. I should have had too easy a life, nearly everything my own way, and my genius would have been destroyed'" (Nehls, 1:71). Hopkin added: "That belief was persistent in him. Even in his teens he allowed nothing to come between him and what he wanted for his writing" (Nehls, 1:71).

Helen Corke's analysis of the conflict between Jessie and Lawrence is illuminating here, for it underscores the importance of Jessie's conventional view of love and marriage:

> Their conflict was inevitable; social principle and the inheritance of a sternly Puritan moral code obliged her to dismiss, as intolerable, the suggestion of a physical intimacy less binding than that of marriage; nor did she lack the desire of a normal woman for a unique personal right in the man to whom she would devote her life. (Corke, 22)

Corke, who knew Lawrence very well at this time (she is the Helena who appears in a number of his love poems and in his second novel, *The Trespasser*), goes on to say that in 1911 Lawrence "was now realizing that marriage with a girl of his mother's world [i.e., Louie Burrows] would never link him safely and permanently into that world; and that his engagement had been a mistake" (28). In short, it would have been a mistake to marry *any* girl who could not free herself from the moral and social codes of the tribe, as it would also have been a mistake to marry one who could not show a wholehearted sexual desire.

When Lawrence told Jessie that he could not marry her because he had always loved his mother "like a lover" (Corke, 41), it seems plausible, then, that Lawrence was exaggerating his mother love in order to ease the pain that Jessie felt at his heartless breaking off. He was concealing the fact that he could not love her because she, like his mother, was at bottom possessed by unexamined middle-class assumptions that he was determined to throw off. Here again, Helen Corke's appraisal of the situation seems shrewd. When Jessie told Helen Corke (after Lawrence's death) that Lawrence's "Golden Age was the time up to nineteen or so, before his fatal self-division began to manifest itself'' (43), Corke observed that Jessie, in her ''possessive love for Lawrence's adolescent self,'' was ''repeating the error of Lawrence's mother, who with similar insistence had claimed the boy as she herself [Jessie] was now demanding the youth'' (Corke, 44). The fatal self-division that Jessie saw in Lawrence was, to a great extent, Lawrence's repudiation of Eastwood and of all that Eastwood held sacred. Jessie knew that the young Lawrence had rejected Christianity and had swallowed materialism ''at a gulp.'' But she did not understand how deeply Lawrence had been *changed* by his opposition to tribal deities. It was not merely an ''intellectual'' opposition; it was a passionate determination to free himself from the tribe itself, with all its massed and fixed expectations and demands. The full extent of Lawrence's ''fatal self-division'' was revealed to Jessie when he told her, ''With *should* and *ought* I have nothing to do.'' She did not understand that this Nietzschean declaration signaled the end of Lawrence's youth and the beginning of his conscious effort to destroy the old, dead world and to create a new, living one.

If Lawrence exaggerated his love for his mother as a pretext to account for his faithlessness to Jessie, it is easy to account for the confusions that have disturbed critics of *Sons and Lovers*. One must recall that as he wrote the novel, Lawrence was sending the manuscript to Jessie for her comments and criticism. Detached, impersonal, he assumed that she could rise to the same level—could see the novel as art, as presenting an essential truth about Miriam that Jessie would be bound to acknowledge. He must have been startled or dismayed by her purely personal response. But he could atone for the pain he had inflicted on her by ''explaining'' Paul's cruelty as the result of his mother love. He could suggest that Paul is incapable of loving any woman—even the sensuous Clara Dawes. The anguish Lawrence expressed when he broke with Jessie testifies to his realization that he was behaving abominably. Hence he *had* to explain and atone. At the same time, he could not disguise the truth of his view of Miriam: the static, spiritual Miriam who continually rubs Paul the wrong way; her clinging, worshipful, lugubrious manner, which the lively Paul finds so offensive. So the novel wavers in its explanation of Paul's conflict. Implicitly, it argues that what Paul needs is freedom to live on his own terms, untrammeled by the possessive love of women and by the restrictions imposed by bourgeois society. Explicitly, it argues that Paul needs to overcome his oedipal conflict. Yet the mother drops out of the novel for most of the second part, as she becomes less and less important for Paul's development, and it is not until she is dying that her effect on Paul is reinstated. Lawrence provides little evidence in Paul's young manhood that the mother prevents him from loving. The truth is, as I have indicated, that Lawrence began fairly early in his adolescence to throw off his mother's influence. Frieda thought that Lawrence had missed the whole point about Paul—the point being that he loved his mother; but Lawrence hadn't missed the point—he had instead exaggerated the point—against his own deepest inclination, which was to dramatize the more general problem of the struggle for freedom.

But how does one explain Lawrence's proposal to Louie Burrows while his mother was dying? If his inclination was to free himself from a stagnant respectability—and this certainly is the message of his first novel, *The White Peacock*, in which, one after another, the males are entrapped and condemned to be servants of the female—why did Lawrence plunge so quickly into a commitment to Louie?

The answer is certainly, in part, that Lawrence felt lost. His mother was dead; he had broken off with Jessie; he had no woman to support him. His letters after his mother's death make abundantly clear that he felt he needed support very badly. On 13 December 1910, he writes: "I want some money to get married. If I can't stick my head in some hole—c'est à dire, a woman's bosom—I shall soon be as daft as Dostoieffsky. I'm fed up" (*L*, 1:199). Ten days later he writes to Sallie Hopkin: "I could adore any maiden just now if she were sufficiently fruitful and resposeful in her being. But God preserve us from the acid sort just now" (*L*, 1:211). And he tells Louie Burrows, in effect, that he needs her to give him peace, rest, solace. On 20 December 1910, he writes: "When we are together, and quiet, it will be beautiful. I do want you to be peaceful with, to grow with, to slowly and sweetly develope with—it's only now and then passionate" (*L*, 1:208). Again, on 23 December 1910, he writes, "I want you to succour me, my darling—for I am used up" (*L*, 1:211). He also tells Louie that Ada needs his support and comfort and that he must try to make Ada cheerful; but that is difficult, for "I want comforting myself, like a kid, and cheering, like a tearful girl. But it is rather despicable" (*L*, 1:212). He wishes to "light myself at [Louie's] abundant life," as he writes to her on 14 December 1910. For a man who felt he was drifting toward death after his mother's death, it is obvious that almost any maiden could provide the maternal comforting that he most deeply needed.

There is another reason for his sudden choice of Louie. In a letter of 3 December 1910, before his mother's burial, he states that "nobody can have the soul of me. My mother has had it, and nobody can have it again." He goes on to say: "Louie—whom I wish I could marry the day after the funeral—she would never demand to drink me up and have me. . . . She will never plunge her hands through my blood and feel for my soul, and make me set my teeth and shiver and fight away. Ugh—I have done well—and cruelly—tonight" (*L*, 1:190–91). After breaking up with Jessie, Lawrence obviously felt that he might be able to have, with Louie, an "impersonal" relationship of the kind that Rupert Birkin insists upon in his resistance to Ursula's possessive love in *Women in Love*. Lawrence repeated this idea in a letter to Helen Corke some seven months later—at a time when he was pressing Helen to become intimate with him:

> Some of you I should always love. Then again, I must break free. And I
> *cannot* marry save where I am not held. Even set me down that
> disgraceful thing, abnormality, so long as you believe me. I love Louie
> in a certain way that doesn't encroach on my liberty, and I can marry
> her, and still be alone. It must be so, if I marry—alone in soul, mostly.
> (*L*, 1:285)

As early as 27 December 1910 he had warned Louie that this would be so:

> Try, will you, when I disappoint you and may grieve you, to think that
> it is the impersonal part of me—which belongs to nobody, not even to
> myself—the writer in me, which is for the moment ruling. When you
> see it in my eyes, take no notice, chatter as if it were not so. Remember I
> love you and am your husband: but that a part of me is exempt from
> these things, from everything: the impersonal, artistic side. (*L*,
> 1:214–15)

No letter testifies more eloquently to Lawrence's deep sense of being the agent of powers beyond himself.

But while Lawrence was aware of this higher commitment during the Croydon years, he did not evidently understand the depth of his fear of "belonging" to a woman, and he tended to blame women for feeling the fear, in his relationships with them, that was patently his own. The deep conflicts that he was experiencing during this critical period of his life—for it *was* critical: his whole future hung on his decision—all center on the potential violation of his mission. Both in his work as a teacher and in his relationships with women he was fighting a battle for freedom: he was struggling to acquire the courage to break with convention and to "trespass" into a new way of life.

Inevitably his job as elementary-school-teacher had a lot to do with his state of mind during the Croydon years (from October 1908 to November 1911). He had begun teaching in 1902, when he was seventeen, and by 1910 he was already an old hand at the job. Confidence he had never lacked, but discipline was a major problem in his classes, and he had to steel himself to impose his will on his students. His "feminine soul"—as the psychologist Trigant Burrow described it—recoiled from the bullying. If one may judge from the vivid account of Ursula's struggles as a schoolteacher in *The Rainbow,* the experience was harrowing. Yet Lawrence was mature and disciplined, and he did what had to be done—as Ursula, gritting her teeth, does what *she* must do to gain control over her class.

If he had ever had any illusions about his mission as a teacher, the reality of his situation quickly became apparent. The elementary-school-teacher, as he observed in his 1918 essay "Education of the People," is "insulted from above and from below." He is "sneered at by the idealists above and jeered at by the materialists below" (*Phoenix,* 589). "Between the disillusion of their scholars' destiny, on the one hand, and the disillusion of their own mean and humiliating destiny, on the other, they haven't much breath left for the fanning of the high flame of noble human existence" (589). Worst of all, perhaps, for the proud young Lawrence, was that "every shred of natural pride is ground out" of the teacher. The contradiction between the teacher's idealism and the *fact* of utter materialism "is absolutely fatal for the manhood of the teacher" (591). If Lawrence had suffered the jeers and taunts of classmates when he was a boy, he did not escape, in his teaching, the contempt of parents who regarded him as their obedient servant whose job was to " 'treat my child properly' " (589).

In many respects, to be sure, he was a born teacher—born to "set others straight." With his clear quick common sense, his vitality, and his maternal affection for his students, he was bound to be successful. He was innovative, especially in his teaching of art, but also in science. (The headmaster of Davidson School in Croydon, P. F. Smith, reported that Lawrence " 'particularly directed the art training of the upper divisions' " and " 'to a great extent influenced the science teaching of the whole school' " [Ada Lawrence, 95]). Lawrence could easily reduce complexity to simplicity and emphasize the essential. As Hilary Gatti has pointed out, Lawrence's biology lessons—an indication of which is provided in the chapter "Schoolroom" of *Women in Love*—appear to have been "models of vividness and clarity" (212). Moreover, Lawrence realized the importance of what he called "dynamic meaning" for the children: not abstractions which kill real experience ("the earth is round") and not "a ramming in of brain facts through the head" (*FU,* 92), but an effort to encourage the student to play with possibilities. "Let a child make a clay landscape if it likes. But entirely according to its own fancy, and without conclusions drawn. Only, let the landscape be vividly made—always the discipline of the soul's full attention. 'Oh, but where are the factory chimneys?'—or else—'Why have you left out the gas-works?' or 'Do you call that sloppy thing a church?' . . . The soul must give earnest attention, that is all." He did not believe in "self-expression": what self had the child to express? But he did believe that the aim of education is not to force all students to become scholars but to recognize "the true nature in each child" and to give the child the opportunity to "come to his own intrinsic fullness of being."

For Lawrence, the teacher's mission was inevitably religious. As he said in "Education of the People," "It is a sacred business," and the teacher must be a "priest of life"—one whose "whole business" is "to estimate the profound life-quality, the very nature of the child, that which makes him ultimately what he is" (*Phoenix*, 606–7). Worshipping the "creative life-mystery," the teacher-priest assumes responsibility for the unfolding of the being of the child—he watches "the *being*" in each student, and allows the child to develop by leaving him alone—that is, by refusing to violate the singleness of the individual. It was inevitable that the necessity of imposing his own will on the children was associated, in his poem "The Punisher," with a desecration of his role as priest of life: "Desolate I am as a church whose lights are put out / And doubt enters in drearness." Thus wrote the priest who had, by punishing, violated his vows (*CP*, 94).

How many of these pedagogical ideas Lawrence had thought out during his years as a teacher is hard to say. His intuitive response to his students—for example, his realization that, for coal miners' sons, all talk about the Ideal was likely to prove hollow or hypocritical—suggests the sort of "quickness" that he felt was indispensable in the teacher-priest. Acutely he realized the folly of trying to teach the same lesson to every student, heedless of the child's dynamic development or interest. He had learned, in reading John Adams's *The Herbartian Psychology Applied to Education,* that it is idle to undertake educating without first considering the nature and the interests of each student. And he realized that education, for the majority of students, was sheer bullying, a violation of their integrity and of their deepest needs. His solution to the almost insuperable problem of mass education was uncompromising: it would be best, he said later, to close the schools altogether. And his serious concern to prevent violations of the child's integrity—chiefly by a brainwashing idealism—testifies to the depth of his religious reverence for life, a reverence that issued from his own deep sense of having been "violated" by the spiritual tyranny of his mother. His bitter opposition to education based on the assumption that man is "an ideal being" or "a pure spirit" whose goal is to identify with the infinite through "self-abandoning love" is the angry issue of his realization that he had been crippled by a mother who insisted on "personal" love and forced him into the abnormal role of a selfless little angel, "a good boy." Good he had been, perhaps "too good to live," as he jeered. And he had also been, contemptibly, Dicky Dicky Denches, playing with the wenches. Hence his tirade against "the self-conscious woman": "Would God a she-wolf had suckled me, and stood over me with her paps, and kicked me back into a rocky corner when she'd had enough of me. It might have made a man of me. . . . Alas, there isn't a wild she-wolf in the length and breadth of Britain'' (*Phoenix*, 632–33).

Raymond Williams, in *D. H. Lawrence on Education,* has argued that there is a contradiction between Lawrence's idea that "men and women should be themselves" and his prescription of "what boys should learn in school and girls should learn in school"—a prescription based on presumptions that are "reproductions of the social and sexual roles which the existing society has forced men and women into" (12). But Lawrence did not believe that society *had* forced men and women into such roles; on the contrary, men had been rendered docile and effeminate, "hensure," while women, inspired by liberal ideals of freedom and rights, had become "cocksure." Biological differences had been suppressed by an education that stressed only the ideals of freedom, love, selflessness, benevolence, and the common welfare. Again and again Lawrence would stress that education, by emphasizing only the mind and mental consciousness, prevented the development of "dynamic consciousness" and narrowed the range of human feeling. "Educated!" he cried. "We are not even *born* as far as our feelings are concerned" (Williams, 9).

His profound disillusionment with the elementary school was matched by his keen awareness of the ignominy of his position as "that public clown, the elementary school-teacher" (*Phoenix*, 595). And the bitterness was intensified by his awareness that he was squandering in the classroom the gifts that nature had intended for a higher mission: discovery of Truth in his art.

It is essential to remember, as one contemplates Lawrence's relationships to women and his decision to commit himself to Frieda and to leave England, how much and for how long he had been forcing himself as a teacher. As early as 13 May 1908 his frustration erupted in a cry that his true gifts were being wasted in teaching. As he wrote to Blanche Jennings, a "wise safe elder" in whom he often confided at that time:

> Eh, my soul is my great asset and my great misfortune. But I am choking it with mud and stones; I am cooling it, or people are cooling it for me, by making it work, when it doesn't want, and for dirt. As true as I am born, I have the capacity for doing something delicately and well. As sure as I am poor, I am being roughened down to a blunt blade; I am already rusting. (*L*, 1:53–54)

Being poor, he felt intensely the pressure to toe the line—to play the academic game and to put himself in line for the appropriate rewards. On 26 October 1908 he wrote to Blanche Jennings from Croydon:

I ought to continue to study for a degree, but I do not want to study. . . . Everybody says study; I say I won't. Do aid and abet me! I dread your giving me more maternal advice—in this vein: "get on— take your degree." (*L*, 1:85)

He was working on *Laetitia*, the early draft of *The White Peacock*. "I want to have my own way somewhere," he pleaded. Yet the pressure of "maternal advice" checked him, and he had to admit that his soul's desire was a "soap-bubble" (*L*, 1:85). Still, the violation of his deepest desire was intolerable. "I had rather endure anything," he wrote on 16 November 1908, "than this continual, petty, debasing struggle. Shortly I shall be good for very little myself" (*L*, 1:93). This letter was written, he said, on one of his "black days," but his frustration is a recurrent theme in his letters. On 15 September 1911 he wrote: "There are so many things I want to do, and can't. . . . I am really rather,—very—sick of teaching when I want to do something else" (*L*, 1:303). After his illness in the winter of 1911 and 1912, he wrote: "But I shan't teach again—no, I'll be a tramp rather. . . . To think of the amount of blood and spirit I sold the Croydon Education Committee for £100 a year makes me wild" (*L*, 1:367). And after fleeing to the Continent he had a recurrent nightmare—"the worst dream I ever had"—that he must be prepared to teach: "Bang-slap went my heart—½ past eight on Monday morning— school! You've no idea what a nightmare it is to me, now I have escaped" (2 Sept. 1912, *L*, 1:446, also 1:455). Indeed, as late as 1927 he had a dream that he had "clean forgotten to mark the register, and the class has gone home! Why should I feel so worried about not having marked the register? But I do" (*CL*, 2:966).

His desire to escape from the prison of the classroom was paralleled by his intense desire for another freedom: freedom from his Victorian pudency and his sexual inhibitions. To understand his inner doubts and anxieties during the Croydon years, one must look not only at his letters but also at several stories that he wrote about that period of his life, notably "Daughters of the Vicar," "The Old Adam," "The Witch à la Mode," and "A Modern Lover." In all of these stories, the male hero, a young bachelor, encounters the sexual problem that Lawrence was facing. The hero is "quite chaste" ("The Old Adam"), or "almost quite chaste" ("Daughters of the Vicar"), or "kept himself virtuous" ("A Modern Lover"). He is attracted to a number of women—surrogates of Lawrence's landlady in Croydon, of Helen Corke, of Louie Burrows, and of Jessie Chambers; but he is so shy and self-conscious that he is incapable of approaching the woman directly, and he feels shame because he is unlike other men—not blessed with the spontaneity or stupidity that "went to its own satisfaction direct." Desperately he needs release, freedom to act without inhibition. And although, in

"Witch à la Mode" and "A Modern Lover," he blames the woman for withholding herself, his own fear of letting go is equally strong.

"Daughters of the Vicar" indirectly dramatizes Lawrence's state of mind after his mother's death. A young collier, Alfred Durrant, loses his mother (she dies of a tumor) and then quickly agrees to marry one of the vicar's daughters, Louisa Lindley, a transparent copy of Louisa Burrows. Like Paul Morel, Alfred is "lost" when his mother dies: "Without knowing it, he had been centralised, polarised in his mother. It was she who had kept him" (*CSS*, 1:176). "Lost in a great, bewildering flood, immense and unpeopled," Alfred turns to Louisa, who, like Louie Burrows, is "impassive and reserved" and has the "repose" as well as the rich abundant hair that Lawrence often remarked in Louie (177). Louisa's parents, the vicar and his wife, strongly disapprove of Alfred—as Louie's parents disapproved of Lawrence. They have a "position to maintain" (184) and can approve their daughter's marriage only on condition that Alfred will not live with her in the parish: they endorse Alfred's idea of emigrating to Canada.

Alfred is not Lawrence, but the depiction of the bachelor's inhibitions and fears mirrors Lawrence's own state of mind during the Croydon period. Alfred, we are told,

> was almost quite chaste. A strong sensitiveness had kept him from women. Sexual talk was all very well among men, but somehow it had no application to living women. There were two things for him, the *idea* of women, with which he sometimes debauched himself, and real women, before whom he felt a deep uneasiness, and a need to draw away. He shrank and defended himself from the approach of any woman. And then he felt ashamed. In his innermost soul he felt he was not a man, he was less than the normal man. (*CSS*, 1:164–65).

If Alfred is Lawrence, the statement "Alfred was *almost* quite chaste" perhaps alludes to the rare sexual experience of 1909, when Alice Dax, a close friend of Sallie Hopkin's, took the initiative and "gave Bert sex." ("'I had to,'" she is reported to have said. "'He was over at our house, struggling with a poem he couldn't finish, so I took him upstairs and gave him sex. He came downstairs and finished the poem'" [Moore, *The Intelligent Heart*, 131].) Just like that! The episode seems hardly to have counted for the young Lawrence. Although there is his art to sustain him (Alfred plays the piccolo, as Aaron Sisson in *Aaron's Rod* plays the flute, and is "considered an expert"), he is torn by "shame":

> . . . at the bottom of his soul was always this canker of shame and incompleteness: he was miserable beneath all his healthy cheerfulness, he was uneasy and felt despicable among all his confidence and superiority of ideas. He would have changed with any mere brute, just

> to be free of himself, to be free of this shame of self-consciousness. . . .
> Anything, he would have given for this spontaneity and this blind
> stupidity which went to its own satisfaction direct. (165)

The shame of prolonged chastity is compounded by the shame of
masturbation, suggested in the phrase "the idea of women, with which
he sometimes debauched himself." And Alfred, like Lawrence in
Croydon after his mother's death, resorts to "work" as a release
because "at work he was all right" (176).

The extreme shyness, the inability to make sexual advances, are
also vividly depicted in "The Old Adam," a story undoubtedly based on
Lawrence's experiences as a boarder in the home of Mr. and Mrs. Jones
in Croydon. The hero, Edward Severn, is, like Alfred Durrant in
"Daughters of the Vicar," "quite chaste."

> At twenty-seven, he was quite chaste. Being highly civilised, he prized
> women for their intuition, and because of the delicacy with which he
> could transfer to them his thoughts and feelings, without cumbrous
> argument. From this to a state of passion he could only proceed by fine
> gradations, and such a procedure he had never begun. (CSS, 1:30)

Edward plays with the landlady's daughter, as Lawrence played with
Hilda Jones; but kissing the child, he becomes aware of the mother's
"heavy woman's breasts" as she bends down. Yet he cannot act
directly; his passion must be translated into poetry or imagery: " 'A
peculiar, brutal, carnal scent, iris,' he drawled at length, 'Isn't it?' "
(1:27). Symbolic lightning flashes in the sky, and he says to the landlady,
" 'You don't like lightning, do you? You'd even have to take refuge with
Kate [the maid] if I weren't here' " (1:28). He smiles at Mrs. Thomas
"with roused eyes," and she tells him that the lightning " 'makes me
feel worked up . . . as if I couldn't contain myself' " (1:30). Then he
smiles "like a man who feels in jeopardy" (1:30). Presently the lightning
bombards the sky, they are both "panting, and afraid, not of the
lightning but of themselves and of each other" (1:30). But the idea of
embracing Mrs. Thomas "would have shocked [Edward] too much had
he formed it. His passion had run on subconsciously, till now it had
come to such a pitch it must drag his conscious soul into allegiance.
This, however, would probably never happen; he would not yield
allegiance, and blind emotion, in this direction, could not carry him
alone" (1:30). The passage is remarkable for its equivocation, because
Edward is always *conscious* of the sexual promise of Mrs. Thomas.
Indeed, it is the intense self-consciousness and the sense of being "in
jeopardy" that prevent him from making a direct sexual advance. When
Mrs. Thomas's husband returns, the two male rivals fight a covert battle
for the female, but the battle ends in the cementing of their friendship,

and Mrs. Thomas treats Severn "as if he were a stranger." He remains, safely, "quite chaste."

In two other stories of this period—"Witch à la Mode," and "A Modern Lover"—it is the woman who is accused of putting out the fires of sexual love, but in both stories the male hero is at least as responsible as the woman for the failure of love. In "Witch à la Mode," the hero, Bernard Coutts, is engaged to "Connie," who, like Louisa Lindley and Louie Burrows, is the daughter of a vicar. But Coutts is also attracted to Winifred Varley, the "witch à la mode," who is surrogate of Helen Corke. Returning to England after a year in France, Coutts stops in East Croydon before proceeding to the home of his fiancée. He feels a "sense of shame," knowing that he is betraying Connie, but he also exults in the prospect of seeing Winifred Varley. At the home of his former landlady, Laura Braithwaite, he finds Winifred. Both women find it hard to believe that he is still engaged to Connie, and Coutts admits to himself that if he were to marry Connie, she "would bore him" (CSS, 1:65). Yet he clings to Connie because

> with Connie he felt the old, manly superiority: he was the knight, strong and tender, she was the beautiful maiden with a touch of God on her brow. He kissed her, he softened and selected his speech for her, he forebore from being the greater part of himself. She was his betrothed, his wife, his queen, whom he loved to idealise, and for whom he carefully modified himself. She would rule him later on—that part of him which was hers. But he loved her, too, with a pitying, tender love. (CSS, 1:64)

The passage conveys exactly what is stated and implied in Lawrence's letters to Louie Burrows: the profound respect, or idealization, that led Lawrence to soften his speech and to act the role of the knight. Yet it is Winifred who fascinates Coutts: "He and she really played with fire. In her house, he was roused and keen." But her passion is "unacknowledged"; she "was not, and never could be, frank" (CSS, 1:65). So a love-hate relationship exists between them. In the main action, Winifred, "witch-like," opposes Coutts's marriage to Connie. She "could not understand how he could marry: it seemed almost monstrous to her; she fought against his marriage" (1:66). Coutts, showing the acquiescence to fate that Lawrence often felt in Croydon, tells her that he will "'marry—settle—be a good husband, good father, partner in the business; get fat, be an amiable gentlemen—Q.E.F.'" (1:66). A relationship with Winifred, he tells her, would drive them both into insanity; and she wants him, he accuses her bitterly, only to be her "crystal-glass." "'My length of blood and bone you don't care a rap for. Ah, yes, you like me for a crystal-glass, to see things in: to hold up to the light. I'm a blessed Lady-of-Shallot looking-glass for you'" (1:67).

Winifred, lifting her arms toward him, tries to win him over to her and then kisses him—"the first kiss she had genuinely given"—but he realizes that she wants no more than that kiss. "This woman gave him anguish and a cutting-short like death; to the other woman he was false" (1:69). Enraged by the coldness of her soul—symbolized in her ivory possessions—he smashes an ivory lamp, and a fire leaps up that burns him. He bolts from the house, "running with burning-red hands" (1:70). The bitterness of an experience similar to this is reflected in the letter in which Lawrence told Helen Corke that he would never again ask anything of women; he would pay their market price. Yet Lawrence *was* engaged, even as he was asking Helen Corke to move "tiefer ins Leben" with him. It seems not to have occurred to him that he was withholding *himself* even as Winifred/Helen withheld *herself*.

Much more painful to the reader—painful because Lawrence is only half-aware of the true nature of his hero—is the depiction in "A Modern Lover" of a return to "Muriel"—Jessie Chambers—after an absence of two years. The hero, Cyril Mersham (cf. the Cyril of *The White Peacock*), returns to the farm after two years "in the large city in the south" (*CSS*, 1:2). The story, like *The Trespasser*, works with a fundamental opposition between fire and water. Returning, Cyril slogs through symbolic mud. He feels that "most folk had choked out the fires of their fiercer experience with rubble of sentimentality and stupid fear, and rarely could he feel the hot destruction of Life fighting out its way" (1:2). In a Nietzschean vein, he wants to "laugh the crystalline laughter of the stars" and to answer the "wild clawings" of the waves "with laughter" (1:2, 3). But the mud and water of Midland inertia frustrate his desire for the *übermenschlich* fire and laughter. At the farm, he feels "a sense of dreariness." Muriel is "submissive," and he shrinks from the submission that "trammelled him, throwing the responsibility of her wholly on him, making him shrink from the burden of her" (1:3). The torpor of the farm causes him to "react," and he uses "exquisitely accurate" English, whose "nicety contrasted the more with their rough, country habit. They became shy and awkward, fumbling for something to say" (1:5). Only half-conscious of the *nastiness* of his hero, Lawrence tells us that Cyril is "lapped in his unbreakable armour of light irony"; he "twinkled playfully" at Muriel, who is, astonishingly, not disgusted, but is much attracted to him, finding him "very much of a gentlemen" (1:9, 8).

Muriel now has an "old-fashioned" beau, Tom Vickers, who is inarticulate, unconscious, direct. But Cyril, the modern lover, is determined to awaken her old love for him; he wants her, he says, to be flint to his steel—"to spurt out red fire for me" (1:9). Like Lawrence's other bachelor heroes, Cyril has "kept himself virtuous," but now "he would wait no longer." So he works to win Muriel away from her old-fashioned lover, using his bright talk of art and philosophy to arouse her. Plagiarizing Walter Pater and Nietzsche, Cyril declares that it is best in life "to roar away, like a fire with a great draught, white-hot to the last bit" (1:16). "And . . . you are washed with the whitest fire of life—when you take a woman you love—and understand" (1:17). Thus Cyril's talk "lifted Muriel as in a net, like a sea-maiden out of the waters, and placed her in his arms, to breathe his thin, rare atmosphere" (1:17).

Lawrence is half-aware of Cyril's affectation but does not fully recognize the ugliness of his vanity, his condescension, and his maneuvering to win the girl. Indeed, Lawrence tries to make Cyril sympathetic by showing him as being aware that Tom Vickers, with his "beautiful lustihood that is unconscious like a blossom," can give Muriel "some glorious hours" (1:18). Cyril recognizes that he, unlike Tom Vickers, is incapable of such unconscious and direct love. " 'I shall never be blindly in love, shall I?' " he asks Muriel; and she answers, " 'You won't be blindly anything.' " (1:20). Yet she is won over to him and his honesty: " 'You have always been so honest. You are more honest than anybody ever—' " (1:20). When Cyril then asks Muriel to take him "naturally"— though without committing himself to marriage—she draws back; and he recognizes "the woman defensive, playing the coward against her own inclinations, and even against her own knowledge" (1:21). Muriel's fears sting him; it is "as if the glamour went out of life" (1:21); and he decides to leave, "unable to gather his energy to say anything vital" (1:22). The wine of his desire has been spilled, and he is emptied of "all his vitality" (1:22).

As in "Witch à la Mode," the woman is blamed for her cowardice, and the reader is asked to forget the conscious, adroit manipulations of the hero as well as his refusal to commit himself to the woman. Nor does Lawrence recognize clearly the insufferable affectation and play acting of this prig, with his puerile advocacy of Fire. It is noteworthy that during the Croydon years, Ada found her brother's affectation disgusting and told Louie Burrows that she wouldn't marry Lawrence if he were the last man that lived!

Yet Lawrence, at twenty-six, was desperately in need of some woman who could release him from "the shame of self-consciousness" and from what seemed "abnormal" in his situation. But as his engagement to Louie continued through 1911, it became increasingly clear that he was forcing himself to honor the agreement. The difference between him and Louie is sharply underscored in the letters in which he alludes to Louie's conventional aspirations. On Christmas Day 1910, he chides her: "A swell has an immense appeal for you. Don't you pray nightly— 'May I live to be a lady, and die in the cream of fashion'? I know you do" (L, 1:213). He knows that his talk about physical intimacy is "very indelicate and immodest and all that." Although he alludes continually to sexual intimacy, he pleads, "I always want to subscribe to your code of manners, towards you—I know I fail sadly" (30 Oct. 1911, L, 1:321). And to Ada he confesses: "I'm afraid [Louie's] one I shan't tell things to—it only seems to bother her. But it's just as well. In the things that matter, one has to be alone, in this life—or nearly alone" (27 Mar. 1911, L, 1:243). Again, he tells Helen Corke on 14 March 1911 that "the common everyday—rather superficial man of me really loves Louie"; but he goes on to say that "the open-eyed, sad critical, deep seeing man of me" must "humble itself pretty sorely to accept the imposition of the masculine, stupid decree [to marry]. There is a decree for each of us— thou shalt live alone—and we have to put up with it. We may keep real company once in our lives—after that we touch [. . .], now and again, upon someone else—but do not repose" (L, 1:240). Yet again, he writes to Louie on 4 April 1911 (L, 1:251): "I expect everything—life almost: but not—and I never know whether to say unfortunately or happily—a companion in my philosophy:—happily, for it's a philosophy that, shared, would be aggravated to abstruseness and uselessness. Forgive me when I'm priggish and superior." It is as if his philosophy is too sacred, too close to him, or too foreign to the "churchy" Louie, to bear sharing of any kind. And one reason for this is that the philosophy, deriving from Schopenhauer, sees women as the blind agent of the life force that, by a "stupid decree," makes man subservient to the will of the species—and so destroys his proud integrity. All this was clear to Lawrence when he wrote *The White Peacock*. But he had imagined that marriage to Louie might not involve this enslavement—at least not his enslavement to a woman who would seek to possess his soul.

It was not until 4 February 1912 that he could bring himself to admit to Louie what he already knew: "I am afraid we are not well suited" (L, 1:361). His extremely serious illness, he went on to say, "has changed me a good deal, has broken a good many of the old bonds that held me. I can't help it. It is no good to go on." It is as if his illness—and his realization that he might die—had driven him at last to recognize that compromise with the "masculine, stupid decree" was no longer possible. And perhaps more to the point, William Heinemann had given him fifty pounds for *The White Peacock*. Financial independence now seemed, for the first time, within reach. He was not doomed to the life of a schoolteacher and to a fatalistic acquiescence to circumstances—the sort of acquiescence dramatized in his story "Witch à la Mode." He had been going against his own grain for years, and now, for the first time, it seems to have struck him that he did not have to acquiesce or compromise. Freedom was within reach.

It was that knowledge, I suspect, that prevented Lawrence from showing much sympathy for Louie when he saw her on 13 February and she began to cry. "I seemed to be a sort of impersonal creature," Lawrence wrote, "without heart or liver, staring out of a black cloud" (L, 1:366). He was by this time totally committed to his new life. Nothing, not even Louie's tears, could sway him. He had confessed that "the fault is all mine" (L, 1:361). But no confession, and no tears of sympathy, could alter the finality of his determination. If Lawrence here looks cruel, his cruelty toward women was not essentially different from that of a Gandhi, for whom any compromise with his mission would have been unthinkable.

But why, only two months after his break with Louie, did Lawrence fall in love with, and commit himself utterly to, Frieda Weekley? The answer is implicit in all that has been said already about his relationships with women. The woman who could help him free himself from the "mind-forged manacles" of the Midlands—and from a demeaning acquiescence to Respectability—must be one who could give him the courage to "trespass." And this the unconventional and uninhibited Frieda would do as no woman Lawrence had ever met before could do.

Like Tom Brangwen in *The Rainbow*, who, when he meets Lydia Lensky, the "foreign" lady from Poland, realizes instantly, "That's her"; so Lawrence seems to have known at once that Frieda was what he wanted: "Mrs. Weekley is perfectly unconventional," he wrote on 17 April 1912, "but really good—in the best sense" (L, 1:384). Perhaps he sensed what David Garnett saw later (Nehls, 1:197)—that Frieda had "a genius" for expressing love and was "more like a noble animal than most women" or was "a force of nature," as Catherine Carswell said (69). She was the gateway to the freedom that Lawrence needed—not only from the inhibitions and pudency that afflicted him in his young manhood, but also from the middle-class morality and the middle-class expectations that had so oppressively burdened him.

To escape with Frieda to Germany was almost too good to be true. It meant love; it meant freedom; it meant the irrevocable commitment to the mission for which he felt destined. "I feel as if I can't breathe while we're in England," he wrote on 30 April 1912 (L, 1:389). But it was absolutely essential for Lawrence that his flight from England not be construed as immoral—the selfish and treacherous snatching of another man's wife. His love had to be translated into religious terms. Frieda must become the gateway to the Infinite, herself the agent of the divine will that makes possible a new peace—the peace that lies behind, or beneath, the strife of the base temporal world. (Lawrence took particular note of the meaning of her name: "The Peaceful.") In embracing this woman, he would embrace the All—all that is "not-I"—and this embrace was a religious consummation because it entailed the death of the old, egoistic self and the birth of a new self, energized through love and ready to do the will of God (instead of the will of the Croydon Education Committee). Thus the sexual "trespass" became a religious triumph—not a step backward, but a step forward in the striving for individual perfection.

Lawrence did not develop his ideas about love as a religious experience until 1912 and 1913, when he began to write *The Rainbow* and to develop the ideas of *Study of Thomas Hardy*. But as early as 1908, when he was twenty-two, he sensed that love is in some way connected with religious feeling. He wrote to Blanche Jennings on 30 July 1908: "But love is much finer, I think, when not only the sex group of chords is attuned, but the great harmonies, and the little harmonies, of what we will call religious feeling (read it widely) and ordinary sympathetic feeling" (*L*, 1:66). Exactly what he meant by "religious feeling" is clarified in a letter of 15 December 1908:

> Come to think of it and it is exceedingly rare that two people participate in entirely the same sensation and emotion; but they do when they kiss as lovers, I am sure. Then a certain life-current passes through them which changes them forever; another such effect is produced in a mother by the continual soft touchings of her baby. Somehow, I think we come into knowledge (unconscious) of the most vital parts of the cosmos through touching things. You do not know how I feel my soul enlarged through contact with the soft arms and face and body of my Hilda Mary [his landlady's daughter]—who is 9 months old today. I know my phraseology is vague and impossible. But there must be some great purposeful impulses impelling through everything to move it and work it to an end . . . the sympathy with and submission to the great impulses comes through *feeling*—indescribable—and, I think unknowable. (*L*, 1:99)

He does not call the "great purposeful impulses" God; rather, he has in mind Wordsworth's idea of "something far more deeply interfused" or Schopenhauer's idea of the Will as the *ding an sich*, acting in and through the phenomenal world, the great Reality known only through feeling. As he said later, "God in me is my desire." It is through feeling that one somehow establishes a connection with the rest of the cosmos, which is also impelled by the same great purposeful impulses. And he was to generalize his remark about touch when, near the end of his life, he called for "the civilisation of touch."

I shall say more about this in the next chapter, when I consider the early development of Lawrence's "philosophy." For the present, it is enough to observe that when Lawrence committed himself to Frieda, he was, in effect, taking a religious vow. He expected to be "changed forever." The religious note was sounded shortly after they met. On 6 May 1912 he wrote to Frieda, "I'm not keen on coming to your place to lunch tomorrow—but I am in your hands—'into thine hand, O Lord, I commend etc.' " (*L*, 1:391). The next day he wrote to her again, saying, "Don't show this letter to either of your sisters—no. Let us be good. You are clean, but you dirty your feet" (*L*, 1:393). It was essential that their love not be subjected to a defiling gossip. It was also important that it must never be debased by an impatient lust. On 14 May 1912 he wrote: "Look, my dear, now the suspense is going over, we can wait even a bit religiously for one another. My next coming to you is solemn, intrinsically—I am solemn over it—not sad, oh no—but it is my marriage, after all, and a great thing—not a thing to be snatched and clumsily handled" (*L*, 1:401). The next day he presses his idea even further, using language that he also used to refer to his relationship with Louie Burrows in his story "Witch à la Mode":

> Do you know, like the old knights, I seem to want a certain time to prepare myself—a sort of vigil with myself. Because it is a great thing for me to marry you, not a quick, passionate coming together. I know in my heart "here's my marriage." It feels rather terrible—because it is a great thing in my life—it is *my life*—I am a bit awe-inspired—want to get used to it. (*L*, 1:403)

Three years earlier, on a visit to Brighton, he had seen "two ruddy clouds flung together . . . like two lovers at last met in a kiss"; and in that image he saw "a promise of the Annunciation of Love for me" (*L*, 1:127–28). When the promise was fulfilled and when Lawrence had broken through the last barrier of his timidities, he announced: "The world is wonderful and beautiful and good beyond one's wildest imagination. Never, never, never could one conceive what love is, beforehand, never. Life *can* be great—quite god-like. It *can* be so. God be thanked I have proved it" (2 June 1912, *L*, 1:414). He had at last "let go," as he had always believed he must. (Almost four years earlier, he had written: "Where there is no 'abandon' in a love, it is dangerous, I conclude" [*L*, 1:103].) Now in love, he experienced that dissolution of his old self and that submission to the great purposeful impulse, which constituted identification with the divine will. It was this experience with Frieda that he drew upon in depicting the feelings of Paul Morel and Clara Dawes when they make love:

> . . . Clara was not there for him, only a woman, warm, warm, something he loved and almost worshipped, there in the dark. . . . It was all so much bigger than themselves that he was hushed. . . . They felt small, half-afraid, childish and wondering, like Adam and Eve when they lost their innocence and realized the magnificence of the

power which drove them out of Paradise. . . . It was for each of them an initiation and a satisfaction. To know their own nothingness, to know the tremendous living flood which carried them always, gave them rest within themselves. If so great a magnificent power could overwhelm them, identify them altogether with itself, so that they knew they were only grains in the tremendous heave that lifted every grass blade its little height, and every tree, and living thing, then why fret about themselves? They could let themselves be carried by life, and they felt a sort of peace in each other. There was a verification which they had had together. Nothing could nullify it, nothing could take it away: it was almost their belief in life. (*SL*, 353–54)

The passage echoes Lawrence's comments in his letters. Glorying in his escape from England, his freedom, and his love, he wrote to Walter de la Mare on 10 June 1912 that "this is rest, sweet rest" (*L*, 1:417). On 19 August 1912 he wrote: "At any rate, and whatever happens, I do love, and I am loved—I have given and I have taken—and that is eternal" (*L*, 1:441). His "belief," which is strongly indicated in the statement that "it was as if [Paul and Clara] had been agents of a great force," was now "verified"; he had "proved" that life could be great and godlike. What was needed was only abandonment with the right woman. He realized now, as he wrote on 19 August 1912, that the cause of failure in love had been his choice of the wrong women. "I think I ought not to blame women, as I have done, but myself, for taking my love to the wrong women, before now. Let every man find, keep on trying till he finds, the woman who can take him and whose love he can take, then who will grumble about men or about women [i.e., the battle of the sexes]" (*L*, 1:440).

The glory of those months is reflected in the *Look, We Have Come Through!* poems that he wrote during this period of splendor. Unlike the "Man Who Is Not Loved," a man like Paul Morel at the end of *Sons and Lovers*, "isolated in the universe," frightened, feeling himself "infinitely / Small" and (like Siegmund of *The Trespasser*) "too / Little to count," Lawrence declares, "I am myself at last; now I achieve / My very self" (*CP*, 222–23, 218). The lovers together become "One rose of wonderment upon the tree / Of perfect life"; they blossom, fanned by "The Great Breath" (*CP*, 219). Lawrence realizes that Frieda is "*Necessary*, and I have no choice!" (*CP*, 215). "Between her breasts is my home" (*CP*, 249); and he who, earlier, when he kissed the woman he loved, "was kissing also myself," has escaped that obscene narcissism; his old ego is dead; he is now "new-risen, resurrected," "new beyond knowledge of newness, alive beyond life, / proud beyond inkling or furthest conception of pride" (*CP*, 259, 258).

Yet one must beware of overemphasizing their happiness. The love is mixed with pain. The quarrels between Lawrence and Frieda began early in their relationship. For the old problem had not, as he thought, gone away: always there was not only Frieda's yearning for her children—a yearning that he could not help seeing as a kind of betrayal—but also the danger that woman, as agent of the life force, would seek to enslave the man and would oppose his concerted effort to carry out his mission. It was essential that his newly won identity as "the priest of love" not be sullied or compromised. (It was at this time that he used the phrase "priest of love," though later he would say that love is a blasphemy against the Holy Ghost, which always seeks a healthy balance of "love" and "power.") Always there was the danger that he might acquiesce to the status quo: to bourgeois marriage, to tribal mores, and to the base egotism of the irreverent and the unclean, living only for themselves in their limited secular world. Conflict with Frieda and with his friends was inevitable, for they all lived in "temporality," they were incapable of living "in the eternal things" (L, 2:358). By 1915 he declared that Frieda "hates the Infinite" (L, 2:359). But the conflicts that developed after his "coming through" must become the subject of a later chapter. In 1912 he was free at last of conventional English life; he had found his mate; he was ready to do his life's work.

3

LAWRENCE'S
EARLY BELIEFS AND NOVELS

1905–6: Reading of Ralph Waldo Emerson, Henry David Thoreau, Leo Tolstoy, Henrik Ibsen, George Robert Gissing, Oscar Wilde, Honoré de Balzac, Guy de Maupassant, John Locke, John Stuart Mill, Joseph Ernest Renan; **1907 or earlier:** pantheism; belief in impersonal god; **1905–8:** reading of materialists—Charles Darwin, Thomas H. Huxley, Ernst Haeckel, Herbert Spencer, William James; is strongly influenced by Arthur Schopenhauer and Friedrich Nietzsche; reading of socialists and liberals—John Ruskin, William Morris, Bernard Shaw, probably Edward Carpenter, others; meetings at home of Willie and Sallie Hopkin, where socialism, the suffragette movement, and other liberal ideas are advocated; **1906–10:** writing of *The White Peacock*: strong influence of Schopenhauer; **1910 or earlier:** reading of Samuel Butler, George Meredith, W. H. Hudson, George Moore, Arnold Bennett, H. G. Wells, John Galsworthy; Fyodor Dostoevsky, Maxim Gorky, Leo Tolstoy, Ivan Turgenev; Paul Verlaine, Charles Baudelaire, Stendhal; Euripides; Walt Whitman.

W hen he was sixteen, Lawrence said, he rejected his Christian faith. Emile Delavenay, using evidence from *Sons and Lovers*, argues that Lawrence's religious crisis occurred between twenty and twenty-two, but one cannot be sure. What is most significant, in any case, is that Lawrence, a child of his age, could not accept a faith at odds with a tough-minded skepticism and the conclusions of science. He had "yearned," he said in 1907 in a letter to the Reverend Robert Reid (*L,* 1:39), for a conversion "like that of Paul's": "I was constantly endeavouring to give myself, but Sir, to this day I do not understand what this 'giving' consists in, embodies, and includes . . . in the moments of deepest emotion myself has watched myself and seen that all the tumult has risen like a little storm, to die away again without great result. . . . Now I do not believe in conversion, such conversion." In language that recalls Wordsworth's "Tintern Abbey," with its moving meditation on "the still, sad music of humanity" and on the "something far more deeply interfused" that rolls through all things, Lawrence went on to say:

> I believe that a man is converted when first he hears the low, vast murmur of life, of human life, troubling his hitherto unconscious self. I

believe a man is born first unto himself—for the happy developing of himself, while the world is a nursery. . . . But most are born again on entering manhood; then they are born to humanity, to a consciousness of all the laughing, and the never-ceasing murmur of pain and sorrow that comes from the terrible multitudes of brothers. Then, it appears to me, a man gradually formulates his religion, be it what it may . . . and one's religion is never complete and final, it seems, but must always be undergoing modification. So I contend that true Socialism is religion; that honest, fervent politics are religion; that whatever a man will labour for earnestly and in some measure unselfishly is religion. (L, 1:39–40)

The Wordsworthian pantheism appears in a later passage of the letter: "Cosmic harmony there is—a Cosmic God I can therefore believe in. But where is the human harmony, where the balance, the order, the 'indestructibility of matter' in humanity? And where is the *personal, human* God?" (L, 1:41). In 1911 he repeated this idea in a letter to his sister Ada, who had suffered her own religious crisis and was struggling for a new faith. With his characteristic "authority," he declared:

There still remains a God, but not a personal God: a vast, shimmering impulse which waves onwards towards some end, I don't know what— taking no regard of the little individual, but taking regard for humanity. When we die, like rain-drops falling back again into the sea, we fall back into the big, shimmering sea of unorganized life which we call God. We are lost as individuals, yet we count in the whole. (9 Apr. 1911, L, 1:256)

According to Jessie Chambers, Lawrence, having rejected the orthodox creed, "swallowed materialism at a gulp." And for a time he showed some of the dogmatism of the new convert to Science. With a sort of intellectual exhilaration, born of his freedom from superstition and his new, tough-minded skepticism, he adopted a familiar argument against religion: that it is based on childish wish fulfillment. "The secret of religion," he wrote to Blanche Jennings in July of 1908, "is, I think, that one can remain a child without losing any of one's importance. As a matter of fact, most folks are afraid to grow up; that's why they defer it so long. Real independence and self-responsibility are terrifying to the majority; to *all* girls, I think." He sneers at phrases like "the everlasting arms" and "safe on Jesu's breast," and ends: "I miss religion for this only; that I have now no season when I can really 'become again as a little child'" (L, 1:62). Thus he anticipates his lifelong attack on the "grown up children" who abandon all responsibility, seeking "infinite comfort" in conventional religion or in the arms of a woman who will nurse, console, and soothe the infantile male.

But Jessie Chambers's unqualified assertion that he "swallowed materialism at a gulp" is misleading. Certainly Lawrence was deeply influenced by skepticism and materialistic science, as he was deeply influenced by Schopenhauer, William James, and Nietzsche. The "materialism" that Lawrence "swallowed" was not irreligious, however. On the contrary, both Herbert Spencer and Ernst Haeckel had argued that from the point of view of the modern scientist, God must be viewed as an immanent force that manifests itself in all parts of nature. According to Spencer, whom Lawrence read during his second year at Nottingham University (1907), theologian and scientist can agree that there is "an Inscrutable Power manifested to us through all phenomena," and this recognition is "an essentially religious [position]— nay, is *the* religious one" (*First Principles*, 118, 119). Ernst Haeckel, in his *The Riddle of the Universe*, which Lawrence read in 1908, makes a similar observation. For Haeckel, substance or nature is identical with God. "We adhere firmly," he declares, "to the pure, unequivocal monism of Spinoza: Matter, or infinitely extended substance, and spirit (or energy), or sensitive and thinking substance, are the two fundamental attributes or principal properties of the all-embracing divine essence of the world, the universal substance" (21). "God" is "an intramundane being . . . everywhere identical with nature itself, and . . . operative *within* the world as 'force' or energy"; from which it follows "necessarily that pantheism is the world-system of the modern scientist" (288–89).

Even more compelling to the young Lawrence was Schopenhauer's idea of the Will. Thomas Mann, who reached intellectual maturity at about the same time as Lawrence, once remarked that he read Schopenhauer "as one reads only once in a life-time." Lawrence appears to have read Schopenhauer in much the same way. To account for the immense appeal of the Schopenhauerian philosophy to these two artists born toward the end of the nineteenth century, one must understand two things: first, almost all of the scientific thinking of the age *converged* to support Schopenhauer's contention that the will—or the "Unknown"—is manifested in instinct or impulse, in a "force" or "energy" that is in the last analysis unknowable; and second, the will is the naturalistic equivalent of "God": it is the ultimate, eternal, indestructible force that lies beyond, or beneath, the succession of temporal appearances in the phenomenal world. It is the unknown power beyond "God," much like the Hertha of Swinburne's poem:

> God changes, and man, and the form of them
> bodily; I am the soul.

The gods shall die (as Swinburne says in "Hymn to Proserpine"), but the reality endures while "all death and all life, and all reigns and all /

ruins, drop through [Hertha] as sands." It is not surprising that the young Lawrence liked Swinburne as well as Schopenhauer.

The Will is known immediately, not by the mind (which always creates an ideal world, a fictive world of time, multiplicity, causality, etc.), but only in *desire*. Thus Schopenhauer opened the door to Lawrence's later contention that "God is my desire in me." The ultimate reality is seen in sexual desire or in the universal desire for union, even in inorganic matter—"a longing for union which proceeds from the very inner nature of bodies" (Schopenhauer, *Will to Live*, 63). The planets are attracted to one another, yet at the same time there is a resistance to dissolution—a centrifugal force that resists the centripetal attraction. The combination of attraction and repulsion is necessary in order to preserve the existence of the object. The will to live is thus objectified in a pattern of oscillation, as it is objectified also in an alternation of life and death, creation and destruction.

I anticipate here much of Lawrence's *later* psychology and philosophy, which he developed after 1913. But it is clear that the young Lawrence, who read Schopenhauer when he was twenty or twenty-one (in 1905 or 1906) had already taken over a part of the Schopenhauerian philosophy and had connected it with ideas in Darwin, Huxley, Spencer, and Haeckel. His reference to nature's concern for the species, in the letter to Ada, shows the influence not only of Schopenhauer but also of Darwin, whom Lawrence read in 1905, or of Thomas H. Huxley, whom Lawrence read in 1907. In addition, during his early twenties he began to accept the Schopenhauerian idea that feeling or desire is prior to reason, and he found authoritative support for this also in Herbert Spencer and in William James, who regarded mental activity as the *effect* of bodily activity, not the cause of it.

In fact, the whole thrust of advanced opinion during this period of Lawrence's intellectual flowering was directed against the received idea that mind or consciousness is an autonomous instrument, a little god in the machine, capable of originating human conduct. Spencer had argued that consciousness is in the service of the organism seeking to adjust its internal needs to the environment. William James, seizing on Spencer's idea, went on to formulate what came to be known as the James-Lange theory of emotions. According to this theory, physiological activity precedes emotional or conscious response. "I do not strike because I am angry, I am angry because I strike; I do not weep because I am unhappy, I am unhappy because I weep." Love and hatred are not "spiritual"; they are, rather, as Ernst Haeckel suggested, at the very physical foundation of life: they exist as the attraction and repulsion of atoms. Consciousness is in the service of the material body; mind, in the service of "impulse."

What is more, consciousness always creates a *belated* picture of reality. According to William James, the origin of the "I" is the body, its actions and reactions. When consciousness seeks to "know" this origin, it discovers that the "I" has already vanished in the flux of bodily feeling states. The stream of consciousness flows on, but at any given moment the "self" is no more than a Thought that appropriates what has gone before. That Thought gives way presently to another Thought. But to find the "true self," one is returned to the body—or to the *unconscious* desires and fears of the organism.

Thus James confirmed indirectly what Lawrence had found in Schopenhauer and Nietzsche: the mind is not the true man; ideas are falsifications of the intellect, which can never know the reality but only its own representations of reality; the visible world of time, multiplicity, and change is an illusion—*Maya*; to find the reality, one must consult, not the mind, but instinct or intuition. Lawrence's grasp of this view is sharply indicated in a letter I quoted earlier (p. 43) written on 15 December 1908, when he was twenty-three.

> Somehow, I think we come into knowledge (unconscious) of the most vital parts of the cosmos through touching things . . . there must be some great purposeful impulses impelling through everything to move it and work it to an end. The world says you feel the press of these impulses, you recognise them, in knowledge—science; but I, joining hands with the artists, declare that also and supremely the sympathy with and submission to the great impulses comes through *feeling*—indescribable—and, I think unknowable." (*L*, 1:99)

The letter reveals not only Lawrence's implicit acceptance of Schopenhauer's idea that reality is known only in desire but also Lawrence's rejection of a purely mechanistic science that would "explain" life as mere "force" or "energy" or chemical interactions. The science that Lawrence encountered as a student at University College in 1908 did not in the least "explain" the underlying reality. And that was one of the reasons for Lawrence's profound disillusionment with the university. As he said in September 1908, "Now though I am conceited, one of the cruellest shocks I ever had was to find that half the professionals in college were not superior to me in intellect or character. I am timid before people whom I respect as my superiors, but I feel confident even to insolence before my inferiors" (*L*, 1:72). The intellectual inferiority of his teachers is vividly suggested in *The Rainbow*, when Ursula makes her first encounter with pedestrian minds that are not philosophical:

> The professors were not priests initiated into the deep mysteries of life and knowledge. . . . This was no religious retreat, no seclusion of pure learning. It was a little apprenticeship where one was further equipped

> for making money. . . . It was a sham store, a sham warehouse, with a single motive of material gain, and no productivity. . . . Had she not gone to hear the echo of learning pulsing back to the source of the mystery? (*R*, 435–36)

Only in botany laboratory does "the mystery still glimmer" for Ursula. Yet the "explanation" of life presented by the woman doctor of physics, Dr. Frankstone (a variant of Frankenstein?), stops short at the purely mechanical:

> "No, really," Dr. Frankstone had said, "I don't see why we should attribute some special mystery to life—do you? We don't understand it as we understand electricity, even, but that doesn't warrant our saying it is something special, something different in kind and distinct from everything else in the universe—do you think it does? May it not be that life consists in a complexity of physical and chemical activities, of the same order as the activities we already know in science? (*R*, 440)

But Ursula knows that something is left out of this explanation. If life is "an impersonal force," "where then was its will? If it was a conjunction of forces, physical and chemical, what held these forces unified, and for what purpose were they unified?" (441). The answer that flashes into her mind, in "an intensely-gleaming light of knowledge," is that life is "not limited mechanical energy, nor mere purpose of self-preservation and self-assertion. It was a consummation, a being infinite. Self was a oneness with the infinite. To be oneself was a supreme, gleaming triumph of infinity" (441).

Behind the visible world of force lies the invisible world of the will—the divine impulse working in and through all things. Self is an expresion of that will. The deep desires of the self are the will itself, objectified in action.

How far Lawrence went in developing this idea before 1913 is difficult to say. In his new, tough-minded mood, he certainly accepted the view of nature as an impersonal will, indifferent to the aspirations of the individual. At the same time, however, he did not view life as necessarily condemned to the blind, mechanical carrying out of this impersonal will. Most men and women were indeed the innocent victims of the Life Force; most could only submit blindly to the great decrees of the will. But Lawrence also felt strongly that in some few individuals there was an imperative desire to rise above the blind submission—those few who, like Nietzsche's Zarathustra, are able to assume responsibility for their lives instead of allowing nature or society to drive them into bondage. Indirectly, he was dramatizing the question that he put to himself as a man conscious of a special mission and responsibility in life: Am I, like all the others, condemmed to submission to the marriage trap and to respectability? Or am I unique? Do I have the courage to break free—to rise above the sad entanglements of a life that has no other purpose than survival?

Here Lawrence's debt to the climate of opinion in the Midlands at the turn of the century cannot be overemphasized. In 1905 he met Alice Dax, a socialist and a suffragette, the emancipated woman who "gave Bert sex." Alice Dax was an intimate friend of Sallie Hopkin, the first wife of Willie Hopkin, a former colliery clerk who had become a county councillor. The "Hopkin-Dax circle," as Emile Delavenay called it, was passionately interested in feminism, socialism, and the opening of the door to a free, wider life. Among those who visited the house of Sallie and Willie Hopkin were Philip Snowden, Ramsay MacDonald, Beatrice and Sidney Webb, Keir Hardie, and Edward Carpenter. In the working Midlands, this vigorous intelligentsia gathered, "mentally evolving," as Emile Delavenay observes, "in the wake of Ruskin and William Morris and Annie Besant, of early Fabianism and of the Fellowship of the New Life, when there began to spread widely among the élite of the working masses ideas of emancipation of the individual not only from political and economic dependence, but from the moral constraints of the Victorian middle class" (*D. H. Lawrence and Edward Carpenter*, 11). Lawrence had read Ruskin and probably the socialist prose of Morris. He liked Shaw's *Man and Superman*. There was a religious fervor in socialist ideas that Lawrence was bound to respond to. As Louis Blanc declared that socialism is the Gospel carried into action, Lawrence found it easy to say that "true Socialism is religion." Evolution and revolution were in the air. Vitalism was pitted against the dismal fatalism of the mechanists. Aspiration or desire, a deep will to perfection, these, as Bernard Shaw believed, could lift humanity up to the new consciousness and the new life and would cleanse England of the corruption and horror of a century of blind and callous industrialism and capitalism.

Of all those whose ideas inflamed the young Lawrence, one of the most appealing was probably Edward Carpenter. It has not been proved beyond doubt that Lawrence read Carpenter, but Emile Delavenay has shown, with his customary thoroughness, that in 1906 Alice Dax lent Jessie Chambers a copy of Carpenter's *Love's Coming of Age*. Delavenay argues persuasively that "the influence of Carpenter's studies and ideas is present from the very first in Lawrence's prose"—an influence that rose to the "high-water mark" between "the end of 1912 and the end end of 1916" (*Lawrence and Carpenter*, 37). According to Delavenay, Carpenter became "an integral part of Lawrence's own thinking" (44), the younger man embracing not only Carpenter's revolt against "the more crushing aspects of Victorian life" but also the psychology and the religious mysticism that Carpenter used to prescribe a "cure" for the disease of civilization.

Internal evidence suggests that Carpenter's influence reached into a number of obscure corners of Lawrence's thinking, but the essential influence—by no means traceable *only* to Carpenter—may be summarized under four headings: (1) Naturalism; (2) the "Fall" from Harmony with Nature; (3) Regeneration through New Love Relationships; and (4) Cosmic Consciousness and the Development of a New Race of Men.

Carpenter's Naturalism—so typical of that post-Darwinian age—is reflected in his wholehearted acceptance of human sexuality as a manifestation of "cosmic energies." Such an idea's appeal to the inhibited Lawrence was comparable to the appeal of Schopenhauer, Nietzsche, or Havelock Ellis, all of whom view human sexuality in the context of animal behavior and of the deep will of Nature. As Schopenhauer had argued that the inner nature of the will is the desire that ensures the perpetuation of the species, so Carpenter, in *Love's Coming of Age*, observes that Nature "has her own purposes to work out, which in a sense have nothing to do with the individual—her racial purposes" (3). When a person is in love, "he feels a superhuman impulse—and naturally so, for he identifies himself with cosmic energies and entities . . . he lets himself go, rejoicing in the sense of limitless power beneath him—borne onwards like a man down rapids, too intoxicated with the glory of motion to think of whither he is going" (3-4). Reading these passages, one recalls not only the dilemma confronted by the lovers in *The White Peacock*—poor, hapless victims of the Life Force—but also the glory of Paul's and Clara's love-making, in which they become agents of the cosmic will. Love *in all its forms*, said Carpenter, is Nature's will and is part and parcel of a healthy life. The only necessity is that love be expressed spontaneously and freely. Given freedom of expression, Love can lead to the building up of a new world with "higher groupings and finer forms of structure" (*Civilization: Its Cause and Cure*, 108).

But the development of civilization has crippled man's capacity to feel spontaneously. With its artificial and life-denying moral and social codes, civilization is "a temporary alienation from true life" (*Civilization*, 160). (In the same vein, Havelock Ellis spoke of "the whole of religion" as a "remolding of nature, a repression of natural impulses" [*Studies in the Psychology of Sex*, 1:98].) In matters of love, civilized man is "for the most part a child" (*Love's Coming of Age*, 25). He is "the ungrown, half-baked," a creature in whom "affection and tenderness of feeling . . . have never . . . been developed" (*Love's Coming of Age*, 28, 29). As Carpenter condemns the ungrown men "who have the sway of the world to-day"—men who "underneath" are no more developed "than a public schoolboy" (30)—so Lawrence in all of his novels, beginning with *The White Peacock*, would attack the "half-created" and infantile men who fail to "come into being"—men like Gerald Crich or Clifford Chatterley or countless members of the accursed bourgeoisie who have gone "soft" beneath an outward show of competence. Carpenter also condemns those who have defiled sex, "slimed over" it by making the object of sex "our own gratification" instead of a religious union; so Lawrence, with the same puritanical fervor, would inveigh against the "Joy-Hogs" for whom "thrills" and "sensations" are the sole object of life. Like Carpenter, Lawrence brought a Victorian piety to his celebration of the sacred mysteries, and he would heartily have agreed with Carpenter's detestation of those who had made sex "a thing covert and to be ashamed of, marketable and unclean" (*Love's Coming of Age*, 15, 19).

The only cure for the sickness of civilization, Carpenter argued (in the vein of Ibsen, whose *Ghosts* sounded the warning with prodigious effect), is "to undo the bands of death which encircle the present society, and open the doors to a new and wider life" (*Love's Coming of Age*, 71). This new life would become possible only when capitalism and property are abolished and replaced by a form of socialism. The entire relationship between man and woman must change. Woman must cease to be "a serf," a chattel, and must acquire a new freedom and dignity. The proper relationship between man and woman must be that of freedom and unity. As Emile Delavenay has pointed out, Carpenter uses, in defining the ideal relationship between husband and wife, a metaphor very similar to the stars-in-conjunction metaphor that Lawrence would use in *Women in Love*: husband and wife would be like "two suns which, revolving in fluent and rebounding curves, only recede from each other in order to return again with renewed swiftness into close proximity—and which together blend their rays into the glory of one double star" (*Love's Coming of Age*, 103–4). The two are together, yet separate. Fulfillment is found not only in the yoke of love but also in the immense enlargement and clarification of selfhood which love makes possible. For Carpenter saw physical love as "an interchange of vital and ethereal elements," including the cells of the body, "so that it might be said there is a kind of generation taking place *within* each of the persons concerned, through their mutual influence on each other" (23). Lawrence was to accept this idea entirely, as he would accept also (in 1914) the notion that "generation is a secondary object or result" of union: the primary object is "non-differentiation—absolute union of being" (*Love's Coming of Age*, 21–22, 20). Carpenter argues, moreover, that sexual love provides, for the male, that rejuvenating energy which is essential to spur him on in his creative effort to build a new world. He states that woman is "nearer" to "the great unconscious processes of Nature," while man is a sort of adventurer who, "after his excursions and wanderings, mental and physical, continually tends to return [to woman] as to his primitive home and resting-place, to restore his balance, to find his centre of life, and to draw stores of energy and inspiration for fresh conquests of the outer world" (*Love's Coming of Age,* 40). No idea was more important in Lawrence's conception of love than this; and as I have shown in the preceding chapter, the vocabulary of "rest" and regeneration was central in Lawrence's conception of his relationship to woman.

Yet the establishing of a satisfactory marriage is not enough. Like Nietzsche, Carpenter inveighs against the spectacle of a host of couples "in pair," the dreadful *"égoisme à deux"* which causes a man to perish "from all manhood and social or heroic uses into a mere matrimonial clothespeg" (*Love's Coming of Age,* 81–82). Marriage "cuts [the pair] off from the world, . . . barring any openly affectional relations with outsiders, and corroborating the selfish sense of monopoly which each has in the other" (89). There is obviously a deep need for a "less pettily exclusive relationship" (100), and Carpenter followed his favorite poet, Whitman, in calling for the love of comrades, a love that Carpenter, with his strong homosexual inclinations, found in the "greatest men" of "the most remarkable society known to history"—Greece.

As early as 1908, Lawrence, with his sense of a higher mission burning in him, was quick to affirm, with Carpenter, that the *égoisme à deux* of marriage is an insufferable negation of one's desire for sympathetic unison with those outside the marriage coop. (In *Women in Love,* Lawrence uses the phrase *"égoisme à deux."*) And with his strong bisexual feelings, Lawrence did not hesitate to argue that the greatest men tend toward homosexuality and tend to endorse an idealized notion of the love of comrades. As Delavenay argues, Rupert Birkin of *Women in Love,* who loves both Gerald Crich and Ursula, becomes the prototype of the future man, the androgynous superman who exhibits the amalgamated or "intermediate" consciousness, both female and male. Delavenay shows convincingly that the characteristics of Carpenter's new human types, "the teachers of future Society," are exactly those of Birkin and of Lawrence. These "Urnings" (men from Uranos) have special psychological powers: they are men in whom intuition is always strong; they are excellent sick nurses; they are by their nature drawn near to women, though not inclined to fall in love with them; and they can interpret men and women "to each other" (Delavenay, *Lawrence and Carpenter,* 210–11). Moreover, Delavenay argues, the action of *The Rainbow,* with its progress from a "Golden Age" through self-consciousness and civilization to a new paradisal state in which a "cosmic consciousness" is acquired, so that all of experience is seen in relation to the "Great Self" of the universe—this is the artistic embodiment of Carpenter's idea of three great stages of consciousness.

If Lawrence did indeed use all of these ideas, his use occurred after 1912, however, and I have violated chronology to emphasize here the depth of the impression that Carpenter—or Carpenter-like thinking—made on Lawrence in his intellectual development. Perhaps the most significant idea, for the younger Lawrence, was that the project of building a new heaven and a new earth could not be confined to political and economic changes, however sweeping. What was needed, if a new, healthy humanity was to arise, was a new consciousness, a new naturalism joined to the religious sense of the unity of all things: *tat tvam asi*. The basis of this cosmic unity was *feeling*, the impulse that attracted one body to another and ultimately to identification with the All. Carpenter, using an idea derived from J. G. Davey's *The Ganglionic Nervous System*, argued that the "Great Sympathetic" (system of nerves) is the seat of emotion. That argument may have provided Lawrence with a physiological center that he could use in developing his theory of the unconscious (see Delavenay, 129–30). Through desire, through sympathetic attraction, one is united with others and ultimately with the whole of the cosmos. The ego, the separate individual self, is an illusion. As Carpenter said, the "Me-conception" had to disappear before the True Self could appear—a self united to others, eternal (quoted in Delavenay, 132).

The mysticism of this last idea probably had only a limited appeal to Lawrence at this early period of his life. Lawrence remained, generally speaking, in the camp of the materialists and the naturalists; and although he was receptive to mystical speculations, he preferred to ground his conclusions on the best scientific evidence of his time. For that reason, the tough-minded Nietzsche was probably at this time (1908–12) a far deeper influence than was Carpenter or any other mystical writer.

How much of Nietzsche he read in 1907 and thereafter is difficult to determine. According to Jessie Chambers, Lawrence began to talk about Nietzsche's ideas after going to Croydon. The Croydon Central Library shelved a generous selection of Nietzsche's works, and we know that Lawrence read *The Will to Power, The Gay Science* (in 1915), and *Thus Spoke Zarathustra*, works that contain everything essential in Nietzsche. In truth, Lawrence's thought corresponds so closely on so many counts to Nietzsche's that it is obvious the German philosopher was one of Lawrence's greatest passions. The reasons for that appeal are innumerable.

Perhaps the most important is that Nietzsche, with his emphasis on the pride of the noble man and his fierce insistence on the mission of the higher man, was in significant ways the sort of radical preacher and proponent of life whom Lawrence wished to imitate. Nietzsche's critical philosophy and his psychology seemed to carry nineteenth-century naturalism to its ultimate conclusions. Following Schopenhauer, Nietzsche argued that man is motivated, not by spirit or mind ("There are no mental causes," he said), but by the deep instinctive will—which is not just a will to live but also a will to power. Unlike Schopenhauer, however, Nietzsche was not pessimistic; on the contrary, he was contemptuous of fatalism and classical pessimism. While rejecting free will and the idea of man's accountability, he nevertheless affirmed the creative force and zest of the higher man, who, feeling "plenitude" and "power which seeks to overflow," is a creator of values. The higher man is a bold and healthy animal-aristocrat-*homo religiosus* who despises a base, plebeian safety and *ressentiment*, a plebeian desire for "narcosis, stupefaction, rest, peace, 'Sabbath' " (*Nietzsche Reader* [hereafter cited as *NR*], 113), just as he scorns the rabble's base desire for money and personal power. In the higher man, the *Wille zur Macht* flowers as a noble wish to destroy what is worn out and hostile to life, and to create a new, vital world in which the instincts are not condemned but rather are joyfully affirmed, with the joy of the Dionysian poet who says yes to life and to eternal recurrence, a joy that also "encompasses joy in destruction" (*NR*, 147). "Everything *good* is instinct"; every error is "a degeneration of instinct" (*NR*, 163).

The liberation that the higher man holds out to the guilt-stricken victims of a life-denying religion and a paralyzing "spirituality" is inseparable from the attack on the received idea that reason and consciousness are originators of action. Consciousness, Nietzsche argues, is "the last and latest development of the organic and consequently also the most unfinished and weakest part of it" (*NR*, 158). "Thinking which has become *conscious* is only the smallest part of [thought]" and "the worst part." "Man, like every living creature, thinks continually but does not know it" (*NR*, 66). Man's deepest and most accurate thought is unconscious. Conscious thought is "an illness" and, as Henri Bergson also held, a falsification of reality.

In Nietzsche's "deconstruction" of the received ideas that dominate in Western civilization, inevitably those ideas that poison life and that seek to destroy the passions were the ones singled out for his most vehement attacks. Thus he argued that Christianity, with its abhorrence of the body and of the world itself, signifies, at bottom, "a will to nothingness, a will directed against life, a rebellion against the most fundamental presupposition of life" (*NR*, 162). The ideas of good and evil express "the herd instinct"; for the herd, with its "slave morality," all the virtues of the powerful, of the noble man, the aristocrat, become evil. In truth, however, "there are no moral phenomena at all, only a moral interpretation of phenomena" (*NR*, 104). Statements like this were what Lawrence had in mind when he said to Jessie Chambers, "With *should* and *ought* I have nothing to do."

In two important respects, Nietzsche's ideas were opposed to those of Edward Carpenter. According to Nietzsche, the ideas of "love" and "love of neighbor" are lies perpetuated by Christianity and by romanticism (*NR*, 172). Behind the teaching of "the sympathetic affections and of pity" and the teaching of Brotherhood and the Common Welfare was a desire for "nothing less than a fundamental remoulding, indeed weakening and abolition of the *individual*" (*NR*, 94). Nietzsche's hatred of a democratic rabble, the "ant-swarm" who seek to stamp out a proud individuality and who insist on submission to the ideals of selflessness and self-sacrifice for the common good, is undoubtedly one of the great sources of Lawrence's thought: and in this, too, Nietzsche differed from Carpenter.

How early Lawrence began to embrace Nietzsche's thinking is difficult to tell. We know that he read Nietzsche in 1907. It was in 1910 that he said to Jessie, "With *should* and *ought* I have nothing to do." And to Louie Burrows, whose prudery he was trying to undo, he said, "I say only that is wicked which is a violation of one's feeling and instinct" (quoted in Delavenay, p. 73). Emile Delavenay has observed that Lawrence at this time was still "paralysed by shyness" (62). Lawrence apparently needed Nietzsche, as he needed writers like Edward Carpenter, to support him in his effort to "come through" and triumph over his Victorian inhibitions. But Nietzschean ideas were at this time "in the air." Anthony West has pointed out that, by the beginning of 1912,

> the young heroes like Ezra Pound and Wyndham Lewis, whom my mother [Rebecca West] was meeting under Ford and Violet's roof at South Lodge, were full of talk of the "morals of masters," the "moral freedom of the Übermensch," and of the necessity for rejecting the slave ethics of Christianity, particularly in the degenerate form they had assumed as part of the ideology of secular humanism.
> . . . My mother, like many others in her age group, was badly taken in by its [Nietzsche's language's] false vigor, and was soon . . . adapting his tropes for her own purposes. ("Mother and Son," *New York Review of Books*, vol. 31, no. 3 [1 Mar. 1984], p. 11)

West adds that his mother wrote in "The Lamp of Hatred": "A strong hatred . . . is the best lamp to bear in our hands as we go over the dark places of life cutting away the dead things that men tell us to revere" (p.

12). Such a passage is useful to remind one that Lawrence's Nietzschean anger—his rage particularly against "the slave ethics of Christianity" in the "degenerate form" of "secular humanism"—was not necessarily an expression of his idiosyncrasy but reflected the rather widely held view that the repression of instinct had indeed been poisonous and that a scalpel was needed to cut away the dead flesh of civilization.

Perhaps Nietzsche's naturalistic acceptance of egoism as a fact of animal and human life—his effort to extirpate the inhibitions that men feel because of their egoism—temporarily encouraged Lawrence to throw off his own "bad conscience." As a young man beginning his first novel, The White Peacock, he was all too conscious of his Nietzschean uniqueness. His letters from 1908 to 1910 often reveal an affected, self-conscious, and egoistical manner that appears in the hero of some of his early stories—the Young Man who has read Nietzsche. He sees himself as witty and sparkling; he is prone to self-conscious attitudinizing. "My nature is versatile and volatile," he writes glibly. And he regurgitates Nietzsche with studied zest: "I never admire the *strength* of mountains and fixed rocks; but the strength of the sea that leaps and foams frantically and slips back in a tame underwash; strength that laughs and winks, that mocks, and mocks; and broods awhile, and is sullen—I am fascinated by that sort" (L, 1:88).

As I observed in the last chapter, it is not surprising that Lawrence's sister found that "his flippant and really artificial manner gets on my nerves dreadfully" (L, 1:361). But if there was considerable self-conscious posing during this period of his early twenties, there was an underlying seriousness in his declarations of belief. When he said, "I believe in life, and am determined not to waste myself battling against the worlds inertia and contrariness. Hurray!" (L, 1:72), the sense of his mission as a spokesman for the life force is linked to his awareness that he must not "waste himself" in futile or irrelevant battles. As he wrote in March 1911: "I must pluck the very concentrated heart out of each of my mysteries and desires. I go straight, like a bullet, towards my aim. I cannot loiter by the way." In this letter he acknowledged: "I am really dangerous in my fixed mad aim. I love my rose, and no other: . . . What I want I want and quarter measures are nothing to me. I am a nuisance and a trouble to everybody. Always I am cursing myself, but it doesn't alter me what I am" (L, 1:237). In his "fixed mad aim" to carry out his appointed task, he was shrewd enough to detect the dangers of an obsession. But nothing must stand in his way. He had to be free to do his work; any interference with his development must be ruthlessly brushed aside.

The theme of freedom to develop and to assume self-responsibility—freedom to break the cords that prevent one from achieving the full development of one's possibilities—is indeed a kind of obsession in his early fiction. True, the imprint of Schopenhauer and of Thomas Hardy is strong in these earliest works, but the courage of the Nietzschean higher man, with his noble will to power, is pitted against a passive, fatalistic acquiescence to the will of blind nature. Like Schopenhauer (and George Bernard Shaw, August Strindberg, and many others), Lawrence sees sex as the great trap in which the aspiring male is caught—and held fast. The Schopenhauerian Will is pitiless. With a blind ingenuity, it throws men and women together. The preservation of the species requires that the "type" be maintained, and as Schopenhauer held, each is condemmed to be attracted to that which he or she lacks: the intelligent woman loves the stupid man; the intelligent man is ensnared by the stupid woman. Caught in the remorseless workings of the Will, generations arise and are cut down. The alternation of creation and destruction goes on, a continuous process that is indifferent to the human aspiration to transcend nature's blind will and to climb up out of the trap.

The young Lawrence, keenly aware of the misery caused by the mismatch of his father and mother, was determined *not* to be caught in a similar trap. As early as 1908 he was taking note of the disastrous consequences of marriage in the lives of his friends. As Schopenhauer had held that the genius of the species is at war with the genius of individuals and as Nietzsche had argued that marriage destroys the integrity of the higher man, so Lawrence, as he wrote *The White Peacock* in 1908, mused: "I am not sure whether the chords of sex, and the fine chords of noble feeling do not inevitably produce a discord; in other words, whether one could possibly marry and hold as a wife a woman before whom one's soul sounded its deepest notes. . . . It is a cruel, stultifying shame when married folk give up their friends" (L, 1:67). With this view of love and marriage, it is hardly surprising that Lawrence could declare, in November 1909: "I do *not* believe in love: mon Dieu, I don't, not for me: I never could believe in anything I cannot experience or, which is equivalent 'imagine' " (L, 1:141).

When Alice Dax, the bright proponent of women's freedom, married and had a baby, Lawrence saw still another evidence of the disastrous effects of the sex drive: "She has no mind left; she has no interest in anything but 'Son'. Hélas" (L, 1:69). Again, even as he was attempting to bed Helen Corke, he was intensely aware of the dangers to the *individual* in an intimate relationship: "We have broken down the bounds of the individual," he wrote to Helen on 14 March 1911, "—it is true—that's why it is perfectly honorable for you to take me: but with the bounds of the individual broken down, there is too deadly concentrated an intercourse not to be destructive" (L, 1:239). As always,

Lawrence fears his own destruction at the hands of the devouring woman. Four months later, on a holiday to Dover, he rejoices in his solitude—and with a particular bitterness, born of Helen's frustration of his sexual desire, repents the ignominy of his pleadings: "I have been extraordinarily happy by myself at Dover. There has been nothing to push back, nothing to get ironic over. . . . I think I can manage to live alone body and soul as long as must be. Never, never,—and I *can* keep my soul's vows—never never will I ask a woman for anything again: I will pay her market price" (*L*, 286). There is a strong suggestion here that any contact with others is defiling: it leads one to "push back" one's deepest feelings or to "get ironic"—and hence to betray the deepest convictions that one holds. Indeed, this theme is implicit in the whole of *Sons and Lovers*, in which Lawrence shows that every contact with women—and with society—is a threat to the free development of Paul's soul.

In *The White Peacock* Lawrence's picture of men and women condemned to carry out the remorseless decrees of nature and of society—and deeply frustrated by their acquiescence to those decrees—is drawn with a detachment remarkable in a young novelist. All the young people whom Lawrence presents yearn for freedom and the fulfillment of their deepest unconscious desires. All but the narrator, Cyril, who is the detached Lawrence, the contemplator of the remorseless process, acquiesce to the pressures of society.

Lettie, "The White Peacock," a spiritual woman who wishes to "break free," is attracted to her opposite, George Saxton, the "primitive man," who is inert and largely unconscious; but she allows herself to be married off to Leslie Tempest, who is conscious and respectable, and the couple are condemmed to live "a small indoor existence with artificial light and padded upholstery" (*WP*, 287). George Saxton is awakened by Lettie to the possibilities of a new life, but when Lettie marries Leslie Tempest, George turns to the sensual Meg, and as Meg becomes "mistress and sole authority," "a beautiful, unassailable tower of strength," George becomes her servant and, unable to make himself "whole and complete," drinks himself toward certain death (272, 289, 235). Other characters are similarly trapped and doomed. The volatile, restless Alice marries a clerk, and "all her little crackling fires were sodded down with the sods of British respectability" (312). Emily, who (like Jessie Chambers) has sought to free herself through her relationship with Cyril (Lawrence), marries a stolid Englishman and retreats into the "shadows" and "ease" of traditional life: thus she escapes from "the torture of strange, complex modern life" (316). As the coal miners of the district are "imprisoned underground," so the middle-class men and women are all imprisoned and "netted" by their submission to social convention and to "Fate." All are passive victims—all, that is, but the narrator, Cyril, who removes himself from the battle, contemplates the spectacle, and is left at the end in an ambiguous position, not subservient to the Magna Mater, who has devoured the other males, but isolated, detached, apparently still yearning to escape his "rooted loneliness." Cyril alone is not a mere victim and pawn of the immanent will. But the unresolved question hovers over the novel: Can *anyone* escape the trap of blind nature and the prison of society? Can anyone "flower"? If so, how?

Indirectly, the novel reflects the great debate in Lawrence's time between deterministic materialism and Bergsonian or Shavian vitalism, which stresses creative evolution and purposive striving as the agent of progress. Lawrence is obviously impressed by *both* points of view. On the one hand, he sees clearly the remorseless process of creation and destruction in which men, like other animals, are caught and held. Life arises, flowers, and is cut down; and men, as part of the universal process, arise and perish without ever realizing their full potentialities. On the other hand, Lawrence sees that acquiescence to the blind will of nature or of society is the result of a failure to accept self-responsibility. Lettie, for example, decides to

> ignore her own self, to empty her own potentialities into the vessel of another or others, and to live her life at second hand. This peculiar abnegation of self is the resource of a woman for the escaping of the responsibilities of her own development. . . . To be responsible for the good progress of one's life is terrifying. It is the most insufferable form of loneliness, and the heaviest of responsibilities. (WP, 280)

Lawrence saw that most men and women are not strong enough to accept "the heaviest of responsibilities"; but the lonely Cyril is different. Although he has no clear idea of how it is possible to "flower" or achieve "maximum of being," he remains detached and self-possessed; at least he has not been trapped, either by blind nature or by social pressures.

Lawrence's treatment of the failure to break free from the sexual trap is equally remorseless in his second novel, *The Trespasser.* Here, as in *The White Peacock*, Lawrence raises the question of whether the hero has the courage to "trespass" against the decrees of society and of nature. The hero, Siegmund, married and the father of two children, is drawn irresistibly to Helena, whom he has arranged to meet on the Isle of Wight for a fortnight of passion. Siegmund's life has gone stale, and he looks on love as his path to a release, a new freedom, and a completion. Yet Helena fears his possessive love—fears that she will be obliterated by it. She is like the "Helen" of several poems that Lawrence wrote at this time—Helen Corke, who provided Lawrence with the materials for this novel. A spiritual or "dreaming woman," she wants a lover who will satisfy her desire for Love without subjecting her to the degrading coarseness of animal sex. She submits to Siegmund, but his confidence and joy, born of his sexual fulfillment, seem to nullify her as an individual. A contest ensues. Each needs the other; but each resents the other's threat to his or her individuality. Siegmund, when Helena turns away from him, feels her indifference, senses that she is only *using* him. A cosmic struggle is reflected in the covert battle of the lovers. The male sun wars with the female moon; fire with water; light with darkness. The male knows that he must have the courage to strive beyond himself—to climb up out of the dark female waters that threaten to engulf him. But he lacks the courage to continue to "trespass," and in the end, broken by his moral failure, he returns to his wife and children—and commits suicide. Helena, however, continues to search for her Ideal Man—a pure spirit, not an animal—and at the end she has singled out a man named Byrne to take Siegmund's place. In the grip of the life force, she is forced into conjunction with another male against her inner desire for independence.

Thus *two wills* are manifested in human behavior: the will to union, and the will to separateness and self-responsibility. Lawrence, with his keen feeling of the necessity to remain inviolate and with his urgent need to do his life's work despite all obstacles, had seen that "love" is countered by the self-assertion of a "power" impulse. All of his later psychology would become a variation on the theme of this fundamental opposition in the human psyche, an opposition even more basic than that of spirit and "the blood."

Even in these early novels, Lawrence's detachment is impressive. In contemplating the plight of men and women impelled by these two great contrary urges, Lawrence generally shows the attitude, remarked later in his life by Earl H. Brewster, of "the doctor who wishes to heal" (Nehls, 3:135). Lawrence's detachment and sympathy are manifested in his keen sense of the ways in which the dignity of his characters is violated by nature and by society. Implicitly, Lawrence asks his reader to view the characters as potential "lords of life." They command his respect. If they fail to break free, Lawrence examines the motives and circumstances that cause their failure; he does not satirize or condemn. His attitude is vividly suggested in a letter of 6 March 1909, in which he attacks H. G. Wells: "One thing Wells lacks—the subtle soul of sympathy of a true artist . . . he doesn't do his people justice. . . . Everybody is great at some time or other—and has dignity, I am sure, pure dignity. But only one or two of Wells' people have even a touch of sincerity and dignity—the rest are bladders" (L, 1:119). In the same vein, he praised Balzac's *Eugénie Grandet:* "Can you find a touch of melodrama, or caricature, or flippancy? It is all in tremendous earnestness, more serious than all the profundities of German thinkers, more affecting than all English bathos" (11 Nov. 1908, *L*, 1:91). In his effort to show "the subtle soul of sympathy," Lawrence brought even to his early art his maternal sense of obligation to recognize the deep needs of people living in "strange complex modern times." And at the same time he brought the objectivity that, according to Helen Corke, he regarded as "the essential of great art" (Page, 74).

His objectivity and the impersonality of his psychological and philosophical vision are reflected in the symbolic scheme that he was building up to present the basic tensions in human relationships and in the cosmos. He had begun in *The White Peacock* with the opposition between the watery valley of Nethermere, in which life stagnates, and the "fire" of a striving consciousness that seeks to rise up out of the valley, escaping the bondage of matter. He had also worked into his first novel the symbolic oppositions of life and death—the great creative and destructive powers of the Unknown, in relation to which human life must be seen. Now, in *The Trespasser*, his symbolism shows a surprising proliferation and refinement. Drawing on various sources—it is difficult to single out the chief ones—he creates the symbolic war of fire and water, sun and moon, day and night, light and darkness, spirit and flesh, male and female. The clash of opposites is a manifestation of the cosmic struggle, the great oscillation of action and reaction that Herbert Spencer had defined, or the Empedoclean "love and hate" of the elements that Ernst Haeckel had updated as a principle of modern science, or the Schopenhauerian and Nietzschean vision of the antinomy of life and mind, which so deeply impressed another symbolist, Thomas Mann. When Helen Corke described Cyril as "the impersonal, bodiless intelligence," she must have realized how prone Lawrence's mind was to view experience in relation to the fundamental elements and rhythms of the cosmos.

As Lawrence developed this symbolism, he was obviously searching not just for artistic design but also for a symbolism to articulate the great insights of science and philosophy. Gradually his symbolic scheme would acquire richer implications. When he read Katherine L. Jenner's *Christian Symbolism* in 1914, he learned that Greek, Egyptian, and Jewish sources had been used extensively in the creation of the Christian symbolism of light, the cross, the soul, and so forth. The insights of many ancient religions could be fused in his symbolism, and to these ancient symbols he could wed "scientific" ideas of the nature of the God-stuff. He was particularly stimulated, as he shows in a letter to Gordon Campbell (*L*, 2:246–50), by the idea of "the mutual love of the Father and the Son" and the conception of the Holy Ghost as "the

Reconciler, the Comforter, the Annunciation.'' Jenner points out that
"the predominant characteristic of Almighty God in the Old Testament
is power" (26); Lawrence, in "The Crown," would figure God the
Father as power, blood, body or matter, darkness, and origin, while
God the Son became love, spirit, light, and "end"—the two Infinites of
Matter and Spirit (or Energy) that are joined by the Holy Ghost in the act
of creation. Again, when Lawrence read the Greek philosophers, he
found that their ideas could be wedded to the insights of Herbert
Spencer and Schopenhauer, so that the opposition of fire and water, of
dry and moist, of day and night, assumed a kind of scientific validity for
Lawrence, not just a poetic coherence. Later on, Lawrence came to view
myth, too, as having a psychological validity of the sort that C. G. Jung
stressed—validity as an expression of the unconscious mind seeking
balance. As Lawrence held in *The Symbolic Meaning*, "Myth is the
utterance of the primary self-knowledge of the dynamic psyche of man"
(Arundel: Centaur Press, 1962, p. 136). Using myths of the death and
resurrection of the god, he could articulate the great truth of eternal
recurrence, the truth of ancient Dionysian affirmation, and the truth of
the indestructibility of man's true nature, which was staunchly argued
by Schopenhauer. At the highest levels of abstraction—the levels at
which the insights of ancient religions, modern physics, and modern
psychology could be equated—Lawrence's mind worked easily and
naturally, always resisting a literalism that would finite experience by
failing to see profound analogies. Lawrence told Bertrand Russell that "
'facts' are quite unimportant, only 'truths' matter" (Page, 117). He saw
through particular versions of fact to the truths behind them.

The acclaim that Lawrence won for his early poems and for *The
White Peacock* (1911) was unprecedented for a coal miner's son, as his
winning of a King's scholarship six years earlier had been unprecedented. The young Lawrence was, for a time, dazzled by his initiation
into the world of literary celebrities. It was a heady experience, and in
the presence of sophisticated Londoners, Lawrence was acutely conscious of his shabby boots, his awkwardness, his anomalous appearance
as a "genius" from the provinces. He obviously *wanted* to make an
impression, and he felt acutely his slightest shortcomings.
At Ford Madox Ford's in July 1910, he was received "open-armed
by a waiter" and lamented: "I was so astonished I could neither find
him a card nor tell him my name. At last he bawled my announcement,
and I found myself in what seemed like a bargain sale" (*L*, 1:170).
Acutely uncomfortable, he could not bring himself to announce his
departure: "When I was coming away, Miss Hunt was talking. She
wouldn't look at me: I dare not for my life interrupt her. I fled. Was that

criminal? I think I am quite out of favour with Miss Hunt. I'm sorry: I wish she liked me" (*L*, 1:171). He saw himself as "ticketed 'genius' as a last resource: just as they call things 'very desirable' when nobody on earth wants them" (*L*, 1:171). His desire to please was mixed with resentment at the indignity of his being on show—the "bargain sale" atmosphere. He had always hated exposure to the eyes of others. It was as if his inviolacy was threatened, just as it was threatened by publication of his writings. ("When I have *finished* a writing, I hate it," he said in June 1910. "In it, I am vulnerable, naked in a thickly clothed crowd" [*L*, 1:167].) And he felt again, perhaps, that the sacredness of writing was defiled by literary small talk. "A book is better than a meeting," he wrote in December 1908. "The essence of things is stored in books; in meetings and speeches the essence is diluted with hot water and sugar, and may be a dash of fire spirits" (*L*, 1:96). Above all, perhaps, he was intimidated by the *worldliness* of the literary community. Perhaps, like George Saxton of *The White Peacock*, when entering a hotel, "he could never get over the feeling that he was trespassing." In the presence of his publisher's representative, Mr. Pawling, "a large and weighty man of affairs" whom he met on 15 July 1910, Lawrence said he felt "like an extinguished glow-worm under a lamp-post: when I think of writing to him, the stopper dives into the neck of my bottle of words, and there sticks firm. I am an ass" (*L*, 1:170).

He was indeed "an ass"—as he frequently reminded himself—in comparison with the practical people with literary know-how. He was continually cursing himself, "inwardly, saying, 'Under the seal of commonsense, my lad, you are a naked fool'" (*L*, 1:167). After indulging in a flight of fancy in one of his letters, he might add: "What an ass I am!" (*L*, 1:146). Not that Lawrence couldn't manage practical affairs; he was extremely efficient in his dealings with his publishers. But he was so far from living on the assumptions of practical, worldly people that he was inclined, whenever he was exposed to their worldliness, to withdraw—or get angry. Saint Bernard once said that every time he had mixed with people he had defiled himself. Lawrence felt some of the same threat. Although he loved conviviality, he was also a bit like the hermit who desired no one to visit him and to speak to no one because "the angels cannot visit us if we consort with men" (Friedenthal, *Luther*, 29). As Lawrence was introduced to an ever-widening circle of intelligent and distinguished writers and intellectuals, it was inevitable that he would vent his wrath on anyone who threatened his inviolacy or the inviolacy of his message. He was not comfortable among these well-to-do worldlings, not only because he was intimidated by them but also because, as he indicated in one of his last poems, "A Rise in the World" (*CP*, 551–52), he sensed a basic triviality in all the chatter:

> I rose up in the world, Ooray!
> rose very high, for me.
> An earl once asked me down to stay
> and a duchess once came to tea.
>
> . . . .
>
> Up there I didn't like it,
> chattering, though not with glee,
> the whole of the time, and nothing
> mattering—at least, not to me.

In 1910 he did not appreciate how little the chatter mattered. It was not until 1912, after his "coming through" with Frieda, that he began to see himself clearly as a man with a religious mission, basically opposed to the world of bright ironic chatterers. Then, as Lady Cynthia Asquith observed, "He wasted no time—he never did—on small talk" (Page, 95). Indeed, he was so earnest and passionate that he could even sardonically welcome the war because it might cause "a slump in trifling"! (Page, 98).

4

LOVE AND REBIRTH:
SONS AND LOVERS AND *THE RAINBOW*

1912: *The Trespasser;* Germany and Italy; Lawrence feeling that he has "come through" after the shyness and "shame of self-consciousness" at Croydon; **1912/13:** reading of Jane Harrison and probably of Houston Stewart Chamberlain; development of idea of male/female collaboration; new religious views influenced by Chamberlain, Carpenter, and Nietzsche; **1913:** *Sons and Lovers* published; *Love Poems and Others* published; begins *The Lost Girl;* begins *The Sisters (The Rainbow* and *Women in Love);* writes "The Prussian Officer"; June to August, in England; meets John M. Murry, Katherine Mansfield, Gordon Campbell, Edward Marsh, the Asquiths; writes *The Widowing of Mrs. Holroyd;* August to June 1914, in Germany, Switzerland, Italy; **1914:** completes *The Sisters; The Prussian Officer;* returns to England in June; living in London, Buckinghamshire, and Sussex: meets Catherine Carswell, Viola Meynell, Amy Lowell, Richard Aldington, Hilda Doolittle, Barbara Low, Dr. David Eder, S. S. Koteliansky, Mark Gertler; marries Frieda; August 4, World War I begins; Lawrence feels entombed; *Study of Thomas Hardy:* early statement of Lawrence's "philosophy."

Sons and Lovers, so sharply different from *The Trespasser,* which worked at the highest levels of symbolic abstraction, is the triumph of the naturalistic method that Lawrence had learned from Gustave Flaubert, Guy de Maupassant, George Moore, Arnold Bennett, and indeed most of the influential writers of his time. Yet unlike many realistic and naturalistic novels, *Sons and Lovers* does not stop with the efforts of the rational ego to solve the problems it encounters; the novel gives the deeper sense of the very life flow of the individual, the deep yearning for spontaneous expression of one's possibilities, and the deep psychic injury that results from the thwarting or clogging of life energies by industrialism, by poverty, by middle-class expectations, and by a repressive spirituality.

I have already pointed out that the oedipal problem does not entirely explain Paul Morel's behavior—that the root of his life problem is Paul's determination to free himself from *all* limitations on his being and from all obstacles to his mission. In its preoccupation with this general problem, as well as with the narrower oedipal problem, the novel is pure autobiography. Paul cannot "flow" spontaneously, in the first instance, because the poverty of his family and his mother's bourgeois expectations force him into the role of the Ambitious Young Conformist. He cannot love spontaneously, not only because his mother does not set him free but also because Miriam, with whom he drifts unaware into a love relationship, is so cramped and stiffened by her abstracted and spiritual nature that she stifles his spontaneity, makes him feel "anxious and imprisoned," kills "the joy and warmth in him," and spoils his "ease and naturalness." Again, Paul's passionate love for Clara does not set him free, because Clara seeks to "absorb" him and makes him "feel imprisoned." Indeed, all three women—the mother, Miriam, and Clara—make Paul feel that he is in bondage. At the end, when his mother is dying, "sometimes he hated her, and pulled at her bondage. His life wanted to free itself of her. It was like a circle where life turned back on itself, and got no further. . . . He could not be free to go forward with his own life" (345). Not his mind, not his conscious will, but "his life wanted to free itself." The deepest desire is beyond egoistic control. He is desperate, with nowhere to turn. When, toward the end of the novel, he is free of the confining women, one has a glimpse of the young Lawrence wandering about the streets of London, conscious of a terrifying emptiness and loneliness and of an irrevocable need for some Absolute in life: "The real agony was that he had nowhere to go, nothing to do, nothing to say, and *was* nothing himself" (412). The world is absurd, like that of Sartre's *Nausea:* "There seemed no reason why people should go along the street, and houses pile up in the daylight. There seemed no reason why these things should occupy the space, instead of leaving it empty" (410). He must create, he must marry, must find someone to "relieve him of the responsibility of himself" (418). But the responsibility is his, and he must fight against "nothingness," must create in "unsponsored" freedom.

Turning from his mother, from Jessie Chambers, and from Louie Burrows, Lawrence set off with Frieda—this different woman—to create his new life; and Frieda became for a time his Absolute. As he would argue in *Study of Thomas Hardy,* it was woman whom man sought for "Eternality, Infinity, Immutability." In *Sons and Lovers,* Miriam/Jessie, unable to trust Paul, had reflected that "he had no religion." She had been right. The author of *Sons and Lovers had* no religion; it was Frieda, the motherly woman, the Magna Mater, whom he embraced as his Absolute. Emile Delavenay says that Lawrence's view of woman as eternal stems "from his own weakness" (*The Man and His Work,* 309). But Lawrence was aware that woman cannot substitute for God; he was acutely aware, too, that weak men put the burden of "life-responsibility" on the woman. Yet it was through woman, through love, that man could be released from himself—from an obscene narcissism—and born again to the "Not-Me," to the Infinite of which he was only a fragment in himself. It was love that gave him freedom to do his life's work—to create his religious art—and to overcome the "halfness" of his male being.

The joy and exhilaration of Lawrence's consummated love for Frieda—and of his consummated freedom—were a "proof" and a "verification." Life could be godlike, and his belief in life—in the creative and regenerative powers of the great Unknown—was ratified in his consciousness that he had become a new man. He had feared that he might be incapable of loving—that his intense Victorian inhibitions and the "mad" fixity of his ambition as an artist would unfit him ever to "let go." But the fears he had had about himself were now revealed as groundless: he was reborn, eager to start again. At this time in his life, love was for Lawrence what the Bible was for Luther: like the monk, Lawrence felt he could speak now "from certain knowledge and not from mere opinion" (Friedenthal, 187). A new confidence, a bold new authority suddenly enters his writing. He had had the courage to "trespass" against society; and he realized that he was a fool to feel guilt for his trespass (L, 2:90). If he and Frieda were "really scapegoats" on whom Ernest Weekley vented all his righteous wrath (L, 2:93), Lawrence knew he could justify his taking of Weekley's wife on the ground of a life impulse that could not *morally* be denied.

Both his trespass and his "coming through" into a new, confident, and responsible male selfhood are dramatized in a story that he wrote in 1913, "The Thorn in the Flesh." The hero, a soldier named Bachmann, is a young man with "a self-conscious strain in his blue eyes," "almost girlish in his good looks and his grace" (CSS, 1:117). He writes a weekly postcard to his mother, and he finds satisfaction "in delivering himself up to his duty" (CSS, 1:118). But his spirit is "clenched apart": he cannot take "the responsibility of himself." Forced, in an army exercise, to climb a ladder, he begins to lose control, he urinates, and in "deep shame and ignominy" must be hauled to the top of the rampart by his sergeant. When the sergeant brutally berates the youth, Bachmann in self-defense raises his arm and pushes the officer off the rampart and into the moat below. Then he bolts, seeking a release from his shame: "He could not take the responsibility of himself. He must give himself up to someone. Then his heart, obstinate in hope, became obsessed with the idea of his sweetheart. He would make himself her responsibility" (CSS, 1:122).

The girl, Emilie, the servant of a baron (surrogate of Baron von Richthofen), is equally unable to take responsibility. Her desire is to serve the baron, she "needed to be in subjection, because she was primitive and had no grasp on civilised forms of living, nor on civilised purposes" (CSS, 1:128). When Bachmann appears and asks her to hide him, she has "the insupportable feeling of being out of the order, self-responsible, bewildered. The control of her life should come from those above her, and she should move within that control" (CSS, 1:129). But the fear of "trespassing" is thrown off when Bachmann embraces her and then makes love to her in her room. He is "restored and completed" and "his pride unconquerable" is roused. They are "one, complete," and she rejoices in "security of service" to *him*. It is love that enables Bachmann to recover his identity and to throw off his shame: " 'What I am, I am; and let it be enough,' he thought" (CSS, 1:131). "He had won to his own being, in himself and Emilie, he had drawn the stigma from his shame, he was beginning to be himself" (CSS, 1:133). The two plan to meet in America. But before Bachmann can escape, he is seized by the army. Yet "he remained true to himself," and the couple know that "they [are] themselves" (CSS, 1:134). Physically caged, Bachmann has "come through" and knows his deep need for "absolute, imperious freedom" (CSS, 1:133). Indirectly the story mirrors Lawrence's own fears before he found the courage to "trespass" with Frieda; and it depicts the powerful birth of a new, strong, responsible self through love. Bachmann's fear of climbing is symbolic: he has been afraid of losing his grip on himself, and it is his submission to the army, to "his duty," that has prevented him from climbing up into the freedom of the self-responsible individual.

Overcoming his own "shame of self-consciousness," Lawrence now saw that suppression of a deep desire inevitably leads to sickness. Within a month after his own liberation, he showed total certainty in his diagnosis of the sickness of his fellow men, as he wrote to Edward Garnett: "I should like to bludgeon them into realising their own selves. Curse you, my countrymen, you have put the halters round your necks, and pull tighter and tighter, from day to day. You are strangling yourselves, you blasted fools. Oh my countrymen!" (8 July 1912, L, 1:424). Weekley's determination to punish Frieda for her infidelity, and William Heinemann's rejection of *Paul Morel* because of its outspokenness, prompted Lawrence to condemn the English wholesale:

> Curse the blasted, jelly-boned swines, the slimy, the belly-wiggling invertebrates, the miserable sodding rotters, the flaming sods, the snivelling, dribbling, dithering palsied pulse-less lot that make up England today. They've got white of egg in their veins, and their spunk is that watery its a marvel they can breed. They *can* nothing but frog-spawn—the gibberers! God, how I hate them! God curse them, funkers. God blast them, wish-wash. Exterminate them, slime. (3 July 1912; L, 1:422)

And in what follows, Lawrence likens himself to the Christ: "Why, why, why was I born an Englishman!—my cursed, rotten-boned, pappy hearted countrymen, *why* was I sent to *them*. Christ on the cross must have hated his countrymen. 'Crucify me, you swine,' he must have said through his teeth" (*L*, 1:422).

His own illness he now blamed on "sheer distress and nerve strain" (*L*, 2:73). He had had "a good old English habit of shutting my rages of trouble well inside my belly, so that they play havoc with my innards." He saw that he was "so damnably violent, really, and self destructive. One sits so tight on the crater of one's passions and emotions. I am just learning—thanks to Frieda—to let go a bit" (*L*, 2:73). And immediately he proceeded to generalize on the basis of his new power to let go: "It is this sitting tight, and this inability to let go, which is killing the modern England, I think. But soon you will see a bust, I believe." He wrote this in September 1913, a year before World War I began. He understood then what he had found in Dostoevsky: "Cruelty is a form of perverted sex. I want to dogmatise. Priests in their celibacy get their sex lustful, then perverted, then insane, hence Inquisitions—all sexual in origin. And soldiers, being herded together, men without women, never being *satisfied* by a woman, as a man never is from a street affair, get their surplus sex and their frustration and dissatisfaction into the blood, and *love* cruelty. It is sex lust fermented makes atrocity" (*L*, 1:469).

His new authority was born not only, however, from his personal experience but from a conviction that his experience far transcended the personal. In a letter to Henry Savage, he makes clear that he views himself as the voice of a truth that transcends his subjective, personal opinion: "I suppose I'm so damned conceited in my belief in myself—it doesn't seem to be myself, really—I think 'here you are, I tell you the truth'—that I don't care whether I impress my neighbours or not—not much" (*L*, 2:73). He would repeat this idea frequently over the years that followed. To his friend Doctor Barbara Low, on 11 February 1915, he wrote: "You see I do believe some things. It is not myself. But Mrs Eder doesn't listen to me. She makes me a *Wunderkind*. It is not *I* who matter—it is what is said through me" (*L*, 2:280). "Not I, But the Wind": the divine voice speaks through him. In March 1915 he again insisted, this time to Gordon Campbell: "It is The Law we must utter—the New, real Law—not subjective experience" (*L*, 2:302). It is because he felt he had had direct "proof" and "verification" of the birth of a new self that he could speak henceforth with an authority that both impressed and dismayed others.

The impersonal student of love—and of the great trap of love—became, almost overnight, "the priest of love." When he wrote on

Christmas Day 1912, "I'll do my life work, sticking up for the love between man and woman. . . . I shall always be a priest of love, and now a glad one—and I'll preach my heart out, Lor bless you" (L, 1:492–93), he was feeling the exhilaration of his discovery of a new identity. As already noted, he would recognize later that "God" is not love, indeed that it is a "*blasphemy* to say that the Holy Spirit is Love" (L, 2:408). The divine will, he would argue (following the hints of materialistic scientists and philosophers) consists in "opposition and attraction both," in "love and hate" (L, 2:408). But in 1912 and 1913, it was the unifying impulse of love, not the divisive impulse of hate, that he stressed. It was having "a woman behind me," "a woman I love," that enabled him to keep "in direct communication with the unknown, in which otherwise I am a bit lost" (L, 1:503).

It was essential that he act directly from the deepest impulse that the Unknown had sent into him. So he declared, on 17 January 1913:

> My great religion is a belief in the blood, the flesh, as being wiser than the intellect. We can go wrong in our minds. But what our blood feels and believes and says, is always true. The intellect is only a bit and a bridle. What do I care about knowledge. All I want is to answer to my blood, direct, without fribbling intervention of mind, or moral, or what not. . . . I am . . . concerned . . . with the mystery of the flame forever flowing, coming God knows how from out of practically nowhere, and being *itself*, whatever there is around it, that it lights up. (L, 1:503)

It is the ultimate reality and selfhood that is manifested in the flame, in the desire of the blood. One must "answer to" that ultimate reality. As Herbert Spencer had maintained, man is "one of the myriad agencies through whom works the Unknown Cause; and when the Unknown Cause produces in him a certain belief, he is thereby authorized to profess and act out that belief" (*First Principles*, 133).

To grasp the truth that is inaccessible to the mind, the artist must find a way to prevent his daily consciousness, his ego, from creating a false picture of the deep reality. "One needs something to make one's mood deep and sincere," Lawrence wrote to the young engraver Ernest Collings in February 1913.

> There are so many little frets that prevent our coming at the real naked essence of our vision. It sounds boshy, doesn't it. I often think one ought to be able to pray, before one works—and then leave it to the Lord. Isn't it hard, hard work to come to real grips with one's imagination—throw everything overboard. I always feel as if I stood naked for the fire of Almighty God to go through me—and it's an awful feeling. One has to be so terribly religious, to be an artist. I often think of my dear Saint Lawrence on his gridiron, when he said "Turn me over, brothers, I am done enough on this side." (L, 1:519)

After a few false starts, he was beginning his great religious work—
The Sisters. It was to be unlike anything ever done before in the novel;
and it would be done in a spirit of reverence. "It just fascinates me to see
art coming out of religious yearning," he wrote in October 1913 when he
read Jane Harrison's *Ancient Art and Ritual* (L, 2:90). He had no use for
the modern art that was "the art of self hate and self-murder" (L, 2:101).
Baudelaire, Verlaine, Flaubert—they all had "got about them, the
feeling that their own flesh is unclean—corrupt." They "denied God,"
unlike David in the Psalms, for whom "God is . . . like a great woman
he adores." They "denied God in heaven, they would not throw out
their unsatisfaction like a dove over the waters. They denied love, and
lived by hate—hate is the obverse of love, the recoil of unsatisfied love.
They *wanted* to love themselves in the flesh—their intellectual dogma
said so 'We are God, all there is of him' " (L, 2:101). It was the vile
narcissism and the negativism of these unregenerate writers that he was
determined to overcome.

His enthusiasm for Harrison's *Ancient Art and Ritual* was consistent
with his desire to affirm life with a Nietzschean vigor. Harrison's main
contention is that both ritual and art "have, in emotion towards life, a
common root" (168): both express "the intense, world-wide desire that
the life of Nature which seemed dead should live again" (26). The ritual
of the May Day, for example, utters "the desire for the joy in life and
spring" (61). And in sacrifice, the aim was not to give a life to the gods
but rather to *gain* "that special life and strength" which was in the
sacred animal. Greek tragedy, according to Harrison, derives from the
ancient rites of the death of the Old Year, or winter, and the renewal of
life in the New Year.

Thus Harrison introduced Lawrence to ideas that were central in Sir
James Frazer's *The Golden Bough* (which Lawrence later read) and that
were directly related to the Nietzschean idea that Dionysian art was the
Hellene's guarantee of *"eternal* life, the eternal return of life; the future
promised and hallowed in the past; the triumphant Yes to life beyond all
death and change; *true* life as the over-all continuation of life through
procreation, through the mysteries of sexuality" (*The Portable Nietzsche,*
561). Tragedy, as Nietzsche said, was a saying yes to life, "the will to life
rejoicing over its own inexhaustibility even in the very sacrifice of its
highest types" (562). It was this religious idea that Lawrence seized
upon when he argued that "the tragic is the most holding, the most vital
thing in life" (Ada Lawrence, 88). And in addition he enthusiastically
propounds another idea found in Harrison: the idea that egotism is "a
danger inherent in all art" and that "all great art releases from self"
(242). At the end of her book, Harrison supports Tolstoy's idea that art is
"social, not individual" and is concerned with "the union of man in a

common brotherhood" (241, 240). This is exactly what Lawrence had emphasized five years earlier, in a Thursday evening Croydon talk entitled "Art and the Individual," which expounds Tolstoy's idea that art is communication and argues that "the mission of Art" is "to bring us into sympathy with as many men, as many objects, as many phenomena as possible. To be in sympathy with things is to some extent to acquiesce in their purpose, to help on that purpose. We want, we are for ever trying to unite ourselves with the whole universe, to carry out some ultimate purpose—evolution, we call one phase of the carrying out" (*Phoenix II*, 226). In 1913 he carried this idea further, contrasting the egotism of the modern pessimists with the selfless and profoundly religious spirit of the writer who exists only to express the divine will behind appearances, the writer who has faith in the Unknown. Such a faith Lawrence saw in the story of Job:

> Whereas Hardy and the moderns end with "Let the day perish—" . . . the real book of Job ends—"Then Job answered the Lord and said:
>> I know that thou canst do everything, and that no thought can be withholden from thee.
>> Who is he that hideth counsel without knowledge? therefore have I uttered that I understood not: things too wonderful for me, which I knew not. . . .
>> Wherefore I abhor myself, and repent in dust and ashes." (*L*, 2:247)

Lawrence, reading the Bible as he worked on *The Sisters*, found in the book of Job "a story of your own soul," even better than Dostoevsky's *Letters from the Underworld*. Following Nietzsche, Lawrence affirmed that "the great souls in all time" did not end their works by "insisting on the sad plight." They did not end with "*Prometheus Bound* and terribly suffering on the rock of his own egotism," but with *Prometheus Unbound* (*L*, 2:248). The great mission was to show that man could free himself to fulfill his desires, could say yes in the face of corruption and death, could assert the primal impulse of vitality in a dead civilization that had waged war against instinct and life for two thousand years.

The affirmative nature of his new work was made possible not only by his use of Harrison and Nietzsche but also, almost certainly, by his appropriation of a number of ideas and hints provided by Houston Stewart Chamberlain in his *Foundations of the Nineteenth Century*. Emile Delavenay has traced in impressive detail many of the resemblances in the thought of Lawrence and Chamberlain, calling attention to "remarkably similar attitudes to nation and to race," to their "religious, mystical approach to nature and art" (301), to their recognition of the dichotomy of Jewish "Law" and Christian "Love," and to their antidemocratic political and social views. Yet Delavenay's analysis of these similarities is strongly colored by "the experience of the years after 1935," when the ideas of Chamberlain "were subsequently mobilized [by the Nazis] in the service of the worst crimes against mankind" (xvi). But although Lawrence accepted the prevalent notion that races, exposed to particular milieus, develop specific character traits (an idea stoutly argued by Hippolyte Taine), Lawrence used Chamberlain's ideas about Teutons and Jews, not in order to praise or to condemn a race, but to develop his own powerful psychology and his conception of the historical transition from a tribal homogeneity of flesh and blood to the antitribal individuality and spirituality of a man like Jesus.

Chamberlain saw Jesus as "positively anti-social" in his departure from his family and his assertion of a spiritual truth which transcended the old conservative law of the Jews. Whereas Judaism laid emphasis, "not upon the individual, but upon the whole nation," Jesus, according to Chamberlain, "represents exactly the opposite principle, namely, that of extreme individualism, the redeeming of the individual by regeneration" (*Foundations*, 1:245). Lawrence had been working with a similar idea in *The White Peacock* and *The Trespasser*, as well as in *Sons and Lovers*, all of which stress the contrast between submission to society (the blind collective will of the tribe) and the upward climbing of the conscious, purposive man, the "trespasser" who wants to defy the tribe and to create a new freedom and a new identity. Chamberlain clarified Lawrence's understanding of this problem and helped the novelist to see the problem in relation to deep impulses—to unite and to separate—which are differentiated in the south and in the "northern races."

According to Chamberlain, the Romans (like the Hebrews, though Chamberlain did not see the connection) created a unified state by submitting to the law and to the universal will. Chamberlain quotes Theodor Mommsen: "The State-idea among the Romans rests upon . . . the submission on the part of each physical member of the community of his individual will to this universal will" (*Foundations*, 1:130). The Romans know how to command and how to obey, and are "all unanimous" (1:128–29). But the Teutons are individualists who are disposed to "fighting," "are continually at feud with one another," love freedom, and show "a passionate revolt against every limitation of the personality" (1:494, 496, 154; 2:150). (Similar ideas can be found in Edward Gibbon and in Hippolyte Taine.) In the Aryan, "that which one might call 'Protestant' sentiment has existed since earliest times" (2:92), and "the revolt of the North" (2:91) against "the civil and ecclesiastical ideals which were incorporated in Rome" inevitably took the form of a destructive "tear[ing] down" (2:93).

The great psychological impulses that were thus isolated by Chamberlain are the impulse to unite sympathetically and the impulse to divide and to "maintain and defend one's own individuality." These ideas are echoed in the beautiful essays that constitute Lawrence's *Twilight in Italy*, a series of reflections on the contrast between southern submission to the old, mindless way of life, and northern individualism, consciousness, and purposiveness. In *The Rainbow*, Tom Brangwen, living in the blood drowse on the Marsh farm, would be much like the Italian peasant who, as Lawrence wrote in *Movements in European History*, "filled his life well enough. Why should he bother with what was beyond?" (268). But the "beyond" beckons, and Tom, like the Italian lad Duccio of *Twilight in Italy*, is tormented by his inability to achieve the spiritual, conscious development of the northern men who hail from "the beyond." In tracing the movement from "Law" to "Love" or from mindless submission to individualistic revolt and spiritual development, Lawrence was looking forward to a great synthesis: the reconciliation of Law and Love, of unison and separateness, of "the blood" and the spirit. Chamberlain provided him with this idea of a synthesis, arguing that two traits of the Teutonic character—loyalty and freedom—work together in a splendid harmony, presumably for the greater glory of the Teuton. Lawrence dropped Chamberlain's racism but held on to the idea of the blending of autonomy *and* loyalty in the choice of a master, and in *Women in Love* he would begin to explore the possibility of a union of men, a *Blutbrüderschaft*, made possible by the free choice of each individual, a sacred self-surrender to the common weal. Chamberlain, in speaking of the "simultaneous sway of the two impulses—to separate and to unite" (*Foundations*, 2:346)—voiced an idea that was central in Lawrencian psychology, but it is not, obviously, Teutonic psychology that Lawrence develops; it is human psychology.

Chamberlain's emphasis on "the sacredness of the Individual" was connected with his rejection of the "unsound doctrine" of evolution, for Chamberlain argued that there is no "advance" from a simpler stage to a higher stage ("Nature never offers an example of development taking place in anything living without entailing a corresponding loss" [*Foundations*, 1:149]); moreover, the idea of a universal advance does serious injury to "the feeling for the Individual," the recognition of the individual's prime role in the shaping of history. Lawrence would seize on this idea, too, emphasizing individual uniqueness and "the heroic soul in the greater man," rejecting evolution, and preferring the idea of the "rainbow change of ever-renewed creative civilization" (*FU*, 14). "The final aim of every living thing, creature, or being is the full achievement of itself," he writes in *Study of Thomas Hardy* (*Phoenix*, 403). He stresses that each individual is *new*: "In its own degree, the prickly sow-thistle I have just pulled up *is*, for the first time in all time. It is itself, a new thing. . . . In its flower it issues something to the world that never was issued before. Its like has been before, its exact equivalent never'' (402). Like Emerson, Lawrence dwells on the finality of the creatively new: ''The lily in blossom is a ne plus ultra: there is no evolving beyond. This is the greatest truth'' (L, 3:139). All universals are false, all language is false, because it strips the individual of its uniqueness. There is a constant need to discard old dead versions of reality and to find new, more accurate truths. Again and again Lawrence condemns the old and dead and calls for a new life, a new feeling, a new knowledge, a new state, for all knowledge, strictly speaking, is of things dead, a dead world. Only in immediacy, in intuition or instinct that is responsive to the changing realities, is there truth.

Above all, perhaps, Lawrence was impressed by Chamberlain's views on religion. Aryan mysticism, said Chamberlain, with its ancient Hindu doctrine tat tvam asi—''Thou art That,'' the Atman is one with the Brahman—this is the religion of the Teuton. The mystic rejects creeds, formalism, and rationalism. His ''cosmic religion'' stresses ''a direct relation between the individual and the divinely superhuman'' (Foundations, 1:435). For a mystic like Francis of Assisi, ''God is a direct perception, not a logical deduction'' (2:402). And mysticism aims solely at the ''transformation of the inner man—that is, at redemption'' (2:50).

All this was in almost perfect accord with Lawrence's own thinking, most particularly the implicit pantheism of this ''cosmic religion.'' Although Lawrence did not like a pantheism which asserts that all is One, preferring to stress the uniqueness of each realization of the God-stuff, he was like Chamberlain's Aryan mystics in identifying nature with God. And like Chamberlain, Lawrence looked forward to a beautiful transformation of life when the falsehood and superstitions of the past would be thrown off and a new mystical religion would be accepted which does not condemn life and nature but celebrates life and redemption: ''The religious craving is growing so great and so imperious in our breasts,'' Chamberlain declared, ''that of necessity a day must come when that craving will shatter the rotten, gloomy edifice [of falsehood], and then we shall step out into the new, bright, glorious kingdom which has long been awaiting us'' (Foundations, 2:292-93). For Lawrence, that new bright kingdom existed in the vision of the rainbow.

It was because his new work was essentially religious in its depiction of the eternal rhythms of life, the eternal quest for an absolute, and its unique definition of that Absolute that Lawrence found it necessary to rewrite extensively. His early draft of The Sisters, he told Edward Garnett (in April 1914), was ''flippant and often vulgar and jeering,'' but he was gradually getting it right. ''Primarily,'' he said, ''I am a passionately religious man, and my novels must be written from the depth of my religious experience. That I must keep to, because I can only work like that" (L, 2:165). It was when his "deep feeling [did not] find its way out" that he became flippant or sentimental or jeering. As he gradually "got it right," he felt that "the Laocoon writhing and shrieking have gone from my new work, and I think there is a bit of stillness, like the wide, still, unseeing eyes of a Venus of Melos. . . . There is something in the Greek sculpture that my soul is hungry for— something of the eternal stillness that lies under all movement, under all life, like a source, incorruptible and inexhaustible. It is deeper than change, and struggling. So long I have acknowledged only the struggle, the stream, the change. And now I begin to feel something of the source, the great impersonal which never changes and out of which all change comes" (L, 2:137–38). By "the eternal stillness" he means a reality in men and women that lies beneath manners or the ego—the masks of the true self. Beneath the ego lie the *deepest* desires of the soul, the self as a manifestation of the greater inhuman will that sweeps men and women together—and then apart. Seen as objectifications of the will, men and women become "unscarred and beautiful," one glimpses "the eternal and unchangeable that they are" (L, 2:138). It is exactly that glimpse of the unscarred and beautiful selfhood beneath the ravages of change that Lawrence provided in his brilliant and moving "Odour of Chrysanthemums," in which a coal miner's wife, who has been fighting her husband for years, discovers, when he is dead, that she has never known the reality of the man:

> . . . as she looked at the dead man, her mind, cold and detached, said clearly: "Who am I? What have I been doing? I have been fighting a husband who did not exist. *He* existed all the time. What wrong have I done? What was that I have been living with? There lies the reality, this man." And her soul died in her for fear: she knew she had never seen him, and he had never seen her, they had met in the dark and had fought in the dark, not knowing whom they met nor whom they fought. And now she saw, and turned silent in seeing. For she had been wrong. She had said he was something he was not; she had felt familiar with him. Whereas he was apart all the while, living as she never lived, feeling as she never felt. (CSS, 2:300–301)

It is one of the finest passages in Lawrence, but it is matched almost everywhere in *The Rainbow*, where Lawrence provides the sense of repose and peace—or stillness—in the contemplation of his characters' timeless aspirations and their timeless effort to find fulfillment in the infinite. Life is not reduced to "plot" with "vivid scenes." The flaw of *Sons and Lovers* was, as Frieda said (echoing Lawrence's views in March 1914), that there was "nothing *behind* all those happenings." In *Sons and Lovers* Lawrence had captured, in his vivid, concrete, virtually imagistic style, a reality so immediate, so sensuous, that it seemed to be life itself.

The artistic problem, as Lawrence saw it, was that the violently sensuous style failed to reveal the deepest unconscious movements of life. The characters were not seen in relation to the underlying Will of the universe. There was "nothing *behind* all those happenings." It was "an irreligious book," Frieda said, again echoing Lawrence, a book that failed to present the essential soul, "the living, striving *she*," instead of the social mask or the manners of a woman (*L*, 2:151).

What was needed for the new book, Lawrence felt, was that it become, not just a man's book, but the product of man and woman together. Neither the male nor the female soul is complete in itself. Both are halves of the deep creative impulse. In uniting, both realize a new and greater selfhood—the male soul fertilized by the female, the female by the male. Each loves what he or she lacks, as Schopenhauer had argued; love is the admission of a deficiency in the self. But when male and female "collaborate" in the making of a book, a new knowledge is revealed. As Lawrence said to his old friend A. W. McLeod on 2 June 1914:

> I think the only re-sourcing of art, re-vivifying it, is to make it more the joint work of man and woman. I think *the* one thing to do, is for men to have courage to draw nearer to women, expose themselves to them, and be altered by them: and for women to accept and admit men. This is the only way for art and civilisation to get a new life, a new start. . . . Because the source of all life and knowledge is in man and woman, and the source of all living is in the interchange and the meeting and mingling of these two: man-life and woman-life, man knowledge and woman-knowledge, man-being and woman-being. (*L*, 2:181)

The idea is restated in a letter to Gordon Campbell in September 1914:

> I believe there is no getting of a vision, as you call it, before we get our sex right: before we get our souls fertilised by the *female*. I don't mean the feminine: I mean the female. Because life tends to take two streams, male and female, and only some female influence (not necessarily woman, but most obviously woman) can fertilise the soul of man to vision or being. Then the vision we're after, I don't know what it is— but it is something that contains awe and dread and submission, not pride or sensuous egotism and assertion. . . . I know, from the Egyptian and Assyrian sculpture—what we are after. We want to realise the tremendous *non-human* quality of life—it is wonderful. It is not the emotions, nor the personal feelings and attachments, that matter. . . . Behind us all are the tremendous unknown forces of life, coming unseen and unperceived as out of the desert to the Egyptians, and driving us, forcing us, destroying us if we do not submit to be swept away. (*L*, 2:218)

Drawing perhaps on Edward Carpenter's idea that physical love is "an interchange of vital and ethereal elements" (*Love's Coming of Age*, 23), Lawrence now felt that his soul had been wonderfully fertilized by the female. But he did *not* mean "the feminine." He meant instead the female principle—the being grounded in the earth or the flesh, in the deep blood knowledge of sympathy with the whole of being. "The female" is the source, the origin, the Magna Mater. She is the darkness, the sensual body, the unconscious. Only by remaining in contact with the physical origin is the male spirit restored to the primal infinite; only through such contact is the male liberated from his "egotism and assertion" and prepared to do his life's work—work founded on the acceptance of, and submission to, the deepest knowledge of Being and of the human place in the scheme of being. Not petty, human goals but the submission to the nonhuman, the divine will is the object of life. Through a woman, man can be "re-born, re-constructed" and thus "free from oneself" (*L*, 2:115). That renewal cannot be obtained from another man, although Lawrence, like Edward Carpenter, felt that "nearly every man that approaches greatness tends to homosexuality" (*L*, 2:115). A man, Lawrence speculated, "projects his own image on another man, like on a mirror"; but to be *reborn*, a man must fertilize his soul in the woman. Art must become "a two person show," not a "one-man show" (*L*, 2:115).

Here it is necessary to emphasize, in opposition to feminists who have attacked Lawrence for his misogyny, that he saw himself as fighting *for* women, not attacking them, because he was departing in important respects from the misogynistic premises of such men as Schopenhauer, Nietzsche, Strindberg, Otto Weininger, and others. Lawrence accepted the general premise that "the female principle" is sexuality itself and that the motherly type is "sole advocate and priestess of the race" (as Otto Weininger said, echoing Schopenhauer). He accepted, too, that there is an implicit struggle between the sexual desire that entraps man and makes him a servant of woman and the family, on the one hand, and the religious, creative desire to depart from woman and the family and to build a new world. He saw this struggle, schematically, as a struggle between unconsciousness and con-sciousness, matter and spirit, sexuality (or "blood") and spirituality, union and separation, darkness and light. But unlike the misogynistic Weininger (for example), who regarded woman as soulless, "non-moral," and possessing "neither ego nor individuality, personality nor freedom, character nor will" (*Sex and Character*, 207), Lawrence viewed woman as striving, like man, not just to reproduce but to achieve wholeness; nor did he view woman as "the sin of man" because man's yielding to woman would mean yielding to unconsciousness and to man's "lower part" (Weininger, 300). On the contrary, Lawrence saw that the male's acceptance of woman and the achieving of the profound wholeness of male and female together was the sole condition of man's own self-realization, making possible the full creation of his identity as male. By the same token, the woman's acceptance of the male is the sole condition of her sense of wholeness and her realization of *her* identity. Identity achieved through sexual fulfillment is a realization not only of one's full being as male or as female but also of selfhood as an expression of the infinite, the unknown that lies behind appearances and that works in mankind as the deep desire to union.

The methods that Lawrence developed in *The Rainbow* to present this new vision of life reveal his firm grasp of the human condition in relation to the divine energies. He begins with man himself and woman herself, living in the cycle of the seasons, accepting their connection with the deep rhythms of life. Their way of life is deeply fulfilling. They feel a oneness with the whole of Being. Yet "nature" is not enough. The women look to "the beyond": they want more than satisfaction of their animal desires: they yearn for education, religion, culture; they want freedom, scope, range. The world beyond is spiritual—a world of knowledge, of expansion. They dream of rising above the drowse and torpor of the blood intimacy—dream of freedom from the inertia of the old way of life. Lawrence thus telescopes the transition from immersion in a tribal unconscious to the birth of consciousness and the recognition of new, spiritual needs born of man's divorce from nature.

In the first generation, Lawrence establishes the essential rhythms of human life regarded as a manifestation of these deep urges. Tom Brangwen dreams of a new, stimulating life; he wants to free himself from the torpor of his unconscious, inarticulate immersion in the natural world. When he sees Lydia Lensky, the widow from Poland, he knows immediately that she is what he wants and what he lacks. She is the embodiment of all his powerful religious urges—his desire to escape his subjugated and incomplete condition and to find a reality beyond himself. Yet he fears that if he commits himself to her, his own individuality will be destroyed. He is attracted; then he withdraws. She, too, is drawn to him, then shrinks away, defending her own integrity. The emotions of the couple are not "personal." They are expressions of the deep, universal will to love and the deep will to independence. A to-and-fro, an oscillation of love and self-defense, takes place.

What is at stake in their courtship is nothing less than the "reality" of the self—the discovery of a permanency, an absolute, in sexual relationships, that gives meaning to existence. Alone, one is nothing. It is only through love that one can escape the terrible separation from the Infinite and come into vital relationship with the rest of the universe. Yet

Tom depends too much on the female for his fulfillment. His love is half worshipful, half fearful: if she should turn against him, he knows he will be lost, destroyed. When she is having a child, he feels nullified and lapses into the "irresponsibility" of his boyhood.

At length, Tom is able to overcome his Victorian fears and his worshipful attitude; he is able to "let go," and his consummation destroys the old self in him. He feels transfigured, glorified; he has a "complete confirmation" that is like the confirmation that Lawrence had experienced with Frieda. Yet the splendor of sensual fulfillment can never satisfy Tom's deep male purposive desire. He knows that he needs "other things than her, other centres of living"; but his creative, purposive self is undeveloped. He stakes everything on Love, and it is not enough. There remains his deep need for a mission in life; but he does not know what it is. The best he can do, being limited, is to seek fulfillment in his daughter, who he hopes will become a lady in fulfillment of his spiritual desires. He turns to Anna, unconsciously seeking in her the female infinite that he has only imperfectly known in his wife. And he dies in the dark floodwaters of the marsh, the female element, never having freed himself for significant life work.

In the second generation, the same powerful desires are manifested in the interaction between Will and Anna. In its psychic development, the ontogeny recapitulates the phylogeny: love is the gateway to the Infinite, the consummation; yet love is again potentially destructive of individuality and cannot provide complete fulfillment until it is joined to a strong creative or religious purposiveness. Again, the novel plays variations on Lawrence's personal life. Again there is the miraculous fulfillment of the marriage bed; but again there is the male's deep uneasiness because he knows he has other things to do, knows that a deeper summons must be obeyed: he must set about the business of creating a new heaven and a new earth.

Will Brangwen, whose religious inclinations are stronger than Tom's, is drawn intuitively to the church. He wants the consummation of the Absolute, the supreme completion in the Infinite, in that which contains life and death, beginning and end, the whole of being. Yet the cathedral is the symbol of the outmoded Absolute. Lawrence recognized that it was once the symbol of "the whole" and that it was built, not out of egotism, but out of a profound submission to a greater order. Man "didn't say 'out of my breast springs this cathedral.' But 'in this vast Whole I am a small part, I move and live and have my being'" (L, 2:248). But for Will Brangwen, born in the nineteenth century, the attempt to find that Whole in the church is futile. Anna mocks his irrational belief in the dead mysteries, and the cathedral collapses—becomes "dead matter" that he cannot believe in. Jeered into "nullity," he can only seek another absolute: the perverse Absolute, the gratification of all his violent sensual desires. There is a release in this. His plunge into perversity frees him from his old, dead mystical self, and gratified sensually, he is able to turn to a purposive activity: he teaches woodworking in the school at Cossethay. Yet he never challenges the dead social system in which he must function. And he ends up living in "red-brick suburbia," an acquiescent citizen in the great machine. Anna, meantime, finds *her* fulfillment in motherhood—rather like Alice Dax, whose militancy was swallowed up in her devotion to her son. The rainbow beckons Anna to journey onward; but she does not heed the summons.

In the third generation, Ursula, the daughter of Will and Anna, continues the timeless quest for fulfillment. Intelligent, sensitive, and forthright, Ursula cannot accept the formulas of Christianity. To turn the other cheek is to violate her intrinsic dignity and her fierce sense of justice. She cannot compromise with a system that demands her submission to intolerable evils. In love, she seeks one of the "sons of God," a man who, as proud as herself, will not submit to a humiliating compromise with society. But she is quickly disillusioned by her first lover, Anton Skrebensky, who turns out to be a functional unit in the society, a military engineer whose only idea of purpose is to serve the state, whatever it commands. Disappointed, Ursula searches for another "centre" of living. She is drawn to Miss Inger, her teacher, who argues that men have lost the capacity for doing. But Miss Inger proves as sterile as Skrebensky. She is another modern nullity whose sole raison d'être is to fit into the industrial system and to profit by her acquiescence to it. Then Ursula throws herself into "the man's world," becoming a teacher, only to discover that teaching means bullying, the assertion of power over children who hate their subjugation. And when she goes to the university, she discovers, not the temple of sacred knowledge, but a warehouse in which the sole purpose is to prepare young men and women to make money and to "succeed."

Recoiling from this disillusionment, she turns again to Skrebensky, who has returned from the Boer War and, as empty as ever, seeks to fill his inner void by plunging into "African" sensation seeking with her. Through sheer sensation, through sexual violence, he hopes to give meaning to his life. But their love becomes a hideous struggle for domination. Drawing upon the psychology of Dostoevsky, Lawrence sees this plunge into "sensationalism" as an effort to achieve the absolute through destruction or "reduction"—the dismemberment of natural organic life and the pitiless assertion of the egoistic will to power. The result of this struggle for omnipotence in love-making is

Ursula's psychic destruction of Skrebensky. For such a struggle leads inevitably to the triumph of one and the destruction of the other.

But it is a horrifying triumph. Ursula, recoiling from herself—from the madness of her own will to power—must seek a new direction. Pregnant, she is tempted to submit to the decrees of society—to marry the man whom she detests. The threat to her creative freedom is symbolized by the herd of horses that seek to trample her in an enclosed pasture—horses that, critics such as Gavriel Ben-Ephraim and Mark Spilka have argued, represent "powerful male sensuality" and prevent the "social, devitalized marriage with Skrebensky" (Ben-Ephraim, *Moon's Dominion*, 178). I would prefer to say that the horses represent the blind, purposeless, and powerful forces or impulses of nature which can prevent human beings from achieving freedom and maximum of development. Ursula, however, *climbs out* of the enclosed pasture in which she is trapped: the climbing is a symbolic movement toward a more conscious or highly developed life. She loses her baby, but she is readied for a new life, uncompromising. At the end of the novel, the vision of the rainbow reappears: she knows now that she can never yield to the ugly mechanical way of life that condemns men and women to an ignominious acceptance of what they hate in their souls.

The ending of *The Rainbow* has seemed contrived to many critics. But the vision of fulfillment in the rainbow—in the rounded arch created by the union of water and sunlight, female and male, flesh and spirit, origin and end, the unconscious and the conscious—this vision hovers over every generation in the novel. The building of the rainbow is the deep unconscious goal: the fulfillment of desire both in the union of man and woman and in the balancing of the deep desires toward union and toward the maximum of individual being. Mankind's timeless struggle for fulfillment of its deepest desires is the essential theme. Lawrence was attempting—as a letter written to Gordon Campbell in March 1915 suggests—to "give expression to the great collective experience, not to the individual" (*L*, 2:301). Lawrence's purpose, unlike that of the lyrical artist, was not to give a personal impression of life: "One is in oneself the whole of mankind. . . . Not *me*—the little, vain, personal D. H. Lawrence—but that unnameable me which is not vain nor personal" (*L*, 2:302). His own experience was important only as a clue to the understanding of what all men felt and needed deeply, unconsciously. His object was to "put into art the new Great Law of God and Mankind—not the empirical discovery of the individual—but the utterance of the great racial or human consciousness, a little of which is in me . . . it is The Law we must utter—the New, real Law—not subjective experience" (*L*, 2:302). The new Great Law was a law true to the deepest psychology, which comprehends not only the need for love and the need for independence but also the creative religious striving for meaning and for an absolute. The rainbow is the new equivalent of the cathedral, symbol of the whole in which psychic integration is inseparable from social integration in a new world based on truth—on acceptance of human desire as the vital manifestation of the divine impulse that works through all things, on submission to that divine will as the condition of health and social progress. In the second half of the novel, Lawrence draws a vivid picture of the ugliness and evil of industrialized England—a system based on the machine and dedicated solely to maximum production and profit. The violation of men's deepest needs is the result of the egotistic will to power; submission to the machine for the sake of power has crippled and poisoned life everywhere. A world of healthy men and women can arise only if the machine is smashed, only if all existing conditions of life are altered radically.

For Lawrence, the solution had to be radical. No compromise with a sordid materialism or a militant egotism was possible. It was, for him, as for a Luther or a Gandhi, a choice between purity and filth, between truth and falsehood, between life and death, between God's way and the way of the world. Now fully conscious of his special mission in life, Lawrence, like Gandhi, had to take a direction that would lead "to all or to nothing" (Erikson, 100). Writing was not enough; he had to create the new heaven and new earth in *fact*—in the building of a new religious society. In this ambition, he seems "hopelessly messianic" to some. But as Kim A. Herzinger has pointed out in *D. H. Lawrence in His Time: 1908–1915:*

> Those, such as Paul Delany in his *D. H. Lawrence's Nightmare,* who see Rananim [Lawrence's city of God] as simply the utopian fantasy of a hopelessly messianic and embittered Lawrence, do not sufficiently take into account the powerful attraction, and general success, of the small enclave-community in early twentieth-century cultural life. With few exceptions, every significant British writer between 1910 and 1930 attached himself more or less intimately to an actual enclave-community (like Bloomsbury or Cambridge or the Kensington Imagists) or to a de facto enclave-community of kindred spirits (like the Georgians). (Pp. 22–23)

In praising the Georgian poets for their overcoming of fear and their "keen zest in life," their affirmation of "joy" and their "warmth of blood," Lawrence was convinced that a new generation had arisen to liberate mankind from the bondage of rationalism, Victorianism, and reaction. What he did not understand clearly in 1913 and 1914 was that most of his contemporaries, in their rebellion against the system, were lukewarm.

5

CONSTRUCTION AND DESTRUCTION: WORLD WAR I AND RANANIM

1915: Meets Ottoline Morrell, Bertrand Russell, Duncan Grant, E. M. Forster, Dorothy Brett, Philip Heseltine, Aldous Huxley, and others; plan for Rananim: an alternative to the madness of the system; reading of early Greek philosophers and Sir James Frazer; quarrels with Russell and others; shocked by encounter with Cambridge homosexuals—Keynes, Birrell; *The Rainbow* published in September; suppressed in November; "The Crown": a full statement of Lawrence's "philosophy," of the need for the right relationship of love and power; moves to Cornwall in December; illness.

Perhaps an even greater impression was made by his warm, sincere approach; it was evident that he expected nothing in return . . . and was also quite prepared to attack his friends if he thought it necessary. Luther always had the gift of winning enthusiastic friends and supporters; many of them he lost again, and cursed roundly.

—Richard Friedenthal, *Martin Luther*

In 1914, in Italy, living first in Lerici and then in the square pink Villino Ettore Gambrosier in Fiascherino on the Gulf of Spezia, Lawrence was "very deeply happy" with Frieda, despite the conflicts that arose because he resented her yearning for her children. Lawrence knew he was doing new, important work; he loved the beauty of Italy and liked the Italians, who were so much less rigid than the English. His faith in his work and his hope for humanity were strong. In his optimism, he could write, "I like people as people anywhere" (L, 2:149). Yet he also felt isolated, cut off from those whom he hoped to rally in an effort to create a "new heaven and new earth." In June 1914 he wrote to Henry Savage: "I *should* like to see a few decent men enlist themselves just as fighters, to bring down this old régime of dirty, dead ideas and make a living revolution" (L, 2:179). A month earlier he had written to John Middleton Murry: "Can you understand how cruelly I feel the want of friends who will believe in me a bit. People think I'm a sort of queer fish that can write: that is all. And how I loathe it. There isn't a soul cares a damn for me, except Frieda—and it's rough to have all the burden put on her" (L, 2:171). When Murry wrote back, saying that Edward Marsh (who had published one of Lawrence's poems in *Georgian Poetry*) and the Irish lawyer Gordon Campbell had said some unpleasant things about Lawrence, Lawrence replied: "Oh, I think to myself, if only one could have a few real friends, who will understand a bit along with one. They are all against one. I feel Marsh against me with the whole of his being: and Campbell would like to be, for he is a perverse devil" (L, 2:161).

His assertion that "they are all against one" suggests paranoia, but one must remember that he had been trying, when he met these people a year earlier, to break through normal self-protectiveness; he felt he could not be his "further self" with Edward Marsh: "One might as well talk to a daisy by the path, as be one's further self with Marsh.— Campbell ought not to misunderstand me" (L, 2:161). What Lawrence wanted, he went on to say, was people "to have *faith*. I am rather great on faith just now. . . . We are so egoistic, that we are shamed of ourselves out of existence. One ought to have faith in what one ultimately is, then one can bear at last the hosts of unpleasant things which one is en route. I seem to spend half my days having revulsions and convulsions from myself. But I do know that Frieda knows I am really decent, and so I depend on her. —It is so horribly difficult not to betray oneself, somehow, with all the different people" (L, 2:160–61).

He identified here the problem that the practical reformer or revolutionist has invariably failed to solve. He wanted friends and believers for his cause, yet he must preserve his own inviolacy in his contacts with others: he must guard against the betrayal of his deep, religious or "further self." And he expected others to have his own daring—the daring, as Ivy Low put it, "to be true to themselves and to their own feelings" (Nehls, 1:218). He expected other people to be cathedrals, Frieda said, and was always dismayed to find that they were just little houses. He was too frank, too direct; he expected others to throw off the armor with which they protected themselves and the guardedness peculiar to social intercourse. Because he dared to expose himself, he expected others to meet him "nakedly" and to join him on the deepest level of commitment. When Rupert Birkin asks Gerald Crich, "What is the aim and object of your life?" he puts the kind of question that Lawrence expected Murry, and all of his friends, to answer at the deepest level of religious conviction. Almost all of the frustration and bitterness that Lawrence suffered during the war was the result of his uncompromising insistence on religious faith and submission. He raged because his friends, as he saw them, were unable to give up their self-defensive egotism for the sake of the higher good. Inevitably, his most constant friends were those who, like Catherine Carswell, "shared a veneration for the religious feeling" (xi); or the Russian Jew S. S. Koteliansky, whom Lawrence called Jehovah and who, according to Leonard Woolf, appealed strongly to Lawrence because of his "passionate approval of what he thought good," his "intense hatred of what he thought bad, the directness and vehemence of his speech, his inability to tell a lie" (Zytaruk, xv); or Aldous Huxley, whose religious feelings were undoubtedly stirred by his contact with Lawrence; or Earl and Achsah Brewster, Buddhists whose doctrines both appealed to and challenged Lawrence.

In early 1914 Lawrence's hopes rode high. It was a time when, as Kim A. Herzinger has pointed out, "hope was in the air" and a rhetoric of "spiritual regeneration and renewed wonder" reflected "the enthusiasm felt by the British intelligentsia for the condition in which they then found themselves" (41). But when Lawrence, with Koteliansky and two other men, returned from a walking tour of the Lake District to find that Britain had declared war on Germany (on 4 August 1914), Lawrence said that "we all went mad," and the "visionary beauty" of the world vanished. His soul lay "in the tomb—not dead, but with the flat stone over it, a corpse, become corpse cold. . . . Yet I was not dead—only passed over—trespassé. And all the time I knew I should have to rise again" (L, 2:268–69). The depth of his emotional devastation can be plumbed only if one understands the full height of his hope for unanimity—for a *vita nuova*, a creative life shared by a company of open-minded individuals who had the courage to break free from the prison of the past. The war was the vivid proof that the Christian era had come to an end. As Catherine Carswell observed, "In the War [Lawrence] came to believe fully in the putrescence—worse because it was denied—of the Christian era" (24). It was necessary for Lawrence to undergo, once again, the sort of death and resurrection that he had experienced after his mother's death and his rebirth through love. Indeed, it was an article of his new faith that all men must "rise again and walk healed and whole and new, in a big inheritance, here on earth" (L, 2:269). As he told Gordon Campbell in a letter of 20 December 1914, death was necessary because the ego "would fain absorb the position of the Eternal god. Therefore it must suffer crucifixion, so that it may rise again praising God" (L, 2:249). A year later (he had been reading Frazer) he looked forward to resurrection in Florida:

> My heart is smashed into a thousand fragments, and I shall never have the energy to collect the bits—like Osiris—or Isis. In Florida I shall swallow a palm seed, ànd see if that'll grow into a new heart for me.

> I want to begin all all again. All these Gethsemane Calvary and Sepulchre stages must be over now: there must be a resurrection—resurrection. (L, 2:454)

And as the war dragged on, he repeatedly urged his friends not only to join him in the effort to create a new society but also to submit to the obliteration of self that would make possible the discovery of a new consciousness. He advised Lady Ottoline to "let go all this will to have things in your own control. We must all submit to be helpless and obliterated, quite obliterated, destroyed, cast away into nothingness. There is something will rise out of it, something new, that now is not" (7 Dec. 1915, L, 2:468). He advised Mark Gertler "to sleep—sleep in your soul—everything will come, and will go, in the end" (L, 3:47). "One ought," he said, "like the fields, to lie fallow during the winter and neither work nor think, but only, in one's soul, sleep" (L, 3:46); for surrender to the unconscious, in imitation of the cycles of the seasons, was the precondition of a new life dedicated to overthrowing the evil system. "One has first to die in the great body of the world," he wrote to Katherine Mansfield in September 1916, "then to turn round and kill the monstrous existing Whole, and then declare a new order, a new earth" (L, 2:658).

The war was the madness of a collective Ego bent on imposing its ugly will on the enemy. Lawrence's call for self-obliteration might suggest to the psychiatrist a regressive or infantile narcissism, a desire for retreat into the safety of the womb. But in Lawrence the idea of destruction was always healthily joined to creation. One must die before one can live. The outburst of mob hysteria during the war—typified by the defiant shout of a woman whom Lawrence observed seeing her sweetheart off at Barrow Station: " 'When you get at 'em, Clem, let 'em have it' " (L, 2:268)—was purely destructive. The collective madness—or the perverted sex that issued in love of cruelty—was a disease that could be resisted only by those who withdrew, found peace and renewal in a deep sleep, and were thus prepared for a new life with a cleansed consciousness. The symbol of that death and resurrection was the phoenix, which, as Lawrence had learned in Jenner's Christian Symbolism, represented the resurrection of Christ.

In September 1914 Lawrence was quickly beginning his destructive and constructive work. The old regime must be destroyed; a new community must be created. Destruction and construction must be joined, for hate and love were the deepest impulses arising from the Unknown.

Out of "sheer rage," he began his essay Study of Thomas Hardy (L, 2:212), which develops from Hardy's idea that the individual who resists society is cast out or destroyed. Implicitly, Lawrence argues, as he had argued in a letter of 13 September 1914 to Edward Marsh, that "if people would see things more from an individual point of view and *be* more individual then they could not have a war" (*L*, 2:215). The imperative need was to resist the herd and to realize that "the final aim of every living thing, creature, or being is the full achievement of itself" (*Phoenix*, 403). Social man has divorced his purpose from the will of life—"the passionate purpose that issued him out of the earth into being" (415). In society as constituted, Lawrence held, man exists only as a prisoner, serving the productive machine and the state. But if the state imprisons him, he must "depart from it. There is no need to break laws. The only need is to be a law unto oneself" (428–29). If "sufficient people came out of the walled defences, and pitched in the open, then very soon the walled city would be a mere dependent on the free tents of the wilderness" (429). The purpose of life is to live, to achieve maximum of being; and this occurs only when male and female, uniting, acquire a dual consciousness, a "complete consciousness," which is the Absolute that man most deeply craves. "The religious effort of Man" is to "recover balance," to "possess that which is missing" (447). Such a balance arises only through love—through the acceptance of the female consciousness of identity in the "oneness of things" (the "undifferentiated") and the male consciousness of a spiritual reality that transcends the "I" and in which the "I" is "nothing": "Man must be born to the [male] knowledge, that in the whole being he is nothing, as he was born to know [as female knowledge] that in the whole being he was all" (453). Whether one asserts "God is with me" or "I am in God," the old law of the body (the "Me") must be joined to the new law of the spirit— love for that which is Not-Me. The antinomy of Law and Love—Flesh and Spirit, Father and Son, selfhood and selflessness—is resolved in the marriage effected by the Holy Ghost. History is the transition from the Epoch of Law to the Epoch of Love, but what remains is "to reconcile the two" (510). Completeness of being, which everyone seeks, is possible only when men and women realize that they are God's in the fulfillment of bodily desire and God's in the fulfillment of selfless love. Lawrence obviously rejects the selfless love of Christianity, which, as he told Catherine Carswell, "is based on re-action, on negation really"; but he also told her that he realized that "the greatest thing the world has seen is Christianity, and one must be endlessly thankful for it" (Carswell, 24, 52–53). His essential point is that the spiritual impulse of sympathy and selflessness must be balanced, in a natural rhythm, by the impulse to sensual fulfillment and the assertion of an individual pride and integrity. Both the Not-Me and the Me, the object and the subject, have claims for the whole person.

The ideas sound mystical, blending psychology and metaphysics in a Joachite conception (probably amplified by ideas in Edward Carpenter and Houston Chamberlain) of historical evolution. It is difficult to see them as arising from Lawrence's rage with the "colossal idiocy" of the war. But Lawrence, like Luther, could approach contemporary events only "from the standpoint of his newly won articles of faith" (Friedenthal, 187). Lawrence had to refer the problem of the war to his grasp of ultimate purpose and ultimate reality. And he had to be sure of where he stood before he could attack his countrymen. The mob spirit of the war is implicitly condemned on the grounds that it is at odds with God's will. It is an expression of the failure to achieve maximum of being by wedding the male impulse to individuality and the female impulse to unison. Men fought because they had cut themselves off from the female—the female conception of God in the flesh; and they fought because they were not brave enough to assert their own individuality against the state that expected their submission.

Lawrence was confident in 1915 that a new beginning could be made. The time had come, he said on 3 January 1915, in a letter to Lady Ottoline Morrell, "to wave the oriflamme and rally against humanity and Ho, Ho, St. John and the New Jerusalem" (L, 2:254). As he considered his alternative to the mobocracy—his "new Jerusalem" that he would call Rananim after the opening of Psalm 33, referring to the rejoicing or flourishing of the righteous—he spoke inevitably in religious terms. On 1 February 1915, he wrote to Lady Ottoline:

> Almost with the remainder of tears and the last gnashing of teeth, I could sing the "Magnificat" for the child in my heart.
>
> I want you to form the nucleus of a new community which shall start a new life amongst us—a life in which the only riches is integrity of character. So that each one may fulfil his own nature and deep desires to the utmost, but wherein the ultimate satisfaction and joy is in the completeness of us all as one. Let us be good all together, instead of just in the privacy of our chambers, let us know that the intrinsic part of all of us is the best part, the believing part, the passionate, generous part. . . . I hold this the most sacred duty—the gathering together of a number of people who shall so agree to live by the *best* they know, that they shall be *free* to live by the best they know. The ideal, the religion, must now be *lived, practised*. We will have no more *churches*. We will bring church and house and shop together. . . . It is no good plastering and tinkering with this community. Every strong soul must put off its connection with this society, its vanity and chiefly its fear, and go naked with its fellows, weaponless, armourless, without shield or spear, but only with naked hands and open eyes. Not self-sacrifice, but fulfilment, the flesh and the spirit in league together. . . . And each man . . . shall submit that his own soul is not supreme even to

himself. . . . The question now, is how shall we fulfil our declaration "God is." For all our life is now based on the assumption that God is not—or except on rare occasions. (L, 2:271–72)

Lawrence's vision of a center or nucleus from which new life could sprout was a natural development of an idea he had held eight years earlier, when he told May Chambers: " 'Don't you think it would be possible, if we were rich, to have a large house, really big, you know, and all the people one likes best live together? All in the one house? Oh, plenty of room inside and out, of course, but a sort of centre where one could always find those one wanted, a place all of us could come to as a home. . . . I know I should love something of the sort. Haven't you often felt sad at the thought of the gradual breakup of families or groups of friends like ours?' " (Nehls, 3:601). May Chambers thought that "it was a beautiful thought, but it seemed impractical to me and on a par with his love of heroines like Dora and Hetty—pretty playmates, but useless wives! Besides, he found fault with those who were very kind to him like my mother, so I had no faith in his success as head of a house full of friends" (Nehls, 3:601–2).

Her misgivings were prophetic. Lawrence's hope for a "gathering together" in a unanimity based on belief in God and the practice of religion was foredoomed in the circle of intellectuals whom he met through Lady Ottoline, despite their opposition to the war. He demanded a submission that was neither intellectually nor psychologically possible for these people. When under the spell of Lawrence's fresh, disarming, spontaneous appeals to their deep religious desires, they were inclined to suspend their disbelief in Lawrence's Messianic appeals; but the beautiful and stirring appeals wore off when they realized that Lawrence expected nothing less than total commitment to his views. Bertrand Russell, when told by Lawrence that "I *must* preach his doctrines and not mine," "rebelled and told him to remember that he was no longer a schoolmaster and I was not his pupil" (Nehls, 1:285). Henry Savage concluded that Lawrence expected one to "efface one's own individuality and consent to become a mere echo" (Nehls, 1:211). David Garnett broke with Lawrence because Lawrence's attack on Grant, Keynes, and Birrell seemed to him "mad" and because Lawrence seemed "determined to interfere in my life" (Nehls, 1:302). Philip Heseltine, who at first deeply admired Lawrence's philosophy, eventually concluded that "all he likes in one is the potential convert to his own reactionary creed" and that "he acts as a subtle and deadly poison" in a "personal relationship" (Nehls, 1:350–51). John Middleton Murry was puzzled by Lawrence's expectation that there should be an *impersonal* bond between them as "servants of the same purpose, disciples of the same idea" (Nehls, 1:276). Only Catherine Carswell and the loyal Koteliansky, from whose Hebrew chant Lawrence had taken the word "Rananim," continued to trust Lawrence. George J. Zytaruk has suggested that "the kind of human relationship that Lawrence envisaged for the inhabitants of Rananim existed between Lawrence and Koteliansky. The mutual trust, dependability, generosity, frankness, and integrity which characterized their relationship, judged by any standard, is indeed worthy of admiration" (xxxv). Lawrence's relationships with many of his other friends quickly deteriorated.

The handwriting was on the wall when Bertrand Russell introduced Lawrence to John Maynard Keynes and Frankie Birrell at Cambridge. In his innocence, Lawrence had speculated that men who are great always tend toward homosexuality; but his conception of homosexuality was idealized and literary; nothing in his experience had quite prepared him for his encounter with the rational, cynical Keynes and Birrell. His immediate response was disgust. It was obvious to him that Keynes and Birrell lacked reverence—a word that Lawrence had used to denounce Flaubert as well as the contributors of war poems to *Poetry* magazine— Richard Aldington and John Russell McCarthy (*L*, 2:232). "To hear these young people talking," Lawrence wrote to Lady Ottoline on 19 April 1915,

> really fills me with black fury: they talk endlessly, but endlessly—and never, never a good or a real thing said. Their attitude is so irreverent and blatant. They are cased each in a hard little shell of his own and out of this they talk words. There is never for one second any outgoing of feeling, and no reverence—not a crumb or grain of reverence. I cannot stand it. I *will not* have people like this—I had rather be alone. They made me dream in the night of a beetle that bites like a scorpion. But I killed it—a very large beetle. I scotched it—and it ran off—but I came upon it again and killed it. It is this horror of little swarming selves that I can't stand: Birrells, D. Grants, and Keyneses. (*L*, 2:319)

The homosexuality of these men seemed to him unclean, defiling: "Men lovers of men, they give me such a sense of corruption, almost putrescence, that I dream of beetles. It is abominable" (*L*, 2:323). Paternally, Lawrence sought to rescue David Garnett from the "blasphemy against love": "You can come away, and grow whole, and love a woman, and marry her, and make life good, and be happy. Now David, in the name of everything that is called love, leave this set and stop this blasphemy against love. It isn't that I speak from a moral code. Truly I didn't know it was wrong, till I saw K. [Keynes] that morning in Cambridge. It was one of the crises in my life. It sent me mad with misery and hostility and rage" (*L*, 2:321). Paul Delany has explained Lawrence's response as "panic and hysteria," arising from a fear of latent homosexuality. This explanation is plausible, especially when one considers the strong feminine inclinations of Lawrence's nature. But the homosexuality that Lawrence encountered was also linked to that irreverence and egotism that he saw as a "blasphemy against love." He felt defiled by contact with men whose love seemed to him pure "sensationalism." He associated their sexual activity with "reduction"—a conscious or egoistic sex whose aim is obscene "knowledge"— the getting of sex in the head. As Lawrence wrote to Philip Heseltine in November 1915:

> When man and woman come together in love, that is the great *immediate* synthesis. When men come together, that is immediate reduction: those complex states, the finest product of generations of synthetic living, are *reduced* in homosexual love, liberating a conscious knowledge of the component parts. This is like Plato. But the *knowledge* is always contained and included within the spirit, the process, of reduction, disintegration.
>
> This may sound wild, but it is true. And it is necessary to overcome the great stream of disintegration, the flux of reduction. . . . Otherwise there is nothing but despair. This is why I am going to Florida. (*L*, 2:448)

His violent attack on the irreverence of the homosexuals is of a piece with his attack on Bertrand Russell. Lawrence and Russell had planned a series of lectures on the bases of social reconstruction. For Lawrence, "reconstruction" could mean only one thing: total revolution, destruction of the false society and the creation of a new, just world. "One must fulfil ones visions, or perish," he wrote to E. M. Forster in February 1915 (*L*, 2:292). It was, as always, a matter of life or death. Compromise was unthinkable. But it quickly became apparent that Russell was incapable of apocalyptic thinking. Lawrence's New Jerusalem had to be established "around a *religious belief which leads to action*. We must centre in the Knowledge of the Infinite, of God. . . . We *mustn't* lapse into temporality" (*L*, 2:359). But Russell, Lawrence saw, "won't let go, he won't act in the eternal things"; "as yet he stands too much on the shore of this existing world. He must get into a boat and preach from out of the waters of eternity, if he is going to do any good" (*L*, 2:358, 362). The draft of the lectures that Russell showed to Lawrence in July 1915 was not "social reconstruction" but only "criticism." What Russell overlooked was the deepest impulse of men: "Primarily, you must allow and acknowledge and be prepared to proceed from the fundamental impulse in all of us towards The Truth, the fundamental passion also, the *most fundamental* passion in man, for Wholeness of Movement, Unanimity of Purpose, Oneness in Construction. *This is the principle of Construction*. The rest is all criticism, destruction" (*L*, 2:361).

Russell's reply to Lawrence's objections was that Lawrence cherished illusions; as Lawrence lamented, "Russell says I cherish illusions, that there *is* no such spirit as I like to imagine, the spirit of unanimity in truth, among mankind. He says that is fiction" (*L,* 2:380). But to deny the deep passion for unanimity was to betray the divine truth: "I've got a real bitterness in my soul, just now, as if Russell and Lady Ottoline were [. . .] traitors—they are traitors. They betray the real truth" (*L,* 2:380). Their error was that they did not really break with the old, evil society. They sought to persist unchanged, their personalities intact, unaltered by the deepest sense of the Infinite:

> All that is dynamic in the world, they convert to a sensation, to the gratification of that which is static. They are static, static, static, they come, they say to me, "you are wonderful, you are dynamic," then they filch my life for a sensation unto themselves, all my effort, which is my life, they betray, they are like Judas: they turn it all to their own static selves, convert it into the static nullity. (*L,* 2:380–81)

He goes on to say: "I don't want any friends, except the friends who are going to *act,* put everything—or at any rate, put *something* into the effort to bring about a new unanimity among us, a new movement for the pure truth, an immediate destructive and reconstructive revolution in actual life, England, now" (*L,* 2:381).

He keeps returning to the Truth—his certain knowledge of the divine will, his certainty that he is the voice of that will: "I am so sure of what I know, and what is true, now, that I am sure I am stronger, in the truth, in the knowledge I have, than all the world outside that knowledge. So I am not finally afraid of anything" (19 July 1915, *L,* 2:367). People must unite "for pure truth in the form of our national and social life" (*L,* 2:368). "But it is killing work trying to get a few people to believe—Frieda, Russell, Lady O. I've only half succeeded as yet with anybody. Yet the truth is the truth" (*L,* 2:369). As always, he insists, "It is no mere personal voice that must be raised: but a sound, living idea round which we all rally" (26 July 1915 to Russell, *L,* 2:371).

The words "dynamic" and "living" are crucial. Lawrence remained convinced that the falsity of all views other than his own arose from the fundamental failure to take into account the deep unconscious desire and hatred that well up spontaneously in the soul. In their souls, he was convinced, men hated the system, hated their submission to a way of life that prevented the fulfillment of their deepest desires. In their souls, men wanted to join together in love and trust. But society has ruthlessly suppressed all natural desire—and men, misled by the humanitarian ideal, have forced themselves to fight and to serve "the common good," which was the negative status quo. In its effort to preserve existing institutions and to perpetrate an evil form of life, society was static, dead. Men were "caught in the clutches of the past, working automatically in the spell of an authorised desire, that is a desire no longer. That *should not be*" (*L*, 2:635). To heed the divine promptings, one must act on one's spontaneous desires, not on the social decrees. "God works in me (if I use the term God) as my desire," he said in July 1916 to Catherine Carswell. "God in me is my desire" (*L*, 2:634–35). But he meant his deepest desire—as contrasted with the shallow, socially conditioned desires expressed in the slogans to which lip service is given. Only the acceptance of dynamic and living desire could save humanity. The forcing of the self from the conscious will— against the promptings of deep organic desire—was the insanity of an age that subscribed statically to democracy and the common good. Russell was "stuck by an old formula, that I hated" (*L*, 2:397); and what Russell really wanted was not fundamental change, not to *submit* to the divine, but to preserve his ego intact: "What does Russell really want? He wants to keep his own little established ego, his finite and ready-defined self intact, free from contact and connection. He wants to be ultimately a free agent. That's what they all want, ultimately" (*L*, 2:378). In the famous letter in which Lawrence decided that it was impossible to continue his association with the "finite" Russell, Lawrence denounced Russell as a liar whose "basic desire is the maximum of desire of war, you are really the super-war-spirit. What you want is to jab and strike, like the soldier with the bayonet. . . . You are simply *full* of repressed desires, which have become savage and anti-social. . . . Your will is false and cruel" (*L*, 2:392). Russell's refusal to put aside his own independence for the sake of the higher good was another instance of the willful egotism that precluded all coming together in ultimate trust and all submitting to a superior authority.

Lawrence felt acutely the impossibility of any reconstruction of society when each individual refused to acknowledge the Infinite—or Lawrence's authority as the spokesman for the Infinite. For nature ratified submission to one's superior. Society must "culminate in one real head, as every organic thing must" (*L*, 2:371). Russell said later that Lawrence's ideas led straight to Auschwitz, but as Vivian de Sola Pinto has observed in his *Crisis in English Poetry, 1880–1940*, several Edwardians held that in order to survive, civilization must "build up a Great Society led by an *élite*" (118). And for Lawrence the idea of a dictator— and a dictatrix—was only "rational sense. The whole thing must be living" (*L*, 2:371). Superiority and inferiority were a law of nature—as Lawrence had learned in Spencer and Darwin. A culture which denied that truth became not a living organism but a swarm of fragmented egos competing for power—base, personal power, the sort that Balzac decried in *Cousin Bette* and that Nietzsche denounced in his vitriolic attacks on the democratic herd. The "free" individual in a "free" society was free to assert his own will over the wills of others, in an anarchy of horrifying competition for power. The only alternative to such anarchy was submission to the religious leader who has a grasp of the impersonal truth that transcends egoistic desire. Lawrence has been accused of bootlicking and overeagerness in his relationships with aristocrats, but it was an article of faith with him that, as he said to Lady Ottoline, "life itself is an affair of aristocrats. In my soul, I'd be as proud as hell. In the state, let there be the Liberté Egalité business. In so far as I am one of the many, Liberté, Egalité—I won't have the Fraternité . . . one doesn't have brothers by arrangement.—In so far as I am myself, Fierté, Inégalité, Hostilité" (L, 2:254). Such a declaration gives a misleading impression, however. Catherine Carswell has stated that Lawrence "provided in general . . . an immediate air of liberty, equality and fraternity such as I never breathed with any man of like gifts" (28). Like Keats, Lawrence was that man who with another man is equal. His belief in a natural aristocracy was not snobbish or megalomaniacal; it was Nietzschean in its recognition of the need for higher men capable of despising their human-all-too-human pettiness. Lawrence took it for granted, I think, that others would recognize that he was incapable of a base snobbery and was concerned only about the good of society, never about his ego's aggrandizement. But others often misunderstood.

In his reaction to the "beetles"—to a whole society of beetles, each encased in the shell of its ego—Lawrence felt the need for a total cleansing and purification. The emphasis he puts on purity and purification is indeed obsessive. The deep guilt he had felt for his own impurities was heightened during the war by his recognition that he, too, in his soul, *wanted* to kill Germans: his hostility cried out for destruction. As he wrote in his poem "New Heaven and Earth" (CP, 257–58),

> War came, and every hand raised to murder;
> very good, very good, every hand raised to murder!
> Very good, very good, I am a murderer!
> It is good, I can murder and murder, and see them fall,
> the mutilated, horror-struck youths, a multitude
>   . . . burned in heaps
> going up in a foetid smoke to get rid of them, . . .

Like Gandhi, Lawrence had an "overweening emotional necessity" to "remain unblemished" and a "fanatic dislike of filth and contamination" (Erikson, 117, 123). The words *pure, clean, cleanse,* and *clear* are recurrent in his letters of 1915 and 1916. *The Rainbow* had to be written "in purity of spirit" (L, 2:435). Men must gather "with one accord and in purity of spirit," must pull down London and "build up a beautiful thing. We must rid ourselves of the idea of money. . . . What good is it to a sick, unclean man, if he wears jewels" (Aug. 1915, *L*, 2:380). There must be "a new heaven and a new earth, a clearer, eternal moon above, and a clean world below. So it will be" (9 Sept. 1915, *L*, 2:390). Men must heed "the pure truth . . . beyond the relative, immediate truths of fact" (9 Nov. 1915, *L*, 2:431). England must "work out the impurity which is now deep-seated in its blood" (7 Dec. 1915, *L*, 2:468). He would like to use insect powder to exterminate the bugs, "only to clear and cleanse and purify the beautiful earth, and give room for some truth and pure living" (4 Sept. 1916, *L*, 2:650). One must "hold up the . . . living truth, of Right, and pure reality, the reality of the clear, eternal spirit" (15 Sept. 1915, *L*, 2:394). When he looks within, he finds "my deepest desire to be a wish for pure, unadulterated relationship with the universe, for truth in being" (16 July 1916, *L*, 2:634). In a beautiful letter to Lady Cynthia Asquith, dated 3 August 1915, he sees the whole of existing society as a corruption to be cleansed away:

> It is a great thing to realise that the original world is still there—perfectly clean and pure. . . .
>
> It is this mass of unclean world that we have super-imposed on the clean world that we cannot bear. When I looked back, out of the clearness of the open evening, at this Littlehampton dark and amorphous like a bad eruption on the edge of the land, I was so sick I felt I could not come back: all these little, amorphous houses like an eruption, a disease on the clean earth: and all of them full of such a diseased spirit, every landlady harping on her money, her furniture, every visitor harping on his latitude of escape from money and furniture: The whole thing like an active disease, fighting out the health. . . . It is a dragon that has devoured us all: these obscene, scaly houses, this insatiable struggle and desire to possess, to possess always and in spite of everything, this need to be an owner, lest one be owned. It is too horrible. . . . One feels a sort of madness come over one, as if the world had become hell. . . . It can be cleaned away. (*L*, 2:375–76)

This sense of a corruption that must be cleaned away became, inevitably, one of the most important sources of his writing at this time. His essay "The Crown," half of which appeared in *The Signature*, a monthly paper founded by Lawrence and Murry and financed by private subscription, was an attempt to lay bare the deep unconscious motives acting in the war—the unconscious lust for cruelty, destruction, and death. Lawrence hoped that the magazine might be "the seed . . . of a great change in life: the beginning of a new religious era, from my point" (22 Sept. 1915, *L*, 2:399). The immediate problem of the war had to be diagnosed, however, in the light of ultimate truth, and the essay is one of Lawrence's fullest and most satisfying articulations of his "philosophy."

Psychology merges with metaphysics in his postulation of two great rivals fighting for the crown—the lion and the unicorn. The lion is the body, the blood, the darkness, the unconscious, the physical origin; it is also the sensual or subjective will to power, the voluntary impulse. The unicorn is the spirit, the consciousness, the light, the "end"; and it is the selfless impulse to love, the sympathetic impulse. Should either of these opposites triumph, Lawrence argues, it must perish. For life is the wedding of the divine darkness and the divine light, the material origin and the spiritual issue. There are two paths to God—the descent into infinite darkness and the ascent into infinite light. But to proclaim either path as an absolute is to mistake the part for the whole and to deny the reality of the relationship—the reality of God and of life itself, which is utter relation between eternal matter and eternal spirit, a flowing together and a flowing apart.

In writing the essay, Lawrence was obviously drawing heavily on a book that Russell had recommended earlier that year—John Burnet's *Early Greek Philosophy*. The reading of the pre-Socratic Greek philosophers, most notably Heraclitus and Empedocles, had so deeply stimulated Lawrence's thinking—and confirmed his earlier thought—that he had declared to Lady Ottoline: "I shall write all my philosophy again. Last time I came out of the Christian Camp. This time I must come out of these early Greek philosophers" (*L*, 2:367). To Bertrand Russell, Lawrence wrote: "I have been wrong, much too Christian, in my philosophy. These early Greeks have clarified my soul. I must drop all about God. You must drop all your democracy. . . . I am rid of all my christian religiosity. It was only a muddiness" (*L*, 2:364–65).

The word *clarified* is important, for the early Greek philosophers confirmed much of what Lawrence had already accepted. They were scientists, as Burnet emphasizes, and their "materialism" seemed to be consistent with that of the nineteenth-century materialists whom Lawrence had read—men like Herbert Spencer and Ernst Haeckel, who regarded "God" as an immanent force in the universe. The Heraclitean idea of the One and the Many also squares with Schopenhauer's idea of the world as Will (the One) and as Idea (the Many); and in Parmenides there is a version of the Kantian idea, accepted by Schopenhauer, that "the appearances of multiplicity and motion, empty space and time, are illusions" (Burnet, 182). Again, the idea of warring opposites in nature seemed consistent with nineteenth-century ideas about attraction and repulsion and homeostasis. Ernst Haeckel, one recalls, had argued that Empedocles' idea of the love and hate of the atoms was borne out by modern science; and Herbert Spencer had argued that oscillation, or action and reaction, is the only form in which the Unknown is cognizable to man. The war of fire and water, sun and moon, and day and night had been one of Lawrence's great themes as early as *The Trespasser*; and the Greek philosophers seemed to confirm that his intuition had been right: the struggle of male and female was not just "personal"; it was a manifestation of the cosmic struggle. The microcosm exemplifies the war of opposites in the macrocosm, and as Burnet interprets Empedocles, in a statement that sounds like pure Schopenhauer, "the very same Love men know in their bodies had a place among the elements" (Burnet, 232). Lawrence's conclusion of 1913—that man must be viewed as the embodiment of a greater, inhuman will—was supported and clarified by thinkers whose minds had not been muddied by Christian religiosity.

Of the many ideas that Lawrence was to use in all of his writings (both before and after this date) perhaps the most important is that "God," or, rather, eternal primary substance, is manifested in the division into opposites—the warm and the cold, the dry and the wet, light and dark, fire and water. In Heraclitus, the world, or "the All" (Lawrence began to use this phrase), is both one and many, the unity of the One being manifested in the "'opposite tension' of the opposites" (Burnet, 143). The life of the All is made possible by a continuous "exchange" of elements—fire becoming water in a downward path; water becoming fire in an upward path. Nature observes "measures," or a balance. Neither fire nor water must triumph; the very life of things depends on an exchange in which the "measures" remain constant.

Lawrence sees this cosmic process, which he continues to call God, as "a flowing together and a flowing apart"—a systole/diastole of creation and destruction, in perfect accord with the ideas of Schopenhauer and Herbert Spencer. Moreover, he picks up Heraclitus's idea that fire is conscious; water, unconscious. Fire is Spirit; water is "Flesh" or "Matter." God *uncreated* is the two "infinites" in separation. God *created* is the two joined together, male spirit and female matter. Creation and destruction go on continually, and death and life are ultimately one—a manifestation of the God process.

Yet again, Lawrence sees the idea of the upward and the downward paths as being related to Empedocles' ideas of union being caused by Eros and of separation or division being caused by Strife. Burnet quotes Empedocles: "These things never cease continually changing places, at one time all uniting in one through Love, at another each borne in different directions by the repulsion of Strife" (207). Attraction and repulsion, Eros and Deros, Love and Strife—these constitute the law of polarity that Lawrence defines in "The Crown" and that he had already worked into *The Trespasser* and *The Rainbow* as well as into his early draft of *Twilight in Italy*. The idea is so central in Lawrence that it constitutes the very foundation of his psychology as well as the foundation of his philosophy of history, which is articulated both in *Study of Thomas Hardy* and in *Movements in European History*. No wonder Lawrence was enthusiastic about the early Greek philosophers! They confirmed and clarified everything he had believed; and they sharpened his thinking about the images or symbols that might articulate his vision.

The argument of "The Crown" is that mankind has ignored the law of nature—the Heraclitean law of "measures." The conscious ego, an "inferior I," sets itself up as an absolute, refusing to recognize that it is "no more than an accidental cohesion in the flux of time" (*Phoenix II*, 384). The reality lies in the great flux of creation and destruction, the passage from origin to end and back to origin. Consummation exists only when origin and end are one, when the union of spirit and matter reaches its maximum of being in a magnificent flowering. But the thrust into fullness of being is prevented when the false I, the ego, is fixed or static, denying the deep reality that demands the death of the old and the birth of the new.

Joining a Dostoevskyan psychology to his metaphysics, Lawrence argues that the ego, setting itself up as Absolute, recognizes "nothing beyond" itself (*Phoenix II*, 391). The ego "secretly hates every other ego" and hates "an unconquered universe" (391). It seeks to triumph at all costs, to reduce everything to its will. There is no "coming together," only the spectacle of going apart, each ego a part of the general disintegration, corruption, and dissolution of the age. "Ego reacts upon ego only in friction" (394). There is a desire to destroy life, even one's own life, because reduction is "progressive": the final satisfaction of the egoistic will is the omnipotence of death itself, the *total* repudiation of all organic synthesis or complex relatedness. By degrees, one reduces oneself back to the inorganic—through sex, alcohol, drugs, war. The passion in the war is a passion "for the embrace with death" (400). Yet if the spirit of destruction can break down the ego, it is divine. From the breaking down, the going apart, there can arise a new creation, provided that the corruption is "pure"—provided, that is, that it destroys the old ego and makes possible a rebirth. The passion for destruction must be balanced by the passion for creation, for "all birth comes with the reduction of old tissue" (405); God is both destructive and creative, the flowing apart and the flowing together. Evil is "this desire for constancy" (414). The only course open to men is to reject the fixed mad aim of the ego and to become the *ding an sich*—identifying one's own desire with that of the Reality of which one is an expression.

The gist of the argument is that the monomaniacal perpetuation of a life-denying system and the insane continuation of the war constitute defiance of the divine will by the egoistic human will. An England habituated to empiricism and utilitarianism could scarcely be expected to heed such Messianic preaching; but "the truth is the truth," and Lawrence had no intention of compromising with secularists. Nor could he stoop to the sentimental cant that Love is All or that people are "angels in disguise" (L, 2:313). In April 1915 he wrote to Lady Ottoline: "I believe you, that love is all. But it is not easy. If I love a man, and a dog bites him, I must hate the dog . . . if I have a toothache I don't depend on hope nor faith nor love, but on surgery. And surgery is pure hate of the defect in the loved thing. And it is surgery we want, Cambridge wants, England wants, I want" (L, 2:318). He was aware that his own hatred might be the counterpart of the hatred he observed all about him. He told Catherine Carswell that action "springing from 'the nervous fire of opposition' " was "secretly part of the evil"; hence "he could but say that he would have no part in it, not even a protesting part. . . . We must not 'adapt ourselves' but rather go apart" (Carswell, 23). Yet hatred of the status quo was essential, for the status quo was persistence in egotism. He thus could announce without apology: "I hate my fellow men most thoroughly. I wish there could be an earthquake that would swallow up everybody except some two dozen people" (10 Feb. 1916, L, 2:531). (There *was*, he concluded, a Devil—the "powers of darkness" had to be fought [L, 2:313].) "In his purest moments, Christ knew that the Holy Spirit was both love and hate—not one only" (7 Oct. 1915, L, 2:408). For both love and hate issued from "the unknown which is the Creator and the Destroyer" (L, 3:141). With Blake, Lawrence might have said, "Jesus was all virtue, and acted from impulse, not rules."

But Lawrence's savage attacks on his Judas friends condemned him to the isolation that he had sought to escape in 1914. Or perhaps it would be more accurate to say that he had never sought entirely to escape his isolation. Although he half wanted to fight with others against the dead system, he had been shrewd when he confessed to Jessie Chambers in 1911 that he was not strong enough to continue a prolonged fight: "I am not strong like you. You can fight your battle and have done with it, but I *have* to run away, or I couldn't bear things. I have to fight a bit, and then run away, and then fight a bit more. So I really do go on fighting, only it has to be at intervals" (L, 1:221). In February 1915, he made a similar remark to John Middleton Murry, saying that he, Lawrence, "was a forerunner, like John the Baptist before the Christ, whose place it was to give up and surrender" (Nehls, 1:279). Lawrence speculated that his achievement began and ended "with preaching the revolution of the conditions of life" and thought that Murry was stronger than he in some respects—presumably in

Murry's ability to sustain his effort (Nehls, 1:279). Lawrence said he hated to fight—"It will be such an awful scrimmage"—and in July 1915, in a letter to Viola Meynell, after she had provided him with a cottage, he referred again to the oscillation of withdrawal and fighting: "I feel as if I had been born afresh there, got a new, sure, separate soul: as a monk in a monastery, or St. John in the wilderness. Now we must go back into the world to fight. I don't want to, they are so many and they have so many roots. But we must set about cleaning the face of the earth a bit, or everything will perish" (L, 2:374).

When he moved to Cornwall in December 1915, he persuaded himself that "this is the first move to Florida"; but he loved Cornwall because it was "a sort of no-man's-land" (31 Dec. 1915, L, 2:494), and he was delighted that it seemed "uncivilised, unchristianised" and made him think of the "pre-christian Celtic flicker of civilisation" (5 Jan. 1916, L, 2:496). He was glad that he had not taken the cottage that Lady Ottoline had offered him, because "I cannot have such a place like a log on my ankle. God protects me, and keeps me free" (L, 2:323). He had felt trapped, with "too great a danger from invasion from the other houses" (L, 2:323), but in Cornwall there was space and a magnificent ocean, and for a time Lawrence persuaded himself that he had "found a place where some of the men and women really love each other" (L, 2:496). They lived "from just the opposite principle to Christianity: self-fulfilment and social destruction, instead of social love and self-sacrifice" (L, 2:505). The women were especially attractive—"so soft and so wise and so attractive—so soft, and unopposing, yet so true: a quality of winsomeness and rare, unconscious Female soothingness and fertility of being" (L, 2:497). Within a month, however, he had concluded that the Cornish were no different from others in the unclean land: only selfish, "with the most ugly, scaly, insect-like unclean *selfishness*" (L, 2:520).

His illness during the winter of 1915/16 could explain some of this vehemence. But the continuation of the war was spurring him into a rage that was as comprehensive as it was savage. Lady Cynthia Asquith wrote: "The war is driving him quite mad with rage—he just sits and gibbers with fury. He sees no hope in the country, nothing but war, and the war he sees as the pure *suicide* of humanity—a war without *any* constructive ideal in it, just pure senseless destruction" (*Diaries, 1915–1918*, 89). In the spring of 1916 the fall of Prime Minister Asquith, who represented for Lawrence "the old, stable, measured, *decent* England" (CL, 1:490), and the accession of David Lloyd George signified for Lawrence "the end of England." As George A. Panichas has observed, a " 'stinking mongrelism' was epitomized by Lloyd George, who, [Lawrence] wrote, 'stands for nothing, and is nothing,' representing 'the Horatio Bottomley Lloyd George world,' 'mean and paltry in spirit' '' (*Reverent Discipline*, 75). The new base spirit of England was the bullying mob spirit of John Bull, the spirit that sought, as Lawrence said in the "Nightmare" chapter of *Kangaroo*, "to break the independent soul in any man who would not hunt with the criminal mob."

England was dead, and there was no alternative but to withdraw from the fray and to seek, in isolation, a measure of equanimity. When *The Rainbow* was suppressed by the authorities in November 1915, Lawrence was in such a state of repudiation that he could not even accept his barrister's counsel to fight the suppression. Early in December, Lawrence wrote: "But my spirit will not rise to it—I can't come so near to them as to fight them. I have done with them. I am not going to pay any more out of my soul, even for the sake of beating them" (*L*, 2:462). He preferred his inviolacy to the fight, and perhaps for a similar reason he did not show great dismay when the Rananim project fell through. On 12 December 1915 he wrote: "I must let things work themselves into being. One can do nothing now, forcing is disastrous. I shall not go to America until a stronger force from there pulls me across the sea. It is not a case of my will" (*L*, 2:474). It is as if any vigorous action had become impossible at that time, as if he had known all along that others would not join him in building the city of God. But possibly he was relieved too, having feared that his inviolacy would be threatened by communal life. "One has to have the essential life indoors," he had said, "quite inside oneself, independent of whatsoever may happen outside. Voilà" (*L*, 1:223). The habit he had formed in his early youth, of withdrawing when in the presence of those he disliked, persisted; and his psychic economy dictated removal from the unclean or the worldly in order to preserve the purity of his deepest self and of his mission.

This constant tendency to avoid complications in order to continue his work explains his relationships with various women during the war years. Cecil Gray complained that Lawrence was "a Jesus Christ to a regiment of Mary Magdalenes" (Nehls, 1:432); and Emile Delavenay, analyzing Lawrence's "method of attracting female sympathy," speculates that in recruiting men and women for Rananim, Lawrence hoped to escape "at least in part from Frieda's all-powerful grasp" and to enjoy the "complex marriage" espoused by John Humphrey Noyes in his Oneida Community—sexual love not restricted to "pairs" (*The Man and His Work*, 286, 288). Certainly the idea of complex marriage interested Lawrence, who, like Noyes, wished to abolish the "I-spirit" in love. In March 1916 Lawrence would write to Middleton Murry and Katherine Mansfield, calling for "a Blutbruderschaft between us all"—"friendship between man and man, between men and women, and between women and women, sworn, pledged, eternal, as eternal as the marriage bond, and as deep" (*L*, 2:570, 3:302). It seems fair to conclude that Lawrence, who never wished to shut the door on new possibilities in life, entertained the idea of new sexual relations in this *Blutbrüderschaft*. (See in this connection Lydia Blanchard's essay "The 'Real Quartet' of *Women in Love:* Lawrence on Brothers and Sisters".) But while Lawrence dallied with the idea and certainly resented the *égoisme à deux* that prevents married people from entering into new relationships in life, it is not surprising that he did not enter into any well-documented affairs with women. His honesty would not permit him to resort to the subterfuge of an affair, and he instinctively protected himself from entanglements that might distract him from his work or trivialize his life. Hilda Doolittle learned that Lawrence's "fiery love letters" were "no more than a mental game," Delavenay says (284). As Lawrence "stimulated and disappointed" Hilda Doolittle, so he perhaps stimulated and disappointed the American journalist Esther Andrews and the American who lodged with H. D., Dorothy Yorke—women whom Delavenay calls "small fry for his net" (285). But the net metaphor is totally misleading. Lawrence could not have permitted himself to "net" a woman for sexual purposes. Any relationship he might enter into would have to be serious and in some sense "religious." He wanted, and he had always enjoyed, warm relationships with women. A woman like Hilda Doolittle—intelligent, complex, subtle, pretty—elicited all his sympathy—and his male charm. But he could not have acted on his feelings without first making a clean break with Frieda (which he contemplated in 1917 and in writing *Aaron's Rod*) and without being sure that his love was not just a form of the "sensationalism" that he abhorred.

The "impersonal bodiless intelligence" that Helen Corke saw in Lawrence's Cyril attended carefully to the music of its own thought and carefully avoided relationships that would cause a serious interruption of its harmonious flow. By the spring of 1916 Lawrence had concluded that self-preservation, in a world that had become "a dangerous farce," was essential: "One has a certain order inviolable in one's soul. There one sits, as in a crows nest, out of it all" (*L*, 2:601). Indeed, self-protection now acquired the force of a moral injunction: "As far as I possibly can, I will stand outside this time, I will live my life, and, if possible, be happy though the whole world slides in horror down into the bottomless pit. . . . As far as I can, I will save myself, for I believe that the highest virtue is to be happy, living in the greatest truth, not submitting to the falsehood of these personal times" (Nehls, 1:372).

Bertrand Russell said that Lawrence wished only to "indulge in eloquent soliloquy," not really to act in the world (Nehls, 1:283). Certainly this deep inclination to withdraw from the fray was to prevent Lawrence from having any real influence on the course of events. By

September 1916 he could only lament that "my 'indignant temperament' has done for me, and I am dead to the world. Like the monks of Nitria, I am buried in the desert of Sahara. . . . But I hate humanity so much, I can only think with friendliness of the dead. They alone, now, at least, are upright and honorable. For the rest—pfui!" (*L*, 2:648–49). Unlike a Luther or a Gandhi, he could not—he did not want to—adjust himself to the empirical realities (for him they were *unrealities*) of his time. The oscillation between fighting and withdrawal was the essential rhythm of his life, as it was the essential rhythm of his heroes and heroines, who oscillate uniformly between love (the spirit of unanimity) and hatred or power (the divisive, separative impulse to preserve their own independence).

The last two years of the war drove him into even deeper isolation. In part he wanted that isolation; it was necessary if he was to continue his life's work. But he was so deeply wounded by his experiences that for a time his self-doubt became obsessive. The failure of Rananim was in part, as he saw it, his personal failure, which, with his characteristic honesty, he would confront directly in *Aaron's Rod*.

6

THE GOING APART:
WOMEN IN LOVE AND
"THE REALITY OF PEACE"

1916–October 1917: Living in Cornwall until ordered to leave by military authorities; **1916–18:** inclination to leave Frieda because he feels she opposes him; reading of E. B. Tylor, Gilbert Murray, W. M. F. Petrie; **1916:** rejected for military service; completes *Women in Love; Amores* (June); *Twilight in Italy* (June); J. M. Murry and Katherine Mansfield join the Lawrences in Cornwall but soon leave; "The Reality of Peace": further statement of his philosophy; begins reading for "The Transcendental Element in Classic American Literature"; breaks with Russell, Heseltine, Lady Ottoline, the Murrys; **1917:** February: is refused passport to America; "England, My England"; begins *Aaron's Rod* (October); is reexamined by the army; revives plan for Rananim, to include the Eders, Cecil Gray, William Henry Hocking, H. D., Dorothy Yorke, the Carswells; *Look! We Have Come Through!;* October: is ordered to leave Cornwall; **October 1917–1919:** living in London, Berkshire, and Derbyshire; **1918:** *New Poems;* essays in *The English Review;* begins *Movements in European History;* first essays of *Education of the People;* writes *Touch and Go* and "The Fox"; 11 November: the Armistice.

The bitterness that grew in Lawrence during the war was exacerbated by his conflict with Frieda. I suggested earlier that this conflict was inevitable, for Lawrence regarded any woman as the potential subverter of his mission and of his inviolacy. He had sought peace in a woman. As early as 1905 or 1906 he had told May Chambers, "I think a man goes to a woman for rest" (Nehls, 3:599). Rest and solace were what he had sought in Louie Burrows; peace was what he thought he had found in Frieda, "the peaceful." But such peace was based on the woman's total and unquestioning submission to the male. He believed, with Nietzsche, that " 'the happiness of man is: I will. The happiness of woman is: he wills . . . woman must obey and find a depth for her surface' " (*Portable Nietzsche*, 179). Woman, he would argue in *Aaron's Rod*, must submit, not to "any foolish and arbitrary will," but to "the soul in its dark motion of power and pride"—"submit livingly, not subjectedly." And like Nietzsche, Lawrence feared the terrible fusion of marriage which obliterated the male's creative powers and made him subject to the female and to a "female" society. Resisting the *égoisme à deux* of couples "insulated in private houses," with "no further life, no further immediate, no disinterested relationship admitted" (*WL*, 226), he expected Frieda to support him in his mission. According to John Middleton Murry (to whom Frieda complained), Lawrence wanted Frieda, not as a person, an individual, "but as a sort of incarnation of the Female principle, a sort of Magna Mater in whom he deliberately engulfed and obliterated himself" (Nehls, 1:257). And the novels tend to bear out this claim: it is the woman who makes possible the male's self-obliteration in the darkness of the infinite and thus his resurrection as a new self with the pride and power to cast off the dead world and to build a new world. Should woman oppose this male purposiveness, should she seek to drag him back into acquiescence to the status quo, a battle of wills breaks out—the sort of battle that Lawrence depicted with incomparable vividness in *The Rainbow* and in *Women in Love*.

When Frieda persisted in clinging to her children, lamenting their loss and longing to see them again, Lawrence began to see her conduct as a betrayal. John Middleton Murry recounts the occasion in 1914 when, after a meal (prepared as usual by Lawrence),

> we were talking gaily enough, when there was a mention of Frieda's children, and Frieda burst into tears. Lawrence went pale. In a moment, there was a fearful outburst. Ominously, there was no physical violence. Lawrence, though passionately angry, had kept control; and it was the more frightening. He had had enough, he said; she must go, she was draining the life out of him. She must go, she must go now. She knew what money he had; he would give her her share—more than her share. He went upstairs, and came down again, and counted out on the table to me sixteen sovereigns. Frieda was standing by the door, crying, with her hat and coat on, ready to go—but where? (Nehls, 1:256)

More revealing than an outsider's account of the conflict, however, is Lawrence's own dramatization of it in his fiction. His story "New Eve and Old Adam," for example, plays variations on themes that are prominent throughout *The Rainbow* and *Women in Love*. The quarrel arises from the wife's accusation that her husband, Moest, resists the commitment of love. " 'You hate it that you have to love me,' " she accuses him (*CSS*, 1:73). He is " 'too paltry to take a woman,' " she says, even when she flings herself at him. He is " 'afraid to trust [himself]' "— he has saved himself " 'for fear [he] might lose something' " (76). She must have rest from him, for " 'You . . . use a woman's soul up, with your rotten life. I suppose it is partly your health, and you can't help it. . . . But I simply can't stick it—' " (76–77). In words almost identical with those of Anna in *The Rainbow*, she accuses her husband of " 'not leaving me *alone*. You give me no peace—*I* don't know what you do, but it is something ghastly' " (77). She reflects:

> He seemed, often, just to have served her, or to have obeyed some impersonal instinct for which she was the only outlet, in his loving her. So at last she rose against him, to cast him off. He seemed to follow her so, to draw her life into his. It made her feel she would go mad. For he seemed to do it just blindly, without having any notion of her herself. It was as if she were sucked out of herself by some non-human force. As for him, he seemed only like an instrument for his work, his business, not like a person at all. Sometimes she thought he was a big fountain-pen which was always sucking at her blood for ink. (CSS, 1:80)

The charge is exactly the one that Frieda leveled against Lawrence: he seemed to her sometimes like "a writing machine." And the passage suggests not only Lawrence's extreme dependence on Frieda—the kind of hovering dependence that gives the woman no rest—but also the deep blow to Lawrence's pride when he realized that Frieda had begun to hate him for his disregard of her:

> Since she had begun to hate him, he had gradually lost that physical pride and pleasure in his own physique which the first months of married life had given him. His body had gone meaningless to him again, almost as if it were not there. It had wakened up, there had been the physical glow and satisfaction about his movements of a creature which rejoices in itself; a glow which comes on a man who loves and is loved passionately and successfully. Now this was going again. All the life was accumulating in his mental consciousness, and his body felt like a piece of waste. (CSS, 1:81–82)

In the paragraphs that follow, Lawrence depicts the husband's suffering—"almost more than he had ever suffered during his life" (83). His "unknown instincts," his "elemental life" "surges backwards and forwards darkly." "His blood, out of whose darkness everything rose, being moved to its depth by her revulsion, heaved and swung towards its own rest, surging blindly to its own re-settling" (83). In his rage, Moest sees his wife with the bitterness that Browning's duke of Ferrara feels for his last duchess: " 'She's got a heart big enough for everybody, but it must be like a common-room; she's got no private, sacred heart, except perhaps for herself, where there's no room for a man in it' " (86). Moreover, Moest loathes "her pity and her kindliness, which was like a charitable institution. There was no core to the woman. She was full of generosity and bigness and kindness, but there was no heart in her, no security, no place for one single man" (87). Like Will Brangwen in *The Rainbow*, Moest feels glad when he realizes that he hates her: "he could even look at her without the tenderness coming. And he was glad. He hated her'' (87). Like Will, Moest has ''built all his life on his marriage'' (89), but now he must either find a new self—tough, cold, beyond love— or consider whether he has *not* loved her but has only wanted ''the peace of heart'' which she has given him. Has he failed as a man?

> She said he did not love her. But he knew that in his way, he did. In his way—but was his way wrong? His way was himself, he thought, struggling. Was there something wrong, something missing in his nature, that he could not love? He struggled, as if he were in a mesh, and could not get out. . . . Wherein was he deficient? . . . No, he could not understand. His heart flashed hot with resentment. She did nothing but find fault with him. What did she care about him, really, when she could taunt him with not being able to take a light woman when he was in Paris? (*CSS*, 1:90)

This brooding would be repeated in *Aaron's Rod*, where Rawdon Lilly reflects that his wife, Tanny, just opposes him, and where Tanny says that a Japanese lover would be exciting, with an implied dig at Lilly's sexual inadequacies.

The story ends in bitter, apparently irreconcilable opposition. Moest's wife, writing to him in Italy, tells him that his idea of his woman is that she is a rib of himself, '' 'without any existence of her own. That I am a being by myself is more than you can grasp.' '' She *has* given herself to him, she says, but he has kept '' 'safely under cover all the time' '' (*CSS*, 1:93). Moest replies that she can love only herself. Both husband and wife are broken by the conflict.

The significance of these passages, and of related passages in other works, is that they reveal both a profound hurt and self-doubt— Lawrence's old doubt that he was not fully a man like other men—and his profound awareness that, as Moest says in the letter that concludes the story, '' 'without you, I am done' '' (*CSS*, 1:94). The debate is not resolved. Lawrence, who, like Moest, had ''built all his life on his marriage,'' could not give Frieda up. Yet he had to remain himself. The love impulse and the power (or voluntary) impulse were at war, and the war could not be ended: there would be periods of truce, but the bliss of the honeymoon could be only infrequently recaptured. The ''priest of love'' could no longer affirm a love that was separable from hatred.

One of Lawrence's deepest grievances was that Frieda was another one of those who ''hate the Infinite.'' She was ''external,'' he said in 1917, and her ''hatred of me'' was, like Cecil Gray's, a ''cleavage to a world of knowledge and being which you [Cecil Gray] ought to forsake, which, by organic law, you must depart from or die'' (*L*, 3:180). (Frieda at this time was probably interested in Cecil Gray, whom she visited in Lawrence's absence when they were neighbors in Cornwall.) In his well-known letter to Katherine Mansfield, written in December 1918,

Lawrence saw Frieda as "the devouring mother" and argued that a man must fight against his desire and tendency "to return unto the woman, make her his goal and end," and to cast "himself as it were into her womb" (L, 3:301–2). Their "fight" arose from Frieda's refusal to follow him "unquestioningly." It was this refusal that led Lawrence, in his depiction of Aaron Sisson in *Aaron's Rod*, to contemplate the possibility of leaving a woman who nullified him and made her children the center of her life. Yet at the same time, Lawrence had to have a woman "at his back." Without Frieda, he would be plunged back into the tormenting isolation of bachelorhood, an isolation not only unendurable but also destructive of all his faith in rebirth through love.

As for Frieda, her plunges into anger and bitterness did not prevent her from surfacing to enjoy a continually interesting life with Lawrence—his tenderness, openness, and honesty, his often buoyant humor, his fierce spontaneous resentments, his unfailing intelligence. Thanks to all these qualities and thanks to Frieda's resilience, her pity for her often-sick husband, and her admiration for his work, the marriage went on. But Lawrence's anger during the war was often so intense that he seemed to be in danger of destroying his very capacity to live—except on the arctic frequencies of rage. As I have suggested, his frequent outbursts suggest paranoia—and perhaps a revival of his childhood antagonism to the bullies who jeered at him and thought him "not right in the head." But if the term *paranoia* applies to Lawrence, one must remember that his fears were those of a religious man who saw all about him a deadly irreverence and a paralyzing acquiescence to the devil (for there *was* a devil, he had decided in 1916). Perhaps John Maynard Keynes touched on the deepest cause of Lawrence's rage when he observed that "Cambridge rationalism and cynicism, then at their height," were "repulsive" to Lawrence and that this "thin rationalism," joined to "libertinism and comprehensive irreverence," justified in part Lawrence's contention that they were " 'done for' " (Nehls, 1:287–88). Lawrence saw this rationalism and cynicism everywhere, and he had no doubt that it was totally destructive.

Throughout 1916 and 1917 he returned repeatedly to his idea that withdrawal was the only way to keep alive the spark of life in a world that was bent solely on destruction and death. On 7 November 1916 he wrote to Catherine Carswell:

> I am glad you are beginning to reject people. They *are* separaters. They *are* a destructive force. They are like acid, which can only corrode and dissolve. One *must* shun them. The spirit they live by is the spirit of destruction and of putting apart. They bring this spirit into the house along with them, and it overcomes one. It is like a poison-gas they live in. And one is so few and so fragile, in one's own small, subtle air of

life. *How* one must cherish the frail, precious buds of the unknown life in one's soul. They are the unborn children of one's hope and living happiness, and one is so frail to bring them forth. Shelter yourself above all from the world, save yourself, screen and hide yourself, go subtly in a secret retreat, where no-one knows you, only Carswell and your own soul, hiding like a bird, and living busily the other, creative life, like a bird building a nest. Be sure to keep this bush that burns with the presence of God, where you build your nest, this world of worlds, hidden from mankind: or they will drag your nest and desecrate all. (*L*, 3:24)

The letter appears to reiterate Lawrence's old conviction, which he shared in adolescence with May Chambers, that the individual is always besmirched by the crowd. But Lawrence's rage carried him further. Now, for the first time, Lawrence had begun to question his belief in unanimity—in the unison of purposive men. On 15 November 1916 he wrote to Lady Cynthia Asquith: "It comes to this, that the *oneness* of mankind is destroyed in me. I am I and you are you, and all heaven and hell lies in the chasm between.—Believe me I am infinitely hurt by being thus torn off from the body of mankind, but so it is, and it is right . . . there is a separation, a separate, isolated fate" (*L*, 3:32–33). He repeated the idea in a letter to Edward Marsh: "One's old great belief in the oneness and wholeness of humanity is torn clean across, for ever" (29 Jan. 1917, *L*, 3:84). The "Florida idea was right"—"all save the people. It is wrong to seek adherents. One must be single" (*L*, 3:25). A month later, he said he found in himself "a curious moral and physical incapacity to move towards the world" (*L*, 3:44). A year after that, he wrote to Mark Gertler: "My heart shuts up against people—practically everybody—nowadays. One has been so much insulted and let down" (*L*, 3:194).

In his bitterness, Lawrence continued to struggle for stoical calm. The creation of a new world was, he concluded, "beyond one's will and one's control, one can only writhe and wait for the process to hurry up in one" (*L*, 2:662). It was necessary to have "patience, always patience" (*L*, 3:58). "One can only wait and let the crisis come and go" (*L*, 3:125). One cannot allow oneself to be "dragged down"; "one should have courage, and stand clear" (*L*, 3:71). "To think of oneself, and cherish one's flame of life, is very necessary" (*L*, 3:89). "Life is what one wants in one's soul, and in my soul I do not want this wretched conglomerate messing, therefore I deny that it is life at all, it is only baseness and extraneous, sporadic, meaningless sensationalism" (1 Apr. 1917, *L*, 3:110). Desperation "comes of submitting and acquiescing in things one *does not vitally believe in*. . . . One should stick by ones own soul, and by nothing else" (Apr. 1917, *L*, 3:118). For himself, he felt that his health was better because he had removed himself from "the bother" of London. As he made a *pouffe*, stitching a green field with a farm scene in "bright coloured stuffs," he was "busy and happy while one's soul of contention sleeps " (L, 3:46).

His view of death, as the war ground remorselessly on, testifies to the depth of his repudiation of a connection with the existing world. "For me," he wrote to Lady Cynthia in November 1916, "it is better to die than to do something which is utterly a violation to my soul." In language that he would use in *Women in Love*, he continued: "Death is no violation nor ignominy, and can be thought of with sweetness and satisfaction" (L, 3:32). Indeed, "only the dead are real" (L, 2:649), he declared in September 1916. "As for the living, they are really the terrible temptation of temporal reality" (L, 2:649). The dead, escaping the violations and ignominy of the terrible temporal world, the "outer" world, had returned to the ultimate reality—the homogeneous source from which the multitude of appearances arose; hence they were "immortal" (L, 2:649, cf. 3:101). Moreover, he was convinced that "the passionate dead act within and with us," as he said in reference to Rupert Brooke (L, 3:358). Following Schopenhauer, who had argued that man's true nature is indestructible, Lawrence could say confidently to Katherine Mansfield, "on ne meurt pas" (L, 3:307).

His reflections on death—on the need to accept death in one's understanding, as a precondition of renewed life—were to work strongly in two of his greatest works written during his stay in Cornwall: *Women in Love* and "The Reality of Peace." He was now in total command of his "philosophy," which he continued to write throughout 1915 and 1916; he was now absolutely sure of himself. *Women in Love*, his sequel to *The Rainbow*, he wrote rapidly, finding "reality in the unreal world. At present my real world is the world of my inner soul, which reflects on to the novel I write. The outer world is there to be endured, it is not real—neither the outer life" (24 May 1916, L, 2:610).

Women in Love is his *Dies Irae*: his picture of a world disintegrating, impelled by a reaction from "the love and benevolence ideal" and plunging into the hell of sensationalism, reduction, and egoistic competition for absolute power. Beneath all professions of love and all allegiance to "higher" things lies the lust for cruelty—the vain effort to find fulfillment in destructive sex and violence. Love has become rivalry for domination; the relationships of lovers are those of "pride and subservience"—sadism and masochism. Only in extremes of sensation or of violence do men and women find any satisfaction of the deep reactive desire for destruction or "putting apart." The war is in the background: the world's plunge into cruelty is the consequence of its total suppression of instinctive desire and of the insane effort to make all of life submit to the control of the egoistic will.

The plot is contrapuntal: the relationship between Birkin and Ursula counterpoints that between Gerald Crich and Gudrun. Both couples seek in love a fulfillment that will enable them to become whole. Both teeter on the brink: they can be swept down the river of dissolution—the flood of egoistic sensationalism and destruction; or they can draw back and save themselves by acting upon their deepest spontaneous desires.

The deepest desire is not simply love, however; it is also hatred of continuance in a life that they know to be dead, static, destructive. Before health and wholeness can arise, the old self, with its allegiance to the dead forms of civilization, must be destroyed. Only Birkin—and then, grudgingly, Ursula—accept the death of their old selves, realizing that the continued fixation of the will upon the authorized goals of society is a living death. Gerald and Gudrun, however, cannot accept this death of the old self. They seek to continue unchanged; but egoistic love is not enough to unloose them and to set them free for a new life.

The novel counterpoints Birkin's and Ursula's gradual overcoming of the conscious resistance to the new life and Gerald's and Gudrun's gradual plunge towards destruction because of their inability to overcome that resistance. Birkin, in the first part of the novel, seeks to free himself from his relationship with Hermione Roddice—a relationship that has become a battle for domination. Hermione, with her superior will power, has subordinated Birkin, "neutralized" him. He reacts violently, denouncing her ugly determination to prolong the affair, and he is drawn to Ursula. Ursula is divided, half wishing to preserve her independence, half wishing to commit herself to Birkin. Seeking to possess him according to the old formula of egoistic love, she is in many ways like the independent Gudrun and Hermione; yet Ursula also recoils from such women, dimly realizing that her independence is only the freedom to impose her own will, not a life-rejuvenating submission to the *deep* love impulse. There ensues a protracted love battle between Birkin and Ursula, and it is not until each accepts the death of the *old* self that a relationship in "ultimate trust" is possible. They need the love relationship as deeply as they need to preserve their own inviolacy as individuals. Birkin understands these deep necessities; and when Ursula at last comes to understand that Birkin exists, not as *her* lover, her possession, but as one of the "sons of God"—having his own integrity and his "otherness" as a unique manifestation of the divine impulse—their fulfillment is made possible.

As Ursula and Birkin move slowly towards health and rebirth, Gudrun and Gerald move slowly in the opposite direction. Gudrun, the artist, the "free spirit," cannot submit to any will greater than her own. Gerald, in reaction to the love and benevolence ideal practiced by his father, seeks in egoistic domination a cure for his inner emptiness. Through "work"—that is, through his modernization of his father's mines and his boosting of productivity—he seeks to assert his egoistic will to omnipotence. "Love" for him means either the conquest of a subservient woman or an infantile regression into the embrace of the *Magna Mater*. Both work and love fail. The effort to possess the beloved culminates in the attempt to destroy her, the destructive and reductive effort to find fulfillment in the total subjugation of the beloved to his own will. When Gerald realizes that Gudrun will leave him, he attempts to kill her; for the process of reduction leads inevitably to cruelty, the egoistic assertion of self as the Absolute over a universe that resists the will. But his attempt to strangle Gudrun fails, and he is driven to self-destruction in the Alpine snow, symbol of the tyranny of the spiritual will. Gudrun, meanwhile, has decided to go with the artist Loerke to Dresden—self-destructively aligning herself with a man who, like Dostoevsky's Svidrigailov, seeks omnipotence in his ravishing and destruction of young girls.

Birkin and Ursula emerge relatively unscathed from the destructive atmosphere of the time. But Birkin's effort to join with Gerald in the creation of a new, inviolable relationship of men dedicated to a reconstruction of life has failed. In the end, Birkin mourns this failure of his effort to form an inviolable bond with another man. Ursula tells Birkin that his commitment to such a bond is "impossible." But she fails to understand that for Birkin the man-to-man relationship, the sacred *Blutbrüderschaft*, is necessary: new human relationships must be built if a vital form of life is to emerge from the destructive atmosphere.

Much criticism has focused on the homosexual suggestions in Birkin's relationship with Gerald. Lawrence has been accused of authorial duplicity; Jeffrey Meyers, Scott Sanders, and many others argue that puritanical repression and cowardice prevented Lawrence from acknowledging the true sexual desire of Birkin for Gerald. But Charles L. Ross, in his essay "Homoerotic Feeling in *Women in Love*: Lawrence's 'Struggle for Verbal Consciousness' in the Manuscripts" (168–84), argues persuasively that "Birkin's unadmitted love for men [is] a symptom of a general failure in human relations" (176). Confronting the disintegration and destructiveness of the age, Lawrence was not trying to conceal Birkin's and Gerald's true feelings; on the contrary, he decided to deal *explicitly* with their evasion of their feelings and with their need to accept their true desires in order to begin a new relationship. But Ross points out that Lawrence strongly insists that "without woman there can be no life": love for a man can only *complement* the heterosexual relationship. A love that tears man from woman is "a love that was perhaps death" (175). The essential point is that Birkin must admit his deepest desires and must open himself to the creative possibilities in a man-to-man relationship; he must overcome the old conventional disbelief in such a union.

Other critics emphasize Lawrence's "ontological insecurity." Judith Ruderman's recent study, *D. H. Lawrence and the Devouring Mother*, suggests that Lawrence's homosexual tendencies are related to his need for a father who could help him to achieve separation and individuation and to overcome the symbiotic unity of mother and child (186). Another recent study, Daniel Dervin's *A "Strange Sapience": The Creative Imagination of D. H. Lawrence*, argues that the homosexuality is "secondary to and an outgrowth of" a desire to incorporate "a hitherto absent or deficient masculine identity." Dervin feels that Lawrence's need to "overcome the conflicts in becoming a complete male was more urgent if not necessarily more basic than the need to love a male" (161). But Lawrence's search for "complete" manhood seems to have been founded on his conception of men's moral deficiencies rather than the putative "ontological insecurity." In considering his relationships with other men, Lawrence acknowledged honestly that he, like most conventional men, was reluctant to accept his true feelings. Birkin had found in certain men a tenderness and warmth that he could not find in "spiritual" women like Hermione Roddice or Gudrun. His desire to overcome the "splitness" in his relationships with such women led him to contemplate a whole relationship, both physical and spiritual, with a man. The further relationship that Lawrence was looking for was also bound up, as were all his ideas of love, with the conception of a trust so sacred that nothing could shake the *Blutbrüderschaft*. Love of man for man was thus Lawrence's effort to realize his full identity as *homo religiosus*, building, with other men, a new heaven and a new earth. The acceptance of a new sacred relationship with other men would make possible a new creative life. The denial of communion with men was a consequence of the modern reaction against the body and, as Lawrence told Catherine Carswell, a cause of "our modern perversions" (Carswell, 89). The cure for modern man's alienation, which is carefully defined at the end of "Education of the People," is "a new, spontaneous relationship, a new fidelity" between men: "Let there be again the old passion of deathless friendship between man and man. . . . Men who can only hark back to woman become automatic, static . . . the extreme bond of deathless friendship supports them [as they move] over the edge of the known and into the unknown" (*Phoenix*, 665).

Women in Love thus dramatizes Lawrence's deepest convictions regarding the relationships of man and woman and of man and man. It calls for a submission to "the unseen hosts"—a "lapsing out" from the known, egoistical self in the surrender to the divine destructive impulse, and a rebirth, through love, to the acceptance of the divine creative impulse. John Middleton Murry and Katherine Mansfield were but the "germ" of the Gerald/Gudrun relationship, but Lawrence could easily trace the failure of his relationship with them to Murry's inability to commit himself to any fundamental change in his life and to the conscious, willful resistance to change in Katherine Mansfield that led her, ironically, to see that she and Lawrence were at bottom the same!

It is a strange, spectral novel, reminiscent of the madness of Van Gogh's last paintings and reflecting much of Lawrence's bitterness and disgust during the war. The imagery builds the sense of horror, and the novel's essential power derives from the strong contrasts between the culture's dead spiritual ideals of love and benevolence and the inevitable demonic reaction from these ideals into sheer perversity and cruelty. In no other novel by Lawrence are the contradictions within "spirituality" exposed with such ruthless and insistent vividness. The violence is always *there*, moving just beneath the surface of civilized life. It breaks the surface repeatedly, in horrifying intimations of some ultimate threat: the War. Gerald digs his spurs into the mare; the rabbit Bismarck rakes its powerful hard foot across Gudrun's arm; Diana Crich drowns in Willy Water, clutching the boy who tried to save her; Gudrun dances before the cattle with their menacing horns; Hermione crashes the piece of lapis lazuli on Birkin's head; in the café called the Pompadour, Minette (whose name alludes to fellation) rakes the arm of Halliday; and the miners are condemned to a subterranean horror by Gerald's new efficiency regime. The normal world slides into abnormality and perversity. All the foreshadowings culminate in Loerke's inhuman abstraction from life—his regarding of people as sheer material to be used for the satisfaction of his power-seeking will.

Colin Clarke, in his *River of Dissolution: D. H. Lawrence and English Romanticism*, has argued persuasively that "in the larger part of Lawrence's fiction the envisaging of a paradisal fulfilment, and the rejection of sensationalism, are always apt to be balanced by an equally decisive, if less direct, *commitment* to sensationalism—that is, to disintegrative sex and the machine-principle" (147). "We revolt from" the snake, as Lawrence says in "The Crown," "but we share the same life and tide of life as he" (Clarke, 78). What this means is not that we must reject the snake but that we must come to terms with it—terms of acceptance within the natural rhythms of life. As Miroslav Beker has pointed out ('' 'The Crown,' 'The Reality of Peace,' and *Women in Love*''), "a natural acceptance of corruption and death could be found, Lawrence thought, among the extinct Etruscans, to whom [death] . . . was just a natural continuance of the fullness of life" (262). But our civilization

> wants to triumph over death and over the concept of man as part of nature. This civilization is showing ominous symptoms of a will to persist, of an obstinate belief in a state and absolute ego which can overcome the rhythms of nature in its life and death duality. It is the cerebral will (as illustrated in Hermione Roddice) and the stubborn resolution to promote mechanical civilization (as illustrated by Gerald Crich) that eventually lead to the hidden process of corruption and decay under a superficially flawless rind which, too, must eventually collapse. (262)

Women in Love digests all of Lawrence's essential feelings during the war. It was written deliberately to be "destructive"; and although the destructiveness is joined (as always in Lawrence) to the hope of reconstruction, the novel reveals that Lawrence's faith in "unanimity" and in "the social passion" had become wistful, nostalgic—like the dream of Rananim. Hope sprang eternal for Lawrence, like his periodic assertions that he was being reborn or entering "a new phase"; but there is not much evidence in *Women in Love* that he thought most men and women were capable of changing fundamentally.

"The Reality of Peace," written in the early part of 1917, was not destructive, like *Women in Love,* but was constructive. Lawrence's application for a passport had been refused in February, perhaps because Frieda was German. Lawrence saw himself condemned to live in the "tomb" and "prison" of wartime England; yet he still hoped to "do something" and believed that his essays could be "effective." "It is time something was done," he wrote to Catherine Carswell on 31 March 1917. "It is time something new appeared on the face of the earth. . . . We must establish ourselves in the absolute truth, and scorn this filthily contemptible world of actuality. We must do something—it is time to move away from our little selves into the flood of a real living and effective truth" (*L,* 3:106). There were "peace demonstrations every Sunday in the Victoria Park," and he thought he was "almost ready to set out preaching also, now: not only cessation of war, but the beginning of a new world" (*L,* 3:106). In fact, for about six months, from the winter of 1916/17 to the early summer of 1917, Lawrence spoke passionately, in almost every letter he wrote, of the need for a new life. It was necessary to "create the new," one must "grow" and "be really free to live and grow" (*L,* 3:39, 58, 81). There is need for "a new spirit," "a new feeling among people," "a new state," "a resurrection in the hearts of people," "a new being" (*L,* 3:107, 108, 110, 116, 134). One must "set out on the new journey," find "a new sky," a "new soil," "move *westwards,*" seek "the ultimate place we call Typee or

Rananim," "a new [world]," "*a new world, a creative peace,*" "a new
spring of hope and reality," "a new dawn" (*L,* 3:106, 69, 80, 78, 87, 92,
102, 100, 104). One must pray to "the good unknown" and have faith in
"the creative unknown" (*L,* 3:90, 98).

But while he preached so passionately to all of his friends and
acquaintances, he also felt that his essays must provide an antidote to
the hysteria and the violent feelings caused by the war. "I am tired of
emotions and squirmings of sensation," he wrote to Mark Gertler. "Let
us have a little pure thought, a little perfect and detached understanding" (*L,* 3:110). It was necessary to view the war in relation to absolute
truth.

Only four of the seven original essays that constitute "The Reality
of Peace" survive, but the premises of the argument are firmly laid
down in these four, and the remaining three probably developed the
implications of these premises. The essays extend, with a directness and
clarity unusual in Lawrence's essentially mystical thought, the philosophy already developed in "The Crown" and earlier writings.

The basic argument is that man must submit to the primal unknown
out of which his deepest desires issue. There is a systole/diastole in the
universe—a to-and-fro of creation and destruction, life and death, love
and hate. To find peace, man must accept both of these primal impulses,
for in man, too, there is the "great desire of creation and the great desire
of dissolution" (*Phoenix,* 678). The "new epoch of the mind" (682)
begins when man accepts *both* desires within himself instead of denying
his desire for dissolution, for one realizes that the egoism of the herd,
the "obscene self-conceit which is the ruling force of the world that
envelops me" (685), is directed towards a mechanical continuation of a
dead form of life. The desire to *destroy* that dead form, and the desire to
create new life, is the deepest will. Peace arises when attraction (or the
creative impulse) is balanced by repulsion (or the destructive impulse).
Love must be in equipoise with hate; selflessness, with self-assertion;
meekness, with power. To balance these two desires is to live in
harmony with the primal creative/destructive forces of the unknown.

The undeveloped implications seem clear: men and women must
have the courage to choose death—death of the old self—if they realize
that persistence in the old way of life is itself a death. They must have
the courage to destroy a civilization that is a lie, a falsification of the
deepest desires. If they do not have this courage, then destructive
impulses will persist beneath the surface of any established peace. As
Lawrence said to Lady Cynthia Asquith in November 1916, "While we
have the vitality to create, we ought to stop the fighting—otherwise,
when the end comes, we are spiritually bankrupt. Which is final
disaster" (*L,* 3:39). And Lawrence predicted, at the very moment when

England was joyously celebrating the Armistice, that "very soon war will break out again and overwhelm you . . . the Germans will soon rise again. . . . This war isn't over. Even if the fighting should stop, the evil will be worse because the hate will be damned up in men's hearts and will show itself in all sorts of ways which will be worse than war. Whatever happens there can be no Peace on Earth" (Nehls, 1:479). One must dare to oppose the mob spirit of the war. One must learn to live in total acquiescence to the greater will behind nature, in total acceptance of the rhythms of love and hate, creation and destruction. To live in such a way, without forcing life to submit to the human ego and will, is to find peace and fulfillment and is to open oneself to renewal in "the bright transition of creation" (*Phoenix*, 697).

There are a poise and an equanimity in the writing which suggest that Lawrence had truly managed, for a time at least, to rise above the "stinking welter of sensations" spawned by the war. He reposes on the eternal rhythms of nature. (The essays "Love" and "Life," which Delavenay thinks may have been part of "The Reality of Peace," reveal a comparable calm.) His readings in anthroplogy and comparative religions had sharpened his awareness of the importance of these rhythms of nature in the life of primitive man, and he saw more clearly than ever that the denial of the fundamental unity of death and life, corruption and creation, was at the root of the Western madness. In this mood of detachment, Lawrence was beginning also, in September 1917, to write *The Transcendental Element in Classic American Literature* (published as *Studies in Classic American Literature*), a book arising from his interest in the possibility of sloughing off an old, dead consciousness and acquiring a new, vital consciousness. Although he spurned the "realists" who believed in "practical" or material means to win a peace and create a new world, as his letter of 25 November 1916 makes clear (*L*, 3:39-40), he was looking for his own kind of practicable, realized alternative to the sickness of the European mind.

His fiction was still realistic, but slowly he was beginning to make use of myth to define his religious alternative. His reading of Jane Harrison had excited his interest in the kinship of art and religious yearning and had introduced him to Frazer. By 1915 Lawrence had read *The Golden Bough* and *Totemism and Exogamy*, and by 1916 he had read E. B. Tylor's two-volume *Primitive Cultures*, Gilbert Murray's *The Four Stages of Greek Religion*, and W. M. F. Petrie's *The Religions of Egypt*. In *Women in Love* Lawrence had drawn not only on Harrison's idea of the ritual dance to ensure success in the hunt (Gudrun's dance before the cattle) but also on Frazer's accounts of the Great Mother goddess, Astarte or Cybele (with whom Ursula is associated), in whose service her priests emasculate themselves; moreover, as I have pointed out, he works with the idea that Ursula and Birkin must accept the death of their old selves before they can be reborn into a new and vital relationship.

The great revelation of anthropology—far more meaningful for Lawrence than for modern writers who use myth without committing themselves to the bases in nature of mythical stories—is that religion is, *ab ovo*, connected with the death and resurrection, not just of the god, but of the corn spirit. At the root of religion lay the actual, the physical, destruction and the deep sense of eternal recurrence. Skeptics might jeer at religious superstitions, but "April's green endures," and the deep joy in the renewal of life is perennial. Thus a whole generation seized upon *The Golden Bough* as a sort of New Testament, bringing the good tidings of primitive religion—that God is real, that his death and resurrection are accomplished in the cycle of the solar year, and that the truth behind the failure and the triumph of the gods is that life itself fails and triumphs—god as Life, as the great creative and destructive power and glory of the universe. Christianity thus rested on ancient foundations, the recognition of man's place in nature and the deep need for the acceptance of the eternal rhythms, the eternal purpose.

Moreover, there was a profound *psychic* truth in myths of the solar year. As the god descended into the underworld (becoming a lord of death) and then returned to the world of light, so one must accept the death of the old self in order to be born again. It was an article of Lawrence's faith as early as 1915, when he wrote "The Crown," and probably as early as 1913, when he was writing *The Rainbow*, that the encounter with death makes possible the release into "positive life," for death may "'break-down that egoistic entity which has developed upon [the soul] from the past. The near touch of death may be a release into life; if only it will break the egoistic will, and release that other flow'" (*Phoenix II*, 399). In such a passage, Lawrence alluded, perhaps, to his own brush with death in 1910 and to his decision not to keep forcing himself as a schoolteacher but to let his deepest desire flow through him—the desire to take, with Frieda, the risk of poverty and of self-reliance. To accept such a death was also to accept the divine will to destroy that which is worn-out or dying. "The spirit of destruction is divine, when it breaks the ego and opens the soul to the wide heavens. In corruption there is divinity. Aphrodite is, on one side, the great goddess of destruction in sex, Dionysus in the spirit. Moloch and some gods of Egypt are gods also of the knowledge of death" (*Phoenix*, 402). Lawrence's knowledge of comparative religions, in 1915, was rather vague; he did not, surprisingly, refer to chthonic deities. But he would later make extensive use of Frazer's vegetation goddesses and gods and would stress the journey to the underworld as the condition for psychic and spiritual renewal. Of particular interest to Lawrence, as his later works make clear, is the idea of becoming a lord of death. Beginning with stories like "The Ladybird," written in 1922, he will develop the idea that a man like Count Dionys, for whom the war has destroyed all belief in love and unanimity, can serve only the god of the underworld—the god of destruction. He is one of the many lords of death in Lawrence's later work—men who have died to this world, have welcomed embrace with death in order that the way will be prepared for the return to the world of light. Aldous Huxley's description of Lawrence as a man who had been "at the brink of death" and had returned from the darkness to find the world unfathomably beautiful, suggests the importance of the knowledge of death in Lawrence's thinking. In Cornwall, according to Catherine Carswell, Lawrence showed a "certainty" that he would not live long and that "time for him might not be lost" (Page, 140–41). Part of Lawrence's "authority" was apparently his knowledge that he had experienced death—he *had* died to this world—and had accepted death in his understanding as one with life. That is the great insight of "The Reality of Peace," as it is the great insight of the mythic imagination.

James C. Cowan has showed how pervasively the structure of myth came to dominate Lawrence's writing during his "American journey" and during the last years of his life. Encountering "the waste land of contemporary life," Lawrence needed "a myth potent enough to transform it" (Cowan, 64). The fairy tale of Sleeping Beauty and the "monomyth" of romance, with its pattern of separation, initiation, and return—these became the structural grids on which Lawrence plotted out many of his most impressive stories, including *The Virgin and the Gypsy*, *The Plumed Serpent*, and *Lady Chatterley's Lover*. In one way or another, as Cowan shows, Lawrence works repeatedly with death and resurrection and with the ancient symbolism of the solar year as manifested in the dying and reviving god.

As for practical political and economic solutions, Lawrence had none, nor did he feel that the social problem could ever be solved by men and women who accept the "system" and seek to make it work by a sort of fine tuning of its machinery. In *Women in Love* he shows powerfully, in some of his most spirited writing, that to accept the industrial system, with its fixed goals, is to destroy all organic relationships:

> There was a new world, a new order, strict, terrible, inhuman, but satisfying in its very destructiveness. The men were satisfied to belong to the great and wonderful machine, even whilst it destroyed them. . . . [Gerald gave them] what they wanted, this participation in a great and perfect system that subjected life to pure mathematical principles. This was a sort of freedom, the sort they really wanted. It

was the first great step in undoing, the first great phase of chaos, the substitution of the mechanical principle for the organic, the destruction of the organic purpose, the organic unity, and the subordination of every organic unit to the great mechanical purpose. It was pure organic disintegration and pure mechanical organisation. This is the first and finest state of chaos. (WL, 223–24)

Lawrence would amplify his argument in *Touch and Go*, the four-act play published in 1920, which may be read as a sequel to *Women in Love*. In this play his choral spokesman, Oliver Turton (who is Rupert Birkin only slightly altered) argues that the social problem is not, finally, a problem of economics and justice but of the general state of mind that produces resentment and the "ghastly tension of possessions, and struggling for possessions" (*Plays*, 347). The problem is not a conflict between socialism and capitalism, for in truth "everybody supports [the system], the poor as much as the rich . . . every man in the hope of getting rich himself at last. . . . [The people] want the system much more than the rich do—because they are much more anxious to be rich— never having been rich, poor devils" (347). The solution is to change men's minds, not to redistribute wealth and power. Men must "[conquer] their mania for money and machine excitement"; then "the whole thing would be solved" (350).

The conclusion of *Touch and Go* is thoroughly dissatisfying on a practical level. The industrial magnate Gerald Barlow (obviously Gerald Crich once again) says that he, too, like the miners, needs and wants "a new way of life" but that he won't be bullied into reaching a solution. The moral of the story is that class conflict over money and power is stupid and that men must realize that "it's living that matters, not simply having money" (384). The logic is dismaying both to socialists and capitalists, just as Birkin's and Ursula's decision to leave England is no solution for the millions who must stay. Yet, for Lawrence, there was simply no possibility of living satisfactorily within a system based on egoistic striving for superiority and domination. In the last analysis, tinkering with the system would not work: men's hearts must change if "a new state of things" is to be created. And men must have the courage to reject all compromise with the system. One of the great obstacles to change was the bourgeois fear of *poverty*. But Lawrence knew that one *can* live on very little, though, as he remarked in "The Flying Fish," "a man who is not rich, and who would live his life under as little compulsion as possible, must calculate keenly with money and its power" (*Phoenix*, 790).

Lawrence's indifference to worldly compromise inevitably caused him to suffer. In October 1917 the police descended on his house and gave notice that he was to leave Cornwall by the next Monday. The blow reignited all his old fury. He saw his move to London as a return to the Inferno (*L*, 3:170). Once again, he revived the idea of fleeing to America—to "our Island," which was to be the Andes (*L*, 3:174). His emotional state was so black that he seemed "very far from normal" to Robert Nichols. He himself was aware of the dangers of his rage when he wrote to Mark Gertler: "My soul, or whatever it is, feels charged and surcharged with the blackest and most monstrous 'temper,' a sort of hellish electricity—and I hope soon it will either dissipate or break into some sort of thunder and lightning, for I am no more a man, but a walking phenomenon of suspended fury" (*L*, 3:239). Later that fall, when he was confronted again by the medical examiners and had to submit to the violation of the examination, he said: "It kills me with speechless fury to be pawed by them. They shall *not* touch me again— such filth" (*L*, 3:287). To S. S. Koteliansky he poured out his need for escape: "If I don't do something I shall burst or go cracked. I *must* move" (*L*, 3:284). "I am at the end of my line. I had rather be hanged or put in prison than endure any more" (*L*, 3:285).

To restore himself to relative equanimity, he had to insist again, and keep insisting, that the "highest virtue" was to live in the truth and to be happy. More important than the fight was life itself—the ability to live and to be. Even his work must be subordinated to living, for work—as he had showed vividly in his depiction of Gerald Crich's reorganization of the mining industry—was another form of contemporary insanity, another escape from the realities of life. In February 1918 Lawrence wrote, in the vein of Richard Jefferies and Thoreau:

> Then, as to work, I *don't* think that to work is to live. Work is all right in proportion: but one wants to have a certain richness and satisfaction in oneself, which is more than anything produced. One wants to *be*. I think we need, not to paint or write, but to have a liberation from ourselves, to become quite careless and free. And we need to go away, as soon as we can, right to a new scene, and at least for a bit, live a new life . . . and in some queer way, by *forgetting* everything, to start afresh. We live now in such a state of tension against everything. (*L*, 3:215)

He had sometimes reached a similar conclusion during the Croydon years, when his prolonged "swotting" made him yearn to be a vagabond. But his awareness of the danger of work suggests the extent to which he felt he had been driving himself during the war. Now he said that his "real after-the-war ideal" was to "have a caravan and a horse, and move on for ever, and never have a neighbour" (*L*, 3:224). By 1919 he had concluded that his efforts in England were a failure and that he could only "cherish life":

The great thing is not to give in—not to lose one's sense of adventure. Truly one is a dead failure at this life over here—I am—but there are lots of lives. I've not lived more than two, out of my nine. That's seven to the good: and life's the only thing that matters, not love, nor money, nor anything else—just the power to live and be one's own Self. Love is heavily overweighted. I'm going to ride another horse. I mean love in general—humanity and all. Life let us cherish. (L, 3:368)

Lawrence urged Douglas Goldring to " 'look after number one and let humanity stew in its own juice' " (Nehls, 1:495). And he did show a surprising return to life in Derby. Perhaps as a result of his isolation, the stay at Mountain Cottage with his father, his elder sister, her little girl, and his younger sister's boy of three seems to have had a tranquilizing effect. "I feel it is good for me for some time to be with people, and en famille. It is a kind of drug, or soporific, a sort of fatness; it saves one" (L, 3:245). Indeed, "for the first time in my life I feel quite amiably towards [Eastwood, the place of his birth]—I have always hated it. Now I don't" (L, 3:250). To his old friends the Hopkinses he said it was "so jolly when we were all together. And it is the human contact which means so much to one, really . . . only the human warmth, when one can get it, makes the heart rich" (L, 3:258). To Catherine Carswell he wrote: "I feel, at this time, it is better to have friends near one—and children—otherwise one thinks too much and is too much exposed" (L, 3:259).

His anger flared up shortly after this because of the medical examination, but by October he was calmer again. When Catherine Carswell visited him, she said that "his prevailing mood was of extraordinary gaiety, serenity and youthfulness, such as we never saw again in him" (Nehls, 1:473). In October 1918 Katherine Mansfield found him to be "his old, merry, rich self, laughing, describing things, giving you pictures, full of enthusiasm and joy in a future where we become all 'vagabonds'—we simply did not talk about people. We kept to things like nuts and cowslips and fires in woods and his black self *was* not" (27 Oct. 1918, Nehls, 1:477). At Chapel Farm Cottage at Hermitage, Lawrence took time to tutor eight-year-old Hilda Brown, showing her "short methods" in math, inviting her to share their meal, teaching her the "Marseilles" in French, and buying her a melon, which he told her to eat with her fingers and "really enjoy it," instead of "daintily cutting it into cubes" (Nehls, 1:499). He enjoyed the presence of Catherine Carswell's baby on walks and was "ready at any time to take a turn in minding John Patrick" (Nehls, 1:489). The teen-aged Cecily Lambert Minchin, who found Lawrence's visitors "rather condescending and aloof," tells of how, in September 1919, Lawrence took her to lunch, helped her when the chain of her bicycle broke, played charades with the family, and inspired her to paint tin boxes and bowls (Nehls, 1:503–5). She found Lawrence and Frieda "so full of fun and life" that she regretted being too busy with her chores to spend much time with them; and when they left, she and her family "missed the Lawrences very much" and she lamented that "we did not take him more seriously" (Nehls, 1:503, 505).

Despite outbursts of Lawrence's "diabolical temper," it was as if he had returned to Haggs Farm and had recovered some of the old joy in sheer play and in warm companionship. No longer a part of the fight, he could let go—particularly in the company of those to whom his ideas were not of much importance.

In his essay "Life," published in February 1918, Lawrence said again: "I must have patience in my soul, to stand and wait" (*Phoenix*, 697). The patience he had lacked throughout much of this period he now saw as the only solution to his personal problems. The world was mad, but it would emerge from the vortex of destruction. It was necessary to gain some "quiet" in one's soul—the quiet that Rawdon Lilly, in *Aaron's Rod*, feels he has achieved. Insisting that "we are not created of ourselves" and that any great change in the world must issue from the unknown, Lawrence realized that he, for several years, had been trying to *force* a change that only the unknown could bring about. It was a small triumph, this gaining of "quiet," but it was an important one. Lawrence's "diabolic temper" could never be subdued; but it might have driven all love and sympathy from his heart. He realized, in writing *Women in Love*, that to attack an ugly, militant society was to become the counterpart of that society: equally willful, equally destructive, acting from a single motive—hate—instead of from the balance that nature required. His failure during the war led to a fresh realization that one is indeed subject to a greater will and that one cannot oppose this will without doing irreparable harm to oneself.

7

THE SEARCH FOR WHOLENESS

1918–19: Living in Derbyshire, Berkshire, London; has severe financial difficulties; 1918–21: publishing essays in *The English Review* on classics in American literature; reads Leo Frobenius; is interested in Atlantis and in primitive peoples; 1919: very ill with influenza (Feb., Mar.); completes *Movements in European History;* "The Two Principles" (June): basic philosophical statement; reading Helena Blavatsky; November 1919 to February 1922: living in Italy, Capri, Sicily; 1920: *Touch and Go* published; *The Widowing of Mrs. Holroyd* produced; *The Lost Girl,* begun in 1913, completed and published; revises *Studies in Classic American Literature; Women in Love* published; reading Trigant Burrow: the idea of a primary consciousness which is unitive and noncompetitive; 1921: finishes *Aaron's Rod,* begun in 1917; *Movements in European History* (Feb.); *Psychoanalysis and the Unconscious* (May)—important statement of the basic principles of his psychology; finishes *Birds, Beasts and Flowers;* first draft of *Fantasia of the Unconscious; Sea and Sardinia* (Dec.); "The Captain's Doll"; meets Earl and Achsah Brewster; 1922: March, to Ceylon, then Australia; *Aaron's Rod;* writes *Kangaroo.*

After the war, Lawrence had to confront the "failure" that he frankly acknowledged in 1919. The plan for Rananim had failed; he was isolated, having lost many of his friends; his inability to publish *The Rainbow* and *Women in Love* had condemned him to obscurity and poverty. His conflicts with Frieda continued.

From 1918 to 1920 he chafed under his poverty. The fact that he was compelled to write for money and was not free to follow his vision made him curse. When he agreed to do a history for the secondary schools (to be entitled *Movements in European History*), he found himself "cursing myself black in the face" (*L*, 3:304). Although he could provide a "deep, philosophic reverence" in education, he complained: "Curse it—why shouldn't one do as one likes" (*L*, 3:269, 308). "I'm supposed to be doing that little European history, and earning my living, but I hate it like poison, and have struck. Why work?" (*L*, 3:309). "I feel caged, somehow—and I *cannot* find out how to earn enough to keep us—and it maddens me" (*L*, 3:313). To S. S. Koteliansky he lamented: "I loathe returning to my vomit: going back to old work. And it won't mean more than £15 . . . I'm awfully mad and rampageous inside myself, but just hold my nose down and grind on at the history etc." (*L*, 3:321).

A terrible reluctance seized him. Again and again he extols the virtue of not being forced: "The first thing is to be a free, proud, single being by oneself: to be oneself free, to let the other be free: to force nothing and not to be forced oneself into anything. Liberty, one's own proud liberty, is worth everything else on earth: something proud within oneself" (*L*, 3:478). But when he was forced, he reacted by showing indifference and apathy: "Don't let the world matter—it doesn't matter" (*L*, 3:481). "What remaining belief I had in Socialism dies out of me more and more as the time goes by. I feel I don't care" (*L*, 3:486). There is a note of fatalism in his letters: "One may as well accept the dribbling inevitable of this pettifogging fate" (*L*, 3:516). "What does [money] matter, so long as one gets along. I can't take anything seriously any more" (*L*, 3:560). "The world isn't worth raging against. After all, if one can rove about a bit, why bother about humanity" (*L*, 3:687). All this time, *Aaron's Rod* "jerks one chapter forward now and then. It is half done. But where the other ½ is coming from, ask the Divine Providence" (*L*, 3:594). His work was "amusing" or "very amusing"—both the work on *Aaron's Rod* and on *The Lost Girl* (*L*, 3:495, 497, 572), the manuscript of which he had received from Germany. But one gathers it is not of great importance. He does *Sea and Sardinia* in 1921.

He casts about for something to do. He considers a farm in Connecticut; then a boat. If one could ship off to the South Seas! One must break with the "last deep land connections: with society, essentially" (*L*, 3:655). With Robert Mountsier, his American friend and agent, he longs to go off with "two *uneducated* sailors" and "clear of the money complex" (*L*, 3:655). "I am feeling absolutely at an end with the civilised world. It makes me sick at the stomach" (*L*, 3:689). Listening to modern music, he asks Francis Brett Young to "imagine sitting there and looking through the broken windows at this coast swerving and swerving south, silvery in the gold of evening, swerving away into God knows what dawn of our world. That coast rouses a nostalgia that is half ecstasy and half torture in me, swooping in the great dim lines to Syracuse and beyond" (*L*, 3:514). It is "the world's morning—that and the wild cyclamen thrill me with this sense" (*L*, 3:498) Always it is the *inhuman* world, or at least the *dusky* world or the *uneducated* world, that he longs for—the world reflected in *Birds, Beasts and Flowers*.

His restlessness was coupled with a deep personal dissatisfaction— a sense of guilt connected, apparently, with the aimlessness and ineffectuality of his life: the all-too-patent purposelessness. It has often been observed that Lawrence was a puritan, but the depth of his puritanism is not always appreciated. After the war, his puritanism was manifested in two ways: in profound, searching self-criticism and self-castigation and in his continued strong determination to keep himself free of all relationships that might force him to break faith with himself.

The self-castigation is often overlooked. So violent were his denunciations of the society that insulted him and of the friends who, he felt, betrayed him that some saw him as a megalomaniac, an insufferable egotist, incapable of self-criticism. Yet his guilt feelings went deep. Rebecca West has suggested, indeed, that Lawrence's "sense of guilt which scourged him perpetually" was "the motive-power of his genius, since it made him inquire what sin it was which he and all mankind have on their conscience"; West also thought that guilt "forbade him either enjoying comfort or having the money to pay for it, lest he should weaken" (Nehls, 2:62). Freudians explain such guilt as arising from an overdeveloped superego, the "introjected father," who destructively attacks the ego; and this explanation would account for the "ontological insecurity" that, according to Marguerite Beede Howe, is revealed in Lawrence's preoccupation with his identity and his fear of losing his identity. It would also account for Lawrence's affinities to that other *homo religiosus* Gandhi, whose sense of guilt and whose fear of weakening led him to constant self-denial and an obsessive concern with cleanliness. If one has failed in one's mission, which is to do one's Father's business, self-hatred and continual self-castigation may become poisonous; every illness may be attributed to a moral failing; every action may be played out for the highest stakes—salvation or damnation; every encounter with others tests one's purity and purpose. Yet in *homo religiosus*, incessant self-surveillance by an unrelenting superego is tied to creative and productive work and to that deep commitment which requires continual self-affirmation as well as continual self-sacrifice. Such a man sees himself as "nothing" or as "zero" in relation to the divine will; it is God's will that he must carry out; he himself is important only as the voice or agent of that will. His conviction that he has a covenant with God—that the "I" is one with God—gives him a strength and courage that psychoanalytic explanations seldom consider.

The intensity of Lawrence's self-doubt at this time is revealed sharply in *Aaron's Rod*, which, as F. R. Leavis has suggested, is a kind of letter written by Lawrence to himself—a letter in which Lawrence dredges up all the insults to his soul and struggles for equanimity in the face of witheringly destructive attacks. If he had imagined himself a noble leader, a Zarathustra, creating a new heaven and a new earth, the reality now was his poverty, his obscurity, his isolation. If he had imagined that his writings would change the world, the devil whispered that he used his talent, as Aaron Sisson uses his flute, only to provide "bread and butter." If he had imagined that his marriage was different from other men's, the reality was that he found himself living in the same *égoisme à deux* that he had condemned in *Women in Love*. Aaron's experiences with his wife recall unmistakably both the love and the conflict between Lawrence and Frieda, and Aaron's decision to leave his wife (and her three children) mirrors Lawrence's own sporadic thoughts of leaving Frieda. As for Rawdon Lilly—the surrogate of the "strong" Lawrence—his relationship to his wife is obviously less than satisfactory, for Tanny "just opposes me," Lilly reflects, exactly as Lawrence had complained about Frieda. Tanny sides with Lilly's opponent, Jim Bricknell, and she jeers at her husband as, in *Kangaroo*, Harriet jeers at Richard Lovat Somers.

Worst of all, Lawrence levels at Aaron and at Lilly, both of whom show many of Lawrence's own deep conflicts, the charge that they are simply escapists. In effect, Lawrence is asking himself whether his withdrawal to Italy after the war is a flight into irresponsibility. Aaron charges that Lilly has just run away to Malta, that Lilly is not "free" or "content," as he claims, but is always "grinding [himself] against something inside him," always "chafing." Nor, Aaron says, will Lilly "change": he is "only killing time, like the rest of folks, before time kills [him]." And finally, Lilly is not "something special"—he's "no more than a man who drops into a pub for a drink, to liven himself up a bit"; "only you give it a lot of names," Aaron says scathingly, "and make out as if you were looking for the philosopher's stone, or something like that." There is a ruthless honesty in this accusation, which is really Lawrence's own cross-examination.

Aaron's charges are so devastating that Lilly's only reply is to assert that he has found a bit of "quiet" in his soul; he holds on tenaciously to his faith in himself—his faith that " 'I am I, and only I am I, and I am only I, and that is my last blessedness.' " That affirmation of a proud, unyielding selfhood was also a part of Lawrence's puritanism—of his old fear that the cynicism and flaccid fatalism of worldly people might lead him to commit the unpardonable sin against the Holy Ghost. Any acceptance of the way of the world—the way of "normal" people bound together by a worldly amativeness and complacent amiability—would be a betrayal of his integrity. Polite self-effacement to preserve social harmony is a conspiracy against deep conviction. Lawrence had to be on guard constantly against the daily temptation to "give himself away" to others.

This fear is sharply underscored throughout the action of *Aaron's Rod*. Aaron struggles to free himself not only from his wife but also from the whole society that subscribes to love, self-sacrifice, equality, and democratic acquiescence to a conformity that threatens to destroy his essential manhood. When Aaron "gives in"—when he acquiesces to the will of the majority or to women who expect his submission to love, the home, and children—he is nearly destroyed. After repeatedly yielding weakly to others, he is able to reach a kind of equanimity only when he vows never again to yield:

> I gave myself away: and there was someone ready to snatch what I gave. I gave myself away. It is my own fault. I should have been on my guard: always, always, with God and the devil both, I should be on my guard. Godly or devilish, I should hold fast to my reserve and keep on the watch. And if I don't, I deserve what I get. . . . Never again. Never expose yourself again. Never again absolute trust. It is a blasphemy against life, is absolute trust. Has a wild creature ever absolute trust? It minds itself. Sleeping or waking it is on its guard. And so must you be, or you'll go under. (AR, 274–75)

The passage echoes Lawrence's angry outburst in April 1917 in a letter to S. S Koteliansky (CL, 3:112): "I cannot cannot cannot bear the feeling of all these canaille yapping and snapping at me—they are too disgusting and insufferable. Why did I give myself away to them—Otts and Murries etc.!—" The lesson had been well learned. "And Aaron never forgot," the narrator comments. His "sentinel was stationed." Experience has taught him that his sentinel must be "stationed for ever."

Some such lesson, strongly inculcated in Sons and Lovers, Lawrence had had to teach himself again, painfully, during the war years. In the years that followed, his vigilance against any compromise that might cause him to break faith with himself was exercised so unremittingly, and was expressed so often in anger and withdrawal, that he seemed to Witter Bynner and others to be "a promiscuous hater." But to Lawrence, any acquiescence to the collective will, on the assumption of a community of shared interests and goals, had come to mean the death of the soul. Again and again, Lawrence voiced the same fears. In Australia, for example, he found that the way of life "makes you so material, so outward, that your real inner life and your inner self dies out" (Nehls, 2:149). In America, it was necessary to "resist them all the time" while watching that "in resisting them one doesn't become hard and empty as they are. I want to keep myself alive inside, for the few people who are still living" (Nehls, 2:252). In England, "it is an awful great struggle to keep one's spark alight and perhaps kindle something new," for the English "have no life of their own, and they want to drag one away from the life one would make" (Nehls, 2:312). American writers lost their creative force because "you can't adjust yourself vitally, inwardly, to a rather scaring world, and at the same time, get ahead" (Nehls, 2:425). To try to "get ahead" is religiously to be destroyed. "One should discipline oneself," Lawrence would write in 1924, "never to do things which one's own self disapproves of—and then one can't go to pieces" (CL, 2:808).

His ongoing fear of being seduced away from himself is reflected in a number of stories written during the later years of the war and immediately after the war. In almost all of these stories, one may find indirect references to his continuing struggle with Frieda, who appears in the role of the strong possessive female, determined to make the male submit to her will. These women recall the powerful Meg of *The White Peacock,* an unassailable tower of strength, who waxes while George Saxton, her husband, wanes. Obliquely, perhaps, the old battle between his mother and father is resurrected, with Lawrencian variations on the Schopenhauerian, Strindbergian, or Shavian theme of the female spider or boa constrictor: in Lawrence that female usually takes the form of the proud, spiritual, or self-conscious woman who is the potential destroyer of the male but who is often conquered by the indomitable plebeian male.

Psychoanalysis would see these stories as a reflection of Lawrence's continuing oedipal fears, the size and strength of the woman corresponding to that of the gigantic mother to the infant. Again the stories may be seen as reflecting Lawrence's "ontological insecurity" and his desire for revenge on the mother who betrayed him by turning him over to the industrial system and failed him in his need to carry out his mission. Whatever the unconscious motives, however, the stories continue Lawrence's preoccupation with the maintaining of his integrity against the threat of the female and the bourgeois.

As I have indicated, the woman in these stories is often very strong—a sort of Amazon like the woman who often appears in the stories of Joseph Conrad (who, like Lawrence, was influenced by Schopenhauer and who, according to the psychoanalyst Bernard C. Meyer, felt betrayed by his mother). In "Tickets, Please" (1918) the strong female is one of a number of "fearless young hussies" (*CSS,* 1:335) who operate the tram service in the Midlands. Her hard name is Annie Stone; "she can hold her own against ten thousand" (335) and is "something of a Tartar" (336) with a tongue sharp enough to keep the phallic hero, John Thomas, at a distance. Annie, like all the girls on the trams, is attracted to John Thomas, however, and when she meets him at a fair, she delights in his company and eventually, feeling she has got him, shows the pride of "the possessive female" (339). John Thomas, however, is determined to be no more than his name indicates, "nocturnal presence" (338), not Annie's intimate, and he leaves her. Thereupon Annie retaliates, leading the other girls in a wild attack on him. His tunic is torn off, he is thrown on the floor; but "he did not give in to them really—no, not if they tore him to bits" (*CSS,* 344). "Cunning in his overthrow," forced by the vengeful girls whom he has courted indiscriminately to choose only one of them, he chooses the leader of the pack—Annie. And his choice, forcing on her the knowledge that she has wanted him, breaks her pride.

In "Monkey Nuts" (1918) the heroine is even more formidable—a buxom "land-girl" named Miss Stokes, who easily drives a team of horses and who, having conceived a desire for the "slender succulent tenderness" of a young soldier named Joe, imperiously telegraphs him: "Meet me Belbury Station 6.00 p.m. today. M.S." (When Joe's older comrade, the corporal Albert, later taunts her with " 'What's M.S.?' " she retorts angrily, " 'Monkey-nuts.' ") The "masterful" Miss Stokes pursues Joe until he yields to her amorous pressure, a pressure that "made all his bones rotten." But he hates being at her mercy and at last summons up the courage to break with her. Albert, taking Joe's place on a date, informs Miss Stokes that Joe doesn't want to see her. The next day she appears with her team, like an angry Brünnhilde, her "war-whoop" ringing out. But Joe, with Albert's help, refuses to heed her imperious summons and mocks her: " 'Monkey-nuts!' " Miss Stokes is vanquished, and the story ends: "And Joe felt more relieved even than he had felt when he heard the firing cease, after . . . the armistice was signed" (CSS, 1:378).

In three stories of this period, "You Touched Me" (1918), "Samson and Delilah" (1916), and "The Fox" (1919), the hero is the proud, indomitable male who, having the courage to act on his desires, conquers the resistant female. "Samson and Delilah" perhaps mirrors the battle of Frieda and Lawrence. A husband who has (like Aaron) abruptly left his wife and child returns fifteen years later, determined to reassert his old role as husband, as if nothing had changed. The woman, "buxom and healthy," "bursting with life and vigour," like "an Amazon," feels a "sightless fury, like a tiger's" when the man tells her that he intends to stay the night, for she is his "Missis." With her great strength, she pins him to a chair and summons the help of some soldiers to bind him. She triumphs, and he is thrown, bound, out of the pub. But after freeing himself, he returns to the bar and finds the door open. The woman, sitting before the hearth with "knees apart" (as Frieda often sat), cannot maintain her anger and resistance. The man does not apologize for deserting her; neither does he blame her for her part in his decision. He does not judge. As Lawrence, according to Catherine Carswell, admired Frieda's womanhood and even her spontaneous vengeance, which sprang from true feeling, so the husband here praises his wife as " 'a darn fine woman, puts up a darn good fight.' " He begins to caress her, and she does not resist. They fought from the start, he reminds her, and he is pleased by " 'a bit of a fight for a how-de-do.' " Nevertheless, she is not to deny that she is his Missis.

The victories in "You Touched Me," "The Fox," and "Fanny and Annie" (1919) are those of indomitable lower-class males over proud "spiritual" women. In "You Touched Me" the hero, Hadrian, who was adopted from a charitable institution, returns after the Armistice to the home of his adoptive father, Ted Rockley, who is dying and is being cared for by his daughters, Emmie and Matilda. Matilda, a lover of painting, music, and novels, is a proud woman of thirty-two. One night, concerned about her father, she goes to his bedroom and touches his face with her hand—only to discover that it is Hadrian, her "cousin" the charity boy, whom she has caressed. The touch awakens Hadrian's desire, and he determines to "make himself master" of this highbred woman. He asks the dying old man to approve Hadrian's marriage to Matilda; and the old man, who loves the boy, consents. Rockley tells his daughter that he will leave all of his money to Hadrian if Matilda refuses to marry the young man. Thus "the indomitable, dangerous charity boy" gains the upper hand: he has a ratlike courage, "perhaps the ultimate courage, the most unquenched courage of all" (CSS, 1:407), for he is able to act on his deep desires. The woman, Matilda, has touched him, and that touch is enough to authorize his desire for her. In the end, Matilda consents to the marriage: the lowbred charity boy triumphs; the proud "spiritual" woman is subdued.

In the same way, March is subdued by the young man in "The Fox," another virile male who has the courage of his desires. The young man is the hunter, the cunning fox; his prey is March, the young woman whose instinctive life has been suppressed and who lives under the thumb of her jealous, possessive, "spiritual" and near-lesbian friend, Banford (who "bans" the way). To win March, the young man must defeat Banford; and he does not hesitate when he has the opportunity to kill this rival. Like Hadrian of "You Touched Me," he will go to Canada, taking March with him. For he is in revolt against this Old World society that seeks to block his freedom; he knows instinctively that he must fight not only Banford but also society itself, which is "on top of him" and condemns his desire for the older woman. He must fight or perish as a man.

Indeed, that is perhaps what Lawrence would call the "under-meaning" of all of these stories, and of several others, such as "The Captain's Doll" and "Fanny and Annie." The male must fight for his freedom and integrity, or he will perish as a man, become the little "doll" manipulated by woman or by society. He must have the courage to be an "outlaw," like Count Dionys in "The Ladybird," the courage to live "outside the law." The Nietzschean commandment proclaimed by Count Dionys is that one must wield a hammer to "destroy the world of man"; one must become a tablet breaker, accepting, not the god of

Love, but the "god of destruction"—a god of male "power" that would destroy all dead or dying forms of social life.

Not surprisingly, Lawrence's preoccupation with male "power" during this period (as well as his preoccupation with his pocketbook) enabled him to finish quickly the novel that he had begun back in 1913 under the title "The Insurrection of Miss Houghton." The germ of this novel, which was published as *The Lost Girl*, was the idea of a violent reversal—"insurrection" against the stale (though very "high minded") English world in which the heroine is trapped. Alvina Houghton is unwilling to play the game of conventional courtship and acquiescence to respectability. Obliquely, perhaps, her plight suggested to Lawrence that of Frieda when she was married to Ernest Weekley. As Frieda turned from Ernest Weekley to Lawrence, Alvina Houghton turns from the cold-blooded Albert Witham to the dark, sensual Cicio. Unconsciously, she seeks "a Dark Master from the Under-World" (*LG*, 65), and Cicio, who acts the part of an Indian in the Natcha-Kee-Tawara Troupe, exerts a magnetic attraction. Alvina is "glad to be an outcast," "outside the pale of her own people," and "she let herself go down the unknown dark flood of his will, borne from her old footing forever" (*LG*, 258, 279). Their journey into the Alban Mountains south of Rome, where Cicio's native village lies, introduces her to a wildness and savagery that "triumphantly refuses our living culture"—the sort of prehistoric "savage hardness" that Lawrence would emphasize in the American Rocky Mountains or in the Mexican mountains where "the gods . . . demanded human sacrifice" (*LG*, 371, 372). This world Lawrence opposes to the sterility of the civilized world that, at the end of the novel, is summoning Cicio to the madness of the war. Alvina, knowing that Cicio loves her "almost inhumanly, elementally, without communication," has passed "beyond herself" (*LG*, 378, 379). Thus she finds fulfillment in a blood consciousness which, unlike the mental and ideal consciousness, is not fixed on goals and triumphs.

So deep was Lawrence's fear of being seduced away from himself by any cooperation with the world he had known, that he developed a number of habits to defend himself against the importunities and pressures of others. His "ever-ready, amused jeer," as Dorothy Brett called it (Nehls, 2:312), parried the sociability that might cause him to suspend his judgment. His beard, which was the symbol of his "isolate manhood," was another defense against a world of amiable clean-shaven "mates." His habit of giggling instead of replying to others (observed by Mabel Dodge Luhan and others) was probably another defense against the pressures of bonhomie. His response to the generosity of others suggests a similar defensiveness. Norman Douglas believed that Lawrence attacked those who befriended him because

Lawrence saw the help of others as "a form of patronage" and resented being placed "in a position of inferiority and subjection" (Nehls, 2:13). Such patronage is compromising: the patronized person must suspend all honest criticism of, or difference of opinion with, the patron. Lawrence was not, I think, as Douglas claimed, "envy-bitten" (Nehls, 2:13), though envy cannot be ruled out as one of his motives; rather, Lawrence was on guard against any attempt to reduce him to a fawning, acquiescent, and forced friendliness.

The wholesale repudiation or renunciation of the world that Lawrence so often advocated was only a negative solution to his problem, however; and there was always the danger, which Lawrence acutely recognized, that in resisting the world he might become as hard and empty, or as obscenely willful, as those whom he opposed. What positive alternatives remained? There were two—one immediate, the other utopian.

The immediate solution was the one that Lawrence had decided on during the war and that he formulated in the example of Rawdon Lilly in *Aaron's Rod*. Lilly seeks to maintain a stoical calm, a calm based on a recognition of eternal rhythms in nature. The lily does not fret, being life-rooted. In the same vein, Lawrence, in 1920 living in the Villa Fontana Vecchia in Taormina, Sicily, counseled himself: "Why should one travel—why should one fret? Why not enjoy the beautiful indifference" (Nehls, 2:44). The south, he told Catherine Carswell, " 'cures one of caring, and a good thing too!' " (Nehls, 2:71). According to Franceso Cacópardo, from whose family Lawrence rented the villa, Lawrence could spend most of the day loitering on a walk, watching peasants at the olive press and taking lunch with the workers (Nehls, 2:32). To Henry James Forman, who visited Lawrence in Taormina, Lawrence seemed to be a man "at peace" (Nehls, 2:109). At about this time, Lawrence told his Buddhist friend Earl H. Brewster: "We should *not* pass beyond suffering: but you can find the power to endure, and equilibrium and a kind of bliss, if you will turn to the deepest life within yourself. Can't you rest in the actuality of your own being? Look deep into the centre—to your solar plexus" (Nehls, 2:60). These words seem to echo an earlier statement in a letter to Dollie Radford: "In the very middle of one's heart, one is happy, apart from all the world of man. That is the only way: to turn to the essential world of the creative spirit, ignoring the chaos of humanity" (28 Apr. 1917, CL, 3:120). The source of the idea could well be the stoic counsel that is quoted in Gilbert Murray's *Five Stages of Greek Religion*, a book that Lawrence liked: " 'In the centre of your being groan not.' Accept the Cosmos. Will joyously that which God wills and make the Eternal Purpose your own" (127). (By the "solar plexus" Lawrence meant the deep center in the unconscious mind that knows one's selfhood as the subject or center into which the whole of being is assimilated.) For all his outbursts against the world, Lawrence did manage to show, as Catherine Carswell observed, "an underlying steadiness that begot trust in the onlooker and was—it seems to me—incompatible with any neurotic condition" (Nehls, 2:301). In a measure, Lawrence had learned to say *"pazienza, sempre pazienza!"* (Huxley, 562). It was now his settled conviction that "the world is as it is. I am as I am. We don't fit very well" (May 1924, Huxley, 610). But he could repose, in his darkest hours, on his sense of the eternal—on his "vivid star-consciousness," as Achsah Brewster called it, his realization of the cosmic vastness that most people hardly noticed, "not realizing that they were star-doomed" (Nehls, 2:127).

His achievement of a relative equanimity and "quiet" is indicated too by the considerable detachment that he showed in writing *Movements in European History* (1919) and *Psychoanalysis and the Unconscious* (1921). He was making, at this time, a concerted attempt to define the great laws of his psychology. These were "deduced," he said, from his novels and poems—from "pure passional experience." The claim is partially supported by what we know of the fiction and the man. For in his psychology the two great primary centers that are the origin of the unconscious exhibit the great split in Lawrence's characters and in himself—the split between the sympathetic impulse to unison or oneness, and the "voluntary" impulse to separateness, self-assertion, and resistance to that which is "not-Me." In the early fiction, as I have observed, the great creative impulse of Lawrence's heroes is to free themselves from the engulfing and obliterating force of the female and of the tribe—the great "sympathetic" pull that drags the individual into passive acquiescence to the status quo and to the female, who is the prime agent of the procreative urge. As Lawrence's fiction matures, this engulfing darkness becomes more and more threatening. The hero, to save himself, reacts. "Reaction," in Lawrence's psychology, is the effort of the organic self to counterbalance the excessively strong pull of the sympathetic center: it is a hostile or destructive resistance to that pull, manifested either in a destructive cruelty, as in the war, or (in a few strong and healthy individuals) in a proud refusal to cooperate with a sick society. Yet Lawrence's hero does not wish merely to destroy the world. He also wishes to create: his sympathetic impulse prompts him to join with other men in a creative effort of construction. In Lawrence's fiction after the war, this hero oscillates between "love" and "power"— between selfless comradeship and stubborn self-assertion.

The great problem for the modern age, as Lawrence defines it in the light of his psychology, is the overemphasis on the spiritual sympathetic centers. In reaction to that overemphasis, the whole society, seeking to right the psychic balance, has become "voluntary" or "willful." But the will of modern man is the "spiritual will"—the aggressive bullying will to force others to submit, the abnormal, one-sided insistence on unity, good will, the love of one's neighbor, equality, and the common welfare. In such a society, the only healthy way to restore balance is to assert a different kind of "power" impulse—the impulse to male authority and mastery against the female homogenization of the world. But Lawrence does not want base, petty egoistic power: this, indeed, is a form of madness, for the conscious, knowing ego is in the service of a purely destructive will to power. The healthy power impulse is that of the religious man, who wants not "power over" but rather "power to"—power to create, to satisfy his deep purposive desires. The basic premise of this whole psychology is that human life is an effort to achieve "maximum of being." Not the pleasure principle, but the aspiration principle, governs. Man, being derived from the great source, can "come into being" only when he fulfills the deep will of that source; and as all of nature is governed by a law of attraction and repulsion, or sympathy and reaction, it is necessary for man to satisfy both his sympathetic and his voluntary urges. "Desire and anger [or love and hate] are from God." But in the healthy person, the spontaneous balancing faculty that Lawrence calls "the Holy Ghost" checks the impulse to overemphasize either love or hate, selflessness or self-ishness; and sympathy is wedded to power in an organic balance. The Holy Ghost is the voice of the whole self—conscious and unconscious, sympathetic and voluntary, sensual and spiritual. If its counsel is not heeded, a disastrous imbalance occurs; and whole societies react in a blind effort to recover what is missing in organic life. The deep needs must be gratified; they cannot be sublimated or renounced without doing incomparable injury to the self and to the world. History, as Lawrence shows in *Movements in European History,* is a record of overemphases, with only rare achievements of balance.

Throughout *Movements in European History,* Lawrence works with Empedocles' (and Herbert Spencer's) idea that love and strife (unitive and divisive, or sympathetic and voluntary motives) oscillate continually: "Mankind lives by a twofold motive: the motive of peace and increase, and the motive of contest and martial triumph. As soon as the appetite for martial adventure and triumph in conflict is satisfied, the appetite for peace and increase manifests itself, and *vice versa*. It seems a law of life" (306). Moreover, these motives are associated with racial types as these have been modified by environment. Drawing on Edward Gibbon, probably on Houston Chamberlain, and perhaps on Hippolyte Taine, Lawrence argues that "from the south come the impulses that unite men into a oneness: from the north come the strong passions which break up the oneness and shatter the world, but which make in the long run for a freer, more open way of life" (206). Thus the Romans, "children of the sun," a sociable "sympathetic" people, establish a unity based on obedience and submission to the empire; but the warlike Germans, "the non-producing, eternally opposing people," resist assimilation, seek separateness, and fight to break down the unity and cohesion of the Romans. The spiritual will of the unsocial Christians also opposes the Roman sensual cohesion, their "blood-sympathy." With the triumph of Christianity, psychic division occurs in Europe—between the Christian desire for selflessness and love, and the old pre-Christian instincts of fighting and war.

In tracing the larger rhythms of history, Lawrence follows the movement that he had already described in *Study of Thomas Hardy* and *Twilight in Italy*—from unity in the Father (the "Law," blood sympathy, mindlessness and submission) to Unity in the Son ("love," spirit, consciousness, individualism, the ideals of the love of one's neighbor and equality). The Renaissance, according to Lawrence, is the dividing line between the ancient world, in which "the passion of pride and power and conquest" was dominant, and the modern world, in which "the passion for peace and production" is dominant. Freedom begins in the Renaissance. The Reformation, led by "the northern Teutonic race," broke "the power of the Roman Papacy" and ushered in the modern world in which liberty, equality, and fraternity are the ideals that men serve. But the new "unity of the labouring classes" denies the old desire for lordship—the deep need, which Lawrence stresses in his Epilogue, for submission to "the leader who is a star of the new, *natural Noblesse*" (*MEH*, 321).

Movements in European History is history tied absurdly to a theory of racial traits and of polarities, but, like Freud's *Civilisation and Its Discontents* (which *MEH* antedates by ten years), it is a work that illuminates the psychic conflict arising from the frustration of men's deepest urges. And both *Psychoanalysis and the Unconscious* and *Fantasia of the Unconscious*, drawing upon the seminal thinking of nineteenth-century materialists and on the insights of Schopenhauer, Nietzsche, and Dostoevsky, present a theory of the unconscious that rivals Freudian theory for its consistency and insight.

A number of critics have found Lawrence's ideas nonsensical, especially whenever he uses notions that are found in the theosophical writings of James M. Pryse and Helena Blavatsky—notions like that of the four "centers" that originate unconscious impulses, the solar and cardiac plexus, the lumbar and the thoracic ganglion. The criticism is often well taken—the ideas do look nonsensical. But Lawrence uses the chakras of Yoga and other mystical or theosophical terms only to designate psychic realities that he had identified much earlier in his life. He professed no "scientific exactitude," he said, "particularly in terminology" (*PU*, 234–35). The terminology probably helped him to clarify his thinking, and always searching for correspondences, he could find in mysticism ideas that seemed entirely compatible with science. For example, Blavatsky's idea of Fohat, "the universal Electric Ocean, which is LIFE," corresponds to the notion of an undifferentiated god stuff from which the differentiated universe issues. Fohat is manifested in polarities of electromagnetic attraction and repulsion and, as we have seen, this idea also appears in Spencer and Haeckel. Blavatsky also develops the "law which the Kabala calls Balance" and sees everything as male and female, a compound of spirit and matter, of the positive and the negative in equilibrium, which is "the resultant of two opposing forces eternally reacting upon each other"; and she develops the antithesis of life, which is spontaneous and unpredictable, and the mechanical universe. All this, as Richard J. Kuzkowski has pointed out in an excellent dissertation, sounds like pure Lawrence. But such mystical conclusions had a basis in the materialistic science of the time. Lawrence's general view of esoteric doctrines, expressed in a letter to Waldo Frank, was that they are "marvellously illuminating, historically," but "part of the past, and part of a past self in us: and it is no good going back, even to the wonderful things" (*L*, 3:143).

Whatever his indebtedness to others in developing his laws of psychology, his own experience provided the basis for his "subjective science." His keen analysis of his own inner life led him to appreciate not only the to-and-fro of love and power but also the existential dilemma arising from man's divorce from nature and his powerful need for meaning. Thus Lawrence's psychology anticipates many existentialist psychologies of today—such as those of Jean Paul Sartre, Rollo May, Viktor Frankl, and Erich Fromm. At the same time, though Lawrence rejected Freud's basic assumption concerning the principle of conservation—the idea that life seeks to avoid extremes of tension and is driven chiefly by the pleasure principle—Lawrence held to the basic tenets of "hormic" psychology. It is impulse or the unconscious will that makes us act as we do, and the two deepest impulses, "love" and "power," are similar to Freud's instincts of love and death. Yet Lawrence does not reduce human behavior to impulse. He clings to the Holy Ghost, the spontaneous balancing center, as an arbitrator directing the self, adjusting life to the demands of the unconscious and to the realities of experience.

The detachment in this writing suggests that Lawrence had, indeed, acquired "a real bit of quiet" within. And his concern and care for others during the postwar years suggest also his healthy ability to free himself from the sort of self-absorption that one would expect in a neurotic. When he encountered the impecunious and self-destructive Maurice Magnus, for example, Lawrence, though financially pinched and his own prospects looking grim, felt "a responsibility" and lent him money that Magnus used to stay "at the best hotel in Taormina" (Nehls, 2:35). In July 1920, Lawrence sent a pound to Hilda Brown, the little girl he had tutored in England (Nehls, 2:47–48). He remembered to bring "something peculiar and humorous—a salamander and a little baby duck as a pet for the children" of Rosalind Thornycroft Popham (Nehls, 2:49); there were also presents for the *contadino* family at Fontana Vecchia (Nehls, 2:77). And Lawrence was on several occasions a gracious host (and a good cook)—for Rosalind Popham, Rebecca West, and the Brewsters.

He could not have contented himself, however, with the "quiet" of his own life. His mission demanded a continual search for the ground of a new society. The goal, as he said to Earl H. Brewster, "is not that men should become serene as Buddha or as gods, but that the unfleshed gods should become men in battle. God made man is the goal" (Nehls, 2:103). In "The Crown" he said: "The true God is *created* every time a pure relationship, or a consummation out of twoness into oneness takes place. . . . And a man, if he win to a sheer fusion in himself of all the manifold creation, a pure relation, a sheer gleam of oneness out of manyness, then this man is God created where before God was uncreated. He is the Holy Ghost in tissue of flame and flesh, whereas before, the Holy Ghost was but Ghost" (*Phoenix II*, 412). In the fusion of flame and flesh—the male spirit and the female flesh—a new consciousness arises; and this consciousness, being the *whole* will of God rather than a part of God's will, is God created.

Lawrence's search for psychic wholeness was both imaginative and physical. Very concerted was his effort, in *Studies in Classic American Literature* and in his two books on the unconscious, to define the nature of wholeness along with the exaggerations or imbalances of the psyche that prevent people from achieving wholeness. Critics like Philip Rieff, Aidan Burns, Elizabeth Brody Tenenbaum, and Eugene Goodheart have argued that Lawrence foolishly advocated acting impulsively, as the unconscious dictates; but Lawrence's thought, stressing man in his wholeness, is far more subtle than many have understood.

Studies in Classic American Literature is not only bold, original literary criticism; it is also bold religious thought. Begun in 1917 and continued into 1922, these essays are the product of five years' work to define the nature of the "whole self"—the IT—that Europeans sought when they emigrated to America. Their deep desire, Lawrence says, was "(1) To slough the old European consciousness completely. (2) To grow a new skin underneath, a new form" (58). Americans wanted to "do away with the old thing," not only the "old authority of Europe" but also the old morality. In their blood, "sensuously, passionally, they all attack the old morality." Yet mentally, consciously, "they know nothing better"; "therefore they give tight mental allegiance to a morality which all their passion goes to destroy. Hence the duplicity which is the fatal flaw in them, most fatal in the most perfect American work of art, *The Scarlet Letter*" (180).

The fatal flaw is seen first in Franklin, who denies the deepest whole self of man and insists on the "barbed wire moral enclosure that poor Richard rigged up." Against Franklin's prudence and common sense, Lawrence devises his own twelve commandments, all of which say, in effect, "Thy will be done," where "Thy" refers to "the dark gods," the voice of the whole self, the Holy Ghost. Men must have the courage to let the gods—the deep impulses—enter "the clearing of the known self," as well as the courage to act on those deep promptings. Franklin, Lawrence thought, never admitted them. He denied the wholeness of the self, as indeed the eighteenth century generally concocted a conception of a "good man" who was "only one-hundreth part of a man" (*Phoenix*, 752). As Lawrence argues in his essay on the duc de Lauzun (*Phoenix*, 751), the idea of the *homme de bien*, with his "reasonable social virtues," denied the "great passions" known only to the religious.

Crèvecoeur made a similar mistake, Lawrence argues in the second essay, by failing to make any adjustment in his white consciousness to the realities that he observed in the New World. Against the evidence, Crèvecoeur continued to believe that "Nature is sweet and pure, that all men are brothers, and equal, and that they love one another like so many cooing doves" (*SCAL*, 36). In effect, Crèvecoeur hated "the dark, pre-mental life" and simply wanted to get the savage life "in the head"—as a thrill of consciousness.

James Fenimore Cooper, too, clung to the idea and the ideal—to the ideal of democracy and equality, even though "his innermost wish was to be: Natty Bumppo"—to slough "the old skin, the old form" of democratic life and to discover "a new human relationship"—that of two men joined in a new comradeship and integrity. In Cooper, Lawrence sees the deep unconscious resistance to the democratic will and the unconscious need for male integrity. In the satisfaction of that need is the potentiality for a new American character, one that will resist all disintegrative forces and keep its moral integrity "hard and intact. An isolate, almost selfless, stoic, enduring man, who lives by death, by killing, but who is pure white" (*SCAL*, 69). Such a man, like the hero of *The Boy in the Bush*, has the courage to obey Lawrence's fourth commandment: "To abide by your own deepest promptings. . . . Kill when you must, and be killed the same: the *must* coming from the gods inside you, or from the men in whom you recognize the Holy Ghost" (23).

In Poe, however, the Holy Ghost is denied, and that denial issues in a desire to kill the quick of life. Poe's morbid preoccupation with spiritual gratification, with Love, and with Knowledge reveals the death of the conscious, nerve-ridden self.

In Nathaniel Hawthorne, Lawrence focuses again on the male loss of integrity—Dimmesdale's loss in *The Scarlet Letter* of "integrity as a minister of the Gospel of the Spirit" and Hester's consequent revenge, the revenge of any woman, as Lawrence sees it, on "the spirit of man, which has betrayed her into unbelief" (*SCAL*, 100). In some of his most eloquent exhortations, Lawrence urges his male reader that to stop the destructive revenge of women "you've got to believe in yourself and your gods, your own Holy Ghost, Sir Man; and then you've got to fight her, and never give in" (100–102). The counsel is not only for others but also for himself:

> Man should *never* do the thing he believes to be wrong. Because if he does, he loses his own singleness, wholeness, natural honour.
>
> If you want to do a thing, you've either got to believe, sincerely, that it is your true nature to do this thing—or else you've got to let it alone.
>
> Believe in your own Holy Ghost. . . .
>
> A thing that you sincerely believe in cannot be wrong, because belief does not come at will. It comes only from the Holy Ghost within. Therefore a thing you truly believe in, cannot be wrong. (*SCAL*, 108–9)

The passage explains Lawrence's decision to ignore scientific teachings, such as evolution, whenever such teachings violate his deep belief in life and in proud integrity. For, as Houston Chamberlain argued, evolution, because it implied "increasing progress towards 'perfection,'" had done a serious injury to "the feeling for the individual," for "individualised nations and great personalities that never recur" (*Foundations*, 1:149). Lawrence seems to have agreed, preferring to believe that cause and effect can never explain the incomparable uniqueness of an individual or a nation.

The "marvellous under-meaning" in Hawthorne is that the suppression of the deep blood urges, both the urge to sensual fulfillment and the urge to integrity, breeds poison and the spirit of revenge. Thus there is "perfect duplicity" in Hawthorne, whose "pious blame is a chuckle of praise all the while." As a psychologist, Hawthorne is greater than as a moralist.

In Charles Dana, too, and again in Herman Melville, Lawrence calls attention to the falsifications of the idealizing consciousness. In Dana, idealism denies the "breath of life"—the "constant vibrating inter-change" that is "positive" or "negative" (*SCAL*, 124). Dana seeks to substitute an idea for the reality of this interchange, for "the natural reciprocity of command and obedience," or for the "spontaneous *passional* morality" evinced in the flogging of a sailor. In Melville, too, a "paradisal ideal" interferes with the acceptance of realities and tortures the writer, who fails to see that the world "ought *not* to be a harmonious loving place. It ought to be a place of fierce discord and intermittent harmonies: which it is" (151–52). Similarly, "Love ought *not* to be perfect." It is only the idealizing spirit which invents these fictions of perfection and seeks to impose them on life. The doom of such a spirit is seen in *Moby Dick*, which depicts "the maniacal fanaticism of our white mental consciousness," seeking to destroy "the deepest blood-being of the white race" (169). If Lawrence's interpretation of Melville's sym-bolism sounds fanciful, one must remember that for Lawrence the deepest blood being is equivalent to the divine, the very ground of being; and Melville's Manichean universe, with the whale at its center, is, like Lawrence's, a world of creation and destruction, love and hate. (There are passages in Lawrence's "The Flying Fish" that read like purest Melville.) The idealizing consciousness would deny and destroy the very nature of the divine reality: that is what Lawrence finds blasphemous—the sin against the Holy Ghost.

In Walt Whitman, finally, Lawrence finds another failure of the ideal consciousness, which falsely proclaims, "We're all One in One Identity" and which, paradoxically in a poem entitled *Song of Myself*, denies the integrity of selfhood. In contrast to Whitman's call for merging and the universal sympathy of love, there is need for "a morality of actual living," for a *true* sympathy, which is both positive and negative: positive in its response to that which the soul loves; negative in response to that which the soul hates: "What my soul loves, I love. What my soul hates, I hate." Thus Lawrence returns to his great theme: Thy will be done, where "Thy," to repeat, means the dark gods, the deepest promptings from the unknown, both love and hate.

In his inquiry into the nature of psychic wholeness and health, Lawrence needed more than literature to direct him, however. He needed to find in experience the realization of the wholeness that he was convinced was attainable—and had been attained prior to the growth of self-consciousness. The question was *where*: where could he find men who acted from the God impulses?

" 'I'm going to find them,' " Lawrence told Compton Mackenzie. " 'I may find them in the South Pacific. I may find them in Mexico.

They're not to be found any longer in Europe' " (Nehls, 2:27). In Europe were "only Christ-like heroes and woman-worshipping Don Juans, and rabid equality-mongrels. The old, hardy, indomitable male is gone. His fierce singleness is quenched" (Nehls, 2:54). The Nordic races were "dead, dead, dead" (Huxley, 626). In a Nietzschean disgust with "the herd-proletariat and the herd-equality mongrelism, and the wistful, poisonous, self-sacrificial, cultured soul" (Nehls, 2:54), Lawrence dramatized in *Aaron's Rod* the search for "the heroic soul in a greater man." He wanted "power": not the base *Wille zur Macht*, but "dark, fructifying power"—the creative and destructive power of Nietzsche's higher man. The society based on the female "love ideal" had to be destroyed; a new balance was needed, a new assertion of the male integrity and individuality against the collective female will. So Lawrence traveled, as Rebecca West said, "to get a certain Apocalyptic vision of mankind" (Nehls, 2:63). According to Frieda, he wanted to visit every continent—perhaps to make his research as complete as possible. And on every continent he looked for evidences of new life—for men who could think from the solar plexus.

In Israel, whose "cruel, naked, sharp" terrain he observed from the ship as it passed through the Suez Canal, he saw the symbol of "the murderous will and the iron of the ideal—iron will and ideal" (Huxley, 114). He was glad to pass Sinai and the Red Sea.

In Ceylon he was profoundly disappointed. He glimpsed "the world before the Flood, . . . the soft, moist, elephantine prehistoric" world which "swamped in over my known world" (Huxley, 551). He felt "the vastness of the blood stream, so dark and hot and from so far off." Like Joseph Conrad, he feared that the natives, who "are *back* of us," were going to "swarm over us and suffocate us" (Huxley, 552). (He had found the same dire warning in the German ethnologist Frobenius.) England, he saw now, remained "the growing tip"; it held "the most living clue of life," and "the great mistake we make is in not uniting together in the strength of this real living clue—religious in the most vital sense—uniting together in England and so carrying the vital spark through" (Huxley, 549). In Ceylon there was "stagnant apathy where one doesn't bother about a thing, but drifts on from minute to minute" (Nehls, 2:130). He preferred a Jesus to a Buddha. "Buddhistic peace is the point to start from," he said, but he could not accept "Buddhistic inaction and meditation" (Huxley, 540), and repeatedly he rebuked his Buddhist friend Earl Brewster for wishing to float off into an "easy ether" (*CL*, 2:933). Why didn't Buddha *stand up*?

As for Australia, it too was a land of apathy—"aboriginal *sympathetic* apathy," as he put it in his novel *Kangaroo*. Democratic Australians were "happy-go-lucky, don't-you-bother":

> There seems to be no inside life of any sort: just a long lapse and drift.
> A rather fascinating indifference, a *physical* indifference to what we call
> soul or spirit. . . . As you get used to it, it seems so *old*, as if it had
> missed all this Semite-Egyptian-Indo-European vast era of history, and
> was coal age, the age of great ferns and mosses . . . as if one resolved
> back almost to the plant kingdom, before souls, spirits and minds were
> grown at all: only quite a live, energetic body with a weird face.
> (Huxley, 555)

Lawrence had finished *Psychoanalysis and the Unconscious* before his
visit to Australia, and now every new land that he encountered he saw
sharply in relation to his conception of balance or wholeness in the
psyche. Love and power must be in equilibrium; spirituality and
sensuality must also balance. A country may be too spiritual or too
sensual, too loving or too willful. Thus Israel was too willful; Semites
acted primarily from the spiritual voluntary center—the murderous
spiritual will. Ceylon was too sympathetic and sensual: the spiritual
centers were undeveloped, and the voluntary centers that prompt one
to be an individual were also undeveloped. Similarly in Australia,
Lawrence held, the sympathetic centers were overdeveloped at the
expense of the centers that prompt one to oppose the collective
democratic will. The integrity of individuals was dissolved in their herd
acquiescence to a democratic society in which political movements—
whether the quasi-fascistic movement of the Diggers or the Communist
cause—were based on the love impulse, on the unanimity of "mates."
In *Kangaroo* Lawrence's hero, Richard Lovat Somers, is attracted sympathetically to both movements; but he recoils from both, fearing that his
integrity and his male power impulse will be destroyed by submission to
any movement based exclusively on love. Though he admires the power
or *Virtus* in Ben Cooley—"Kangaroo," the leader of the reactionary
Diggers—Somers realizes that Cooley's acceptance of the love ideal is
one-sided. The only alternative is a political and social movement that
takes into account the deep will to power, the will that seeks to destroy,
not to perpetuate, the love ideal: love of one's mates must be balanced
by the "God passion"—the passion to displace old and dead forms of
life and to create new, living forms.

Both Kangaroo and the communist Willie Struthers serve the dead
gods of Idealism and Spiritual Will. Both fail to realize that the forcing of
society in the sympathetic direction breeds a reaction into violence and
hatred. As in *Aaron's Rod* the proponents of love unconsciously *want* a
bloody and destructive revolution, so in *Kangaroo*, men acting in the
name of love and unanimity are brought to murder. Kangaroo, the
strong leader who preaches the doctrine of love, is shot; and Somers,
realizing at last that any movement based exclusively on the love ideal or

the female sympathetic will is bankrupt, sees that nature always corrects an overemphasis and restores balance. Disillusioned, but still holding on to his "God-passion" and his hope for a community based on submission to the deep impulses that work throughout nature, Somers leaves Australia.

At the end, Somers realizes that there is, in Australia, a "call" that is still waiting for an "answer." European ideals and a European consciousness have been imposed on the country, but there remains, beneath the surface, a deep summons to create a new culture based upon a new, non-European constructive effort. Somers, the Englishman with his Old World consciousness, cannot accept the promiscuous democracy that destroys individualism and dissolves civilized consciousness. He knows that a male authority is needed to balance the collective female will, just as consciousness is needed to balance and check the blind, unconscious apathy of the fern world. But he does not know *how* such a society can be created in this new land. His vision remains to be translated into practical terms, and Lawrence is aware that Somers is, from the viewpoint of others, only a preacher and a blatherer who, like Aaron Sisson, oscillates between extremes of love and power and cannot commit himself to *any* practical solution to social problems.

Kangaroo does not succeed because Lawrence asks for Somers a sympathy that he does not *earn:* Somers is always in danger of becoming only an escapist, a man who *dabbles* in politics and then runs away from any commitment. Lawrence's psychological realism, both in *Aaron's Rod* and in *Kangaroo,* compelled him to face objectively, and with some detachment, his own vacillations and his inability to find or to create the vital life that he had imagined when he planned Rananim during the war. In many ways, Aaron Sisson and Richard Somers are anti-heroes. Their weaknesses are Lawrence's. Their inability to commit themselves is the result of their refusal to heed the voice of the Holy Ghost—that voice of the *whole self* which insists on balance and on uncompromising action based on the deepest promptings of the soul. Thus Lawrence's self-castigation in these novels is severe. The novels lay bare the weaknesses of their protagonists with a relentless and savage objectivity. That is a chief reason for their ineffectiveness as art: Lawrence's unwillingness to suppress material that works *against* our sympathy for his heroes. To create the veritable religious and political hero that he wanted, he had to invent more freely—and had to find a world in which the religious leader might plausibly win support. Or else he needed to place his hero in a less artificial situation—a real person in a real community, like Mellors in Tevershall Village.

When in September 1922 Lawrence arrived for the first time in America, he was prepared for Mabel Dodge Luhan, that epitome of the spiritual will which he had denounced in his portrait of Lady Ottoline. In April 1922 he had written: "I wish I could come to America without meeting the awful 'cultured' Americans with their limited self-righteous ideals and their mechanical love-motion and their bullying, detestable negative creed of liberty and democracy." He found himself in "diametric opposition to every American—and everybody else, besides Americans—whom I come across" because he believed "in actual, sacred, inspired authority: divine right of natural kings . . . the sacred duty to wield undisputed authority" (Nehls, 2:122). He was hardly surprised, then, to find that "America lives by a sort of egoistic will, shove and be shoved" (Nehls, 2:185). As Maurice Lesemann reported, Lawrence argued: "All that a sensitive person could do now was to live totally to himself. 'He must be himself,' Lawrence said. 'He must keep to *himself* and fight against all that. There is nothing else to do. *Nothing.*'" Indeed, Lawrence thought that Americans were " 'dangerous as a race. Far more dangerous than most of the races of Europe' "; "he felt revolution" (2:194)—the sort of "death-happening" that might precede the creation of a new world (2:211). Despite the uniformity on the surface, there was a spirit of resistance, of opposition in the land: "the resistance of all things to all things" (2:385), "inhuman *resistance* to the Divinity," which reminded him of the murderous will of Israel, of a "stiff-necked and uncircumcised generation" (Huxley, 565). The power impulse was dominant, and the inner life was crushed: "*Innerlich*, there is nothing. It seems to me, in America, for the inside life, there is just blank nothing. All this outside life . . . people inside dead, outside bustling (sometimes)" (Huxley, 566).

Yet the marvellous landscape made him pay attention. New Mexico he called "the greatest experience from the outside world that I have ever had . . . it was New Mexico that liberated me from the present era of civilization, the great era of material and mechanical development. Months spent in holy Kandy . . . had not touched the great psyche of materialism and idealism which dominated me. . . . But the moment I saw the brilliant, proud morning shine high up over the deserts of Santa Fé, something stood still in my soul, and I started to attend" (*Phoenix*, 142).

Lawrence always *wanted* to believe in fresh starts in his life; and the recurrent metamorphoses of his psyche may strike the skeptical as forced or rhetorical. Yet he did find in the American Indians much that corresponded to his idea of the health and wholeness that had existed in primitive men unwarped by the ideal consciousness; and in their religion he found a sanity, a reverence for life, that exceeded anything he had ever encountered.

The deep impression made by New Mexico—and the richness of Lawrence's thought under the stimulus of this new experience—must be the subject of the next chapter, in which I trace Lawrence's prolonged efforts to depict the positive alternative to the diseased life of Europe and of white America.

8

Blood Consciousness

1922: (September) Arrives in Taos, meets Mabel Dodge Luhan, Tony Luhan, Witter Bynner, Willard Johnson; winters at Del Monte ranch with Kai Gótzsche and Knud Merrild; rereads Frazer; *Fantasia of the Unconscious;* 1923: completes *Birds, Beasts and Flowers;* "England, My England"; "The Ladybird"; "The Fox"; "The Captain's Doll"; March: travels to Mexico, settles in Chapala and begins *The Plumed Serpent; Studies in Classic American Literature* (August); December–March 1924: to England, France, Germany; 1924: March to September: in New Mexico and Mexico; writes "St. Mawr"; *The Boy in the Bush* (with Mollie L. Skinner); meditations on the Indian blood consciousness; 1925: *Mornings in Mexico;* serious attack of tuberculosis; returns to Kiowa Ranch from Mexico; writes *David;* completes *The Plumed Serpent; St. Mawr together with The Princess;* September: leaves for England; then to Spotorno, Italy; *The Virgin and the Gipsy; Reflections on the Death of a Porcupine.*

It was, initially, the space and the startling inhuman splendor of New Mexico that moved him. The land was "so open, so big, free, empty, and even aboriginal" (*CL*, 2:721). "The sun leaps like a thing unleashed in the sky," he wrote in his poem "Men in New Mexico." The man who in England felt like "an animal in a trap" found that it was "very fine indeed, the great space to live in" (Sagar, *D. H. Lawrence and New Mexico,* 23).

As I noted earlier, he felt, too, that the land had "a sort of shutting-out quality, obstinate." Goaded by the example of Mabel Dodge Luhan, he generalized: "Everything in America goes by *will.* A great negative *will* seems to be turned against all spontaneous life—there seems to be no *feeling* at all—no genuine bowels of compassion and sympathy" (*CL*, 2:721). The spirit of New Mexico—and by extension that of the entire American continent—was willful, negative, obstinate, resistant, "voluntary" rather than sympathetic: a lesson in the aboriginal *power* of the god stuff.

Yet the Indians, while hostile, were different from the bullying whites, and Lawrence meditated at length on the nature of the Indian consciousness as opposed to that of the white, egoistic consciousness. Listening to the Indians singing, he felt "an acute sadness, and a nostalgia, unbearably yearning for something, and a sickness of soul"

(Sagar, 3). The rootless Englishman, the man without a country, felt acutely the yearning to belong to a tribe and to feel the unanimity of men who were "not individualized," men whose songs spoke of "no individual, isolated experience" but of the "generic, non-individual" experience. With "unbearable yearning," Lawrence meditated on the Indian's ability to feel a perfect identification with his tribe and with the "great central source where is rest and unspeakable renewal." The white consciousness was cut off from that experience of identification, an experience "of the human blood-stream, not of the mind or spirit" (Sagar, 33). Lawrence knew he could never belong to the Indian way, could never "cluster round the drum." He recognized sharply that "the consciousness of one branch of humanity is the annihilation of the consciousness of another branch." A white man with an Indian consciousness was a contradiction in terms, a chaos. Yet one could make the effort to "see again as they see, without forgetting we are ourselves," and so one could try to overcome the limitations of the white consciousness.

With an immense intuitive sympathy, Lawrence sought to recreate the richness of this Indian consciousness, which still possessed what the white man had lost. It was part of his religious mission that he should assimilate the ancient way of thinking and make it available to the diseased consciousness of the white man, cut off from the cosmos and from the divine. And his reading in anthropology gave him strong support. Ethnologists like James Frazer and E. B. Tylor emphasized that for "the primitive mind" or "the savage mind" the notion of an immaterial god—and indeed the notion of one God—was utterly alien. According to Frazer, "the savage has no god at all" in the sense in which civilized people use the word *god* (93). Gilbert Murray emphasized that for "primitive man" the idea of an unsubstantial god is hard to grasp; rather, "god" is found in the *mana* or the medicine of the medicine chief. Likewise, E. B. Tylor, in his *Primitive Cultures*, pointed out that "the later metaphysical notion of immateriality [of the soul] could scarcely have conveyed any meaning to a savage" (1:457). For the Indians of North America "there is always something actual and physical to ground an Indian fancy on" (1:298). Animism was "an ancient and world-wide philosophy" (1:427), and "the savage mind" had created "the groundwork of the Philosophy of Religion" (1:426) by seeing life or spirit in everything, even in the inorganic world.

Thus anthropology supported an idea that Lawrence was to develop in *Etruscan Places* and in *Mornings in Mexico*—that the "vast old religion of the prehistoric world" was a religion, not of "gods and goddesses," but of "the elemental powers in the Universe, the complex vitalities of what we feebly call Nature" (*EP*, 20). The "primitive mind" was in accord with the pantheism of the stoic, although it rejected that modern pantheism which asserts that "God is everywhere, God is in everything." Instead, Lawrence concluded, for prehistoric man there was not One Great Soul of the Universe but a soul in each individual thing, each cause or effect. As he had learned in John Burnet's *Early Greek Philosophy*, it was possible to say that "every thing was *theos*. . . . Even to the early scientists, or philosophers, 'the cold,' 'the moist,' 'the hot,' 'the dry' were things in themselves, realities, gods, *theoi*. And they *did things*" (*A*, chap. 9). "God" was the animating power, like the Schopenhauerian Will, that causes phenomena to move; but God was in the physical world; and the ancient religion, as Lawrence would stress in *Etruscan Places*, was "a physical religion." It had not made the profound error of separating body and spirit, matter and mind; it had not committed the sin of "abstraction." And it had affirmed man's relationship to the surrounding world that Christianity has denied: it saw man as a part of nature, his being derived from the source and his life absorbing the energies of other living things, clouds, trees, rocks, animals, the All. Man was part of "the old connexion, the old Allness" ("Pan in America," *Phoenix*, 29).

In New Mexico, Lawrence found for the first time, in "the terrible proudness and mercilessness" of the land, a "permanent feeling of religion"; and this feeling he connected with "the old human race-experience there"—the experience of the Red Indian, who was "religious in perhaps the oldest sense, and deepest, of the word" (*Phoenix*, 143, 144). Lawrence felt "the old, old root of human consciousness still reaching down to depths we know nothing of" (145). "In the oldest religion, everything was alive, not supernaturally but naturally alive" (146). The "whole life-effort of man was to get his life into direct contact with the elemental life of the cosmos, mountain-life, cloud-life, thunder-life, air-life, earth-life, sun-life. To come into immediate *felt* contact, and so derive energy, power, and a dark sort of joy. This effort into sheer naked contact, *without an intermediary or mediator*, is the root meaning of religion" (146–47).

The Indian consciousness accordingly shows, in a very pronounced degree, what one might feebly call "empathy," or what Keats called "negative capability"—the sort of consciousness that, as I noted in the first chapter, was inborn in Lawrence. In New Mexico, Lawrence thought he had discovered a land so alive, so brilliant with sun, that one could not help feeling the vital energies rushing through all things. The blood consciousness responded directly, without mediation, to the physical-divine realities. It felt no separation between itself and the "external" world. Indeed, Lawrence was to argue in *Apocalypse*: "We and the cosmos are one. . . . The sun is a great heat whose tremors run through our smallest veins. The moon is a great gleaming nerve-centre from which we quiver forever" (29). Thus all of the external world might be "introjected"—the pride of the lion, the cruelty of the snake, the gentleness of the lamb, the power of the bull. Man might draw these energies, these great psychic and physical impulses, into himself, and gain greater life by the contact. Man's life is not identical with that of lower animals, for man *has* a mind, yet neither can man's life be thought of as distinct from the lives of other creatures and things. On the contrary, man is the master of the world precisely because he is able to assimilate the energies or qualities of all other forms of being. As Lawrence wrote in "Pan in America": "Man, defenceless, rapacious man, has needed the qualities of every living thing, at one time or other. The hard, silent abidingness of rock, the surging resistance of a tree, the still evasion of a puma . . . man can be master and complete in himself, only by assuming the living powers of each of them, as the occasion requires" (*Phoenix*, 29). In such a passage, Lawrence strove to recreate "the savage mind"—to show what the white consciousness has lost:

> In the days before man got too much separated off from the universe, he *was* Pan, along with all the rest.
> As a tree still is. A strong-willed, powerful thing-in-itself, reaching up and reaching down. With a powerful will of its own it thrusts green hands and huge limbs at the light above, and sends huge legs and gripping toes down, down between the earth and rocks, to the earth's middle. (*Phoenix*, 24)

All is "godly," the "wonder and fascination of creation shimmers in every leaf and stone, in every thorn and bud, in the fangs of the rattlesnake, and in the soft eyes of a fawn" (*MM*, 52). The Indian, not cut off from the Pan powers, could absorb or assimilate these powers by entering into a relationship of respect and reverence for the cosmos. So Lawrence felt that he himself could absorb the "fierce and bristling" resistance of the great Ponderosa pine outside his ranch house and become "a degree more like unto the tree, more bristling and turpentiney, in Pan. And the tree," he averred, "gets a certain shade and alertness of my life, within itself" (*Phoenix*, 25).

Such a consciousness, responding to the physical-divine reality, does not ignore time and process. It is sensitive to the vital flow or resistance of things, aware of their "sympathetic" attraction or their "voluntary" resistance, as "intuition" in Henri Bergson knows a reality beyond the fixed and frozen counters of the abstractive intellect. The blood consciousness recognizes the ebb and flow, the warmth and coldness, of vital energies. And it is both sympathetic and antipathetic or resistant. It is a "sacral-sexual consciousness," as Lawrence says, "sexual" or "phallic" in its attraction toward and its warmth for other forms of being, "sacral" in its resistance to that which threatens the pride and integrity of the organism.

As early as *Sons and Lovers*, Lawrence had worked extensively with metaphors that show an intense awareness of the life flow or the life constriction in other human beings. Now, as he was finishing up the volume of poems that he called *Birds, Beasts and Flowers*, his ability to enter into the "souls" of other living things and to register as sensitively as possible the uniqueness of each individual consciousness seems greater than ever. As Blake argued against the folly of "general nature," Lawrence insisted that "Abstraction is the only evil," and in these poems he insists on a scrupulous respect for the otherness of each life. His native gift for intuitive sympathy ("phallic consciousness") combines with the breadth and depth of his mature vision, and the poems are veritable revelations of being.

Again and again, one is startled by the exactness of the observation—or the intuition?—of another life. In "Grapes" (*CP*, 285), for example, he finds

> Audile, tactile sensitiveness as of a tendril which orientates and reaches
> out,
> Reaching out and grasping by an instinct more delicate than the moon's
> as she feels for the tides.

There is the peach ("Peach," *CP*, 279):

> Why so velvety, why so voluptuous heavy?
> Why hanging with such inordinate weight?
> Why so indented?
>
> Why the groove?
> Why the lovely, bivalve roundnesses?

The crocus ("Purple Anemones," *CP*, 309):

> Aha, the stripe-cheeked whelps, whippet-slim crocuses. . . .

The cyclamen ("Sicilian Cyclamens," *CP*, 310):

> Slow toads, and cyclamen leaves
> Stickily glistening with eternal shadow
> Keeping to earth.
> Cyclamen leaves
> Toad-filmy, earth-iridescent. . . .

There is man ("St. Matthew," *CP*, 320):

> I am man, and therefore my heart beats, and throws the dark blood
> from side to side.

There is the bull ("St. Luke," *CP*, 325):

> And glistening, adhesive muzzle
> With cavernous nostrils where the winds run hot. . . .

Like Huxley, we half expect Lawrence to tell us exactly what the other creatures are conscious of. A bat ("Man and Bat," *CP*, 344):

> It was the light of day which he could not enter,
> Any more than I could enter the white-hot door of a blast furnace.

A snake ("Snake," *CP*, 349):

> He lifted his head from his drinking, as cattle do,
> And looked at me vaguely, as drinking cattle do, . . .

Unlike so many who write about animals, Lawrence is never sentimental or condescending, and his occasional flashes of amusement show no disrespect for the animal. Always he follows the first commandment of the Red Indian, "Thou shalt acknowledge the wonder." In "Baby Tortoise" (*CP*, 354):

> Alone, with no sense of being alone,
> And hence six times more solitary.

The "Turkey-Cock" (*CP*, 370):

> Your brittle, super-sensual arrogance
> Tosses the crape of red across your brow and down your breast
> As you draw yourself upon yourself in insistence.

"The Blue Jay" (*CP*, 375):

> Whose boss are you, with all your bully way?

His response to creatures and plants in these poems is of the kind that he admired in the Etruscans, who he believed had a "profound physical religion," a "religion of life" (*EP*, 49) like that of the Red Indian. *Etruscan Places*, written in 1927, can perhaps best be understood in connection with Lawrence's experience in New Mexico, for the book is a prolonged effort to show what it means to live in full possession of the blood consciousness, as this is exhibited in Etruscan paintings. There is "the natural beauty of proportion of the phallic consciousness," says Lawrence, "contrasted with the more studied or ecstatic proportion of the mental and spiritual Consciousness we are accustomed to" (10). The "true Etruscan quality" is "ease, naturalness, and an abundance of life, no need to force the mind or the soul in any direction" (12); thus the Etruscan was able to capture the *horsiness* of a horse far better than "Rosa Bonheur or Rubens or even Velazquez" (72). Moreover, there is "in the Etruscan instinct a real desire to preserve the natural humour of life" (26). And there is "sensitiveness" and a "sense of touch": "the people and the creatures are all really in touch. It is one of the rarest qualities, in life as well as in art" (45–46). The Etruscans, dancing their sacred dances, "were always kept *in touch*, physically, with the mysteries" (52). They felt "the three compelling emotions" of "wonder, fear and admiration" (69). (Love, Lawrence adds, was "only a subsidiary factor in wonder and admiration" [70].)

For the Etruscans "the cosmos was alive, like a vast creature" and "had a great soul, or *anima:* and in spite of one great soul, there were myriad roving, lesser souls: every man, every creature and tree and lake and mountain and stream, was animate, had its own peculiar consciousness. And has it to-day" (49). In this living cosmos, "the active religious idea was that man, by vivid attention and sublety and exerting all his strength, could draw more life into himself, more life, more and more glistening vitality, till he became shining like the morning, blazing like a god" (50).

In passing, one must note that both the New Mexican Indian and the ancient Etruscan, "blazing like a god," drew this life from physical worlds that were linked in Lawrence's mind. As he indicates in his "Introduction to *Mastro-don Gesualdo* by Giovanni Verga," the Mediterranean world was (like New Mexico) one of "light and marvellous open country." "Practically the whole day-life of the people passes in the open, in the splendour of the sun and the landscape, and the delicious, elemental aloneness of the old world." In such a world, "the great freshness keeps the men still fresh" (*Phoenix II*, 286).

In the ancient religion, a great duality in the cosmos corresponded to the great duality in man's consciousness. There was not only the duality of sex—of male fire and female water—but also the duality of gentle creatures like the deer or the lamb and of powerful creatures like the lion. "There were different currents in the blood-stream, and some always clashed: bird and serpent, lion and deer, leopard and lamb. Yet the very clash was a form of unison, as we see in the lion which also has a goat's head" (*EP*, 67). The blood consciousness is not only phallic; it is also sacral: it accepts and reconciles the duality, and thus expresses the divine will working throughout the cosmos:

> Every consciousness, the rage of the lion, and the venom of the snake, *is*, and therefore is divine. All emerges out of the unbroken circle with its nucleus, the germ, the One, the god, if you like to call it so. And man, with his soul and his personality, emerges in eternal connection with all the rest. The blood-stream is one, and unbroken, yet storming with oppositions and contradictions. (69)

Thus the blood consciousness embraces both lamblike gentleness and lionlike power. Or to return to the language of *Psychoanalysis and the*

Unconscious, it is both "sympathetic" and "voluntary." The sympathetic impulse prompts one to be attracted to the rest of the cosmos in wonder and admiration. The voluntary impulse, arising from the lumbar ganglion, a center of willful resistance or self-assertion, prompts one to assert one's independence and integrity, or to "recoil" or "react" against a world that causes one to feel fear or dread. It is an impulse associated with male pride—the desire of the male to preserve his selfhood inviolate, without yielding in his soul to others, without making what Lawrence calls, in *The Boy in the Bush,* the "compromise of amiability and casual friendship" (362).

Thus the Etruscans, like Lawrence's Indian or Mexican males, are both gentle or "delicately sensitive" and powerful. "It was by seeing all things alert in the throb of inter-related passional significance that the ancients kept the wonder and the delight in life, as well as the dread and the repugnance. They were like children: but they had force, the power and the sensual *knowledge* of true adults. They had a world of valuable knowledge, which is utterly lost to us" (*EP,* 70). That "knowledge" is also seen in a character like Don Ramón in *The Plumed Serpent*—a man who is proud and resistant (acting from the voluntary center) but also gentle and tender (acting from the sympathetic center). Similar characteristics are observed in the Indians of *Mornings in Mexico,* in whom Lawrence observes both the sympathetic or centripetal impulse and the voluntary or centrifugal impulse: they "flow together" sympathetically into the marketplace, then separate "voluntarily" on a "swerve of repulsion"; or they seek union with the cosmos in the round dance, but defend their own isolation in the mime dance (42, 48–49). In acting "from the source," they are instruments through which the great will of life is expressed: "Not I, But the Wind. . . ." As Lawrence said in "Introduction to Pictures," "the spontaneous self with its sympathetic consciousness and non-ideal reaction [its voluntary resistance or repulsion] is the original reality, the old Adam, over which the self-aware-of-itself [i.e., the conscious ego] has no originative power" (*Phoenix,* 768).

To the blood consciousness, the world with its opposing voluntary and sympathetic forces—"the fangs of the rattlesnake, and . . . the soft eyes of a fawn"—elicits only wonder or fear; but as Lawrence had learned in Tylor's *Primitive Cultures,* the old animistic religion is non-retributive and amoral: "There is no judgment" (*MM,* 52, 53). The words *good* and *evil* are the products of the ideal consciousness. For the Etruscans, "The leopard and the deer, the lion and the bull, the cat and the dove . . . do not represent good action and evil action. On the contrary, they represent the polarised activity of the divine cosmos, in its animal creation" (56). In other words, they represent "the sway of passional action and reaction" that Lawrence sees in the whole of the universe, a to-and-fro of sympathy and power, attraction and repulsion. Those who act from the blood consciousness do not judge others: they defend themselves with a healthy, instinctive "voluntary" reaction against that which threatens their existence, but they do not invent a world of devils whom they single out for perpetual torture. In *Mornings in Mexico*, Lawrence argues that the mind of the Indian "bows down before the creative mystery, even of the atrocious Apache warrior. It judges, not the good and the bad, but the lie and the true. The Apache warrior in all his atrocity, is true to his own creative mystery. And as such, he must be fought. But he cannot be called a *lie* on the face of the earth" (53). (In the same vein, Nietzsche's Zarathustra counseled: " 'Enemy' you shall say, but not 'villain'; . . . 'fool,' you shall say, but not 'sinner' " [*Portable Nietzsche*, 150].) As for the Etruscans, whose sympathetic or phallic impulses were presumably stronger than those of the Apaches (products of the willful or resistant continent), Lawrence rejects the Roman contention that the Etruscans were cruel. Cruelty he saw as arising from the damming up of the life instinct. Where the flow of life is strong, there is "delicate sensitiveness." Thus Lawrence thought that the Etruscans would not have practiced slavery. Etruscan peasants, he thought, "were serfs rather than slaves," were "half-free, at least, and had a true life of their own, stimulated by the religious life of their masters" (77). He also believed that men acting from a phallic consciousness would not wage war. In "Introduction to Pictures" he says:

> I believe that there was a great age, a great epoch when men did not make war: previous to 2000 B.C. Then the self had not really become aware of itself, it had not separated itself off, the spirit was not yet born, so there was no internal conflict, and hence no permanent external conflict. The external conflict of war, or of industrial competition, is only a reflection of the war that goes on inside each human being, the war of the self-conscious ego against the spontaneous old Adam. (*Phoenix*, 769)

It is the tyrannical spiritual will, forcing life always in the ideal direction, that causes the prolonged reaction of violence and destructiveness, as exemplified in *Women in Love* and, Lawrence believed, in World War I. The blood consciousness can *hate:* for the vital energies of the cosmos are destructive as well as creative; but prolonged or "permanent external conflict" would be impossible to such a consciousness, for the natural rhythms of life necessitate an oscillation of voluntary destructive feeling and sympathetic creative feeling. Hatred, like love, is part of life, which is "a flowing together and a flowing apart and a flowing together again" (*Phoenix II*, 541).

Lawrence's stories of the Southwest and Mexico are read variously
as expressions of a violent misogyny or of an anti-Oedipal reaction or of
an infantile regressiveness or of an "ontological insecurity." Such
readings tend to reduce the stories to the ingenuous outpourings of a
compulsive, unstable author. The stories acquire an altogether different
meaning and significance if we see them as the product of a religious
man seeking to provide, for a sick humanity, a guide to what it means to
think from the blood.

The male heroes in these stories show the same essential qualities.
On the one hand, they are resistant (voluntary), maintaining their pride
and "isolate manhood" against a society that would demean them and
reduce them to servility. On the other hand, they can show a gentleness
or tenderness for others that is conspicuously lacking in European or
white North American males, who are both bullying egotists and base
conformists, passively accepting either the spiritually dead "love and
benevolence ideal" or the perverse idea of fun and sensation as a reason
for living. These dark-skinned male heroes are all natural aristocrats,
who have what Lawrence, in *Apocalypse,* called "the tenderness and
gentleness of *strength*" (11).

The action in these stories is built on a simple paradigm: the
spiritual-mental white woman (perhaps a surrogate of Mabel Dodge
Luhan) encounters a Mexican or Indian for whom (as in "The Princess")
"the phallic mystery was still the only mystery" (*CSS,* 2:477). The
woman is ambivalent, scorning the "low" uncultured man, yet attracted to him because her life is cold and empty and she needs his
warmth and strength. The action tests her ability to break free from the
nullity of her static egoistic condition.

In "The Princess," for example, the heroine, reared on the idea of
her superiority, feels, after her father's death, that she is "an empty
vessel" (*CSS,* 2:480). At a ranch in New Mexico, she is attracted to
Domingo Romero, a guide whose family once owned miles of land in
the area. Although Romero shows the "fatal inertia" of a man who has
no raison d'être—a man "waiting either to die or to be aroused into
passion and hope"—there is "at the centre of [his] hopelessness . . . a
spark of pride, or self-confidence, or dauntlessness" (483). Thus
Romero acts from the voluntary center, which asserts pride and separate
individuality against the collective will of the gringo mob. At the same
time, Romero is "sympathetic." He helps the Princess, "and she felt in
his presence a subtle, insidious male *kindliness* she had never known
before waiting upon her" (484). "It was curious no white man had ever
showed her this capacity for subtle gentleness, this power to *help* her in
silence across a distance. . . . It was as if Romero could send her *from his*

heart a dark beam of succour and sustaining" (485). A "peculiar subtle intimacy of inter-recognition" arises between them.

When the Princess and Romero ride up into the Rockies, where she wants "to see the wild animals move about in their wild unconsciousness," she is frightened by the inhuman mountains and by "the dread and repulsiveness of the wild" (*CSS*, 2:487–88, 501). That night, in the miner's shack that Romero has made ready, she dreams of snow falling—symbolic of the murderous spiritual will by which she has lived; and she turns to Romero for "warmth, protection, she wanted to be taken away from herself" (503). He takes her "with a terrible animal warmth." But she has *not* wanted any violation of her virginal self, she decides, and next day she tells Romero that she doesn't " 'care for that kind of thing' " (506). Yet the woman's invitation has given Romero "a curious joy and pride" (504), and now her sudden denial of the emotional connection crushes his spirit and awakens his anger. Deeply injured in his pride, he says he will make her respond. He disposes of all of her clothing and holds her prisoner. Her calling to him, he says, has given him "some right." He wants to marry her. But she refuses, and he, retaliating, violates her repeatedly. Yet she remains "hard and flawless as a diamond," even though "he had got hold of her, some unrealised part of her which she never wished to realise" (509). In the end, Romero is killed by rangers who have come in search of them; and the Princess struggles to recover "herself entirely," "a virgin intact"— though she is "slightly crazy" because her self-possession has been broken.

Many readers are dismayed or disgusted by Lawrence's justification of "rape" and male "power" in this story. Baruch Hochman, for example, speaks of Lawrence's " 'demonism' and his exultation in evil and destruction, as manifested in stories like 'The Princess' and 'The Woman Who Rode Away' " (256–57). R. E. Pritchard sees Romero's acts as illustrating "brutal male primitivism" (164). Graham Hough sees "The Princess" as "a product of the sort of doctrinaire cruelty that possessed Lawrence for at least a part of this period" and, like Hochman, finds a "suppressed sexual malice in the tale" (Hough, 179). But such responses ignore the intuitive relatedness or "inter-recognition" that Lawrence emphasizes. Romero's cruelty is provoked by the Princess's cruel rejection. When the Princess denies her feelings, Romero's response is the immediate, unpremeditated response that arises directly from "the source": " 'You Americans,' " he tells her, " 'you always want to do a man down' " (*CSS*, 2:505). The Princess's rebuff tips the balance in his soul, which has waited "either to die or to be aroused into passion and hope." In his vengeance, he acts from "a demonish desire for death" (506). (In Lawrence, the life or death of the

soul is always at stake in a passional encounter.) The Princess's denial
of her own desire and her indifference to Romero's pride reveal the
failure of the ideal consciousness to enter into sympathetic union with
another person. She is more cruel than is Romero. Her wickedness is
"to prostitute the creative wonder to the . . . individual conceit":
thus Lawrence defined wickedness from the Indian point of view
(Sagar, 36).

"The Woman Who Rode Away" is another story in which Lawrence seems cold-bloodedly to sanction male "mastery" and "power."
But here, too, he exhibits the instinctive-intuitive recognition of primal
realities that are inaccessible to the ideal, rational modern consciousness. The heroine, kept "morally" in "an invincible slavery" by
her idealist husband, who lives only to work, is driven in desperation
and by "a foolish romanticism" to ride off alone in search of the
Chilchui Indians, who are said to keep up the ancient religion of the
Aztecs, with its human sacrifice. When she encounters the Indians and
delivers herself up to their direction, she knows she is powerless and
already "dead." She dreads, but wants, the death of her old self.

Taken to the Indian village, she is treated with a "curious impersonal solicitude," an "utterly impersonal gentleness, as an old man
treats a child." She talks to a young Indian who is both "still and
gentle" and "darkly and powerfully male" (CSS, 2:576). Indeed, there
is "something womanly" in the "soft, insidious understanding" of
these men, yet they are also "primitively male and cruel" (576). They do
not love their enemies, though they can be kind to them, and the white
woman is one of their enemies. When she watches the Indians dancing,
Lawrence observes: "Her kind of womanhood, intensely personal and
individual, was to be obliterated again, and the great primeval symbols
were to tower once more over the fallen individual independence of
woman. The sharpness and the quivering nervous consciousness of the
highly-bred white woman was to be destroyed again, womanhood was
to be cast once more into the great stream of impersonal sex and
impersonal passion" (569).

The young Indian explains that white people " 'know nothing.
They are like children, always with toys. We know the sun, and we
know the moon' " (CSS, 2:570). Living in a vital relatedness to the
cosmos, the Indians have never acquired the personal, egoistic consciousness that divides sun and moon, male and female. Because the
divisive egoism of the white consciousness has triumphed, the Indians
have lost their power with the sun and moon; it is necessary to recover
the ancient relationship that will "make the world again" (571, 570).

Gradually, the white woman begins to lose "her ordinary personal
consciousness" and to go into "that other state of passional cosmic

consciousness, like one who is drugged" (*CSS*, 2:574). But she does not understand the impersonal hatred of the young Indian, and as she is prepared for the sacrifice that will restore life to the Indians, she feels that they are driven by "passions too remote for her to grasp" (577). Just before her death, she sees, in the eyes of the oldest man, "power, power intensely abstract and remote, but deep, deep to the heart of the earth, and the heart of the sun" (581). This power, Lawrence concludes, is "the mastery that man must hold, and that passes from race to race" (581).

It is not egoistic male power. It is the power that derives from the "passional cosmic consciousness," the power to act from the source, in accordance with the deepest promptings of the source. These, as I have indicated, are both sympathetic and voluntary: they are "desire" and "power," or, more simply, "love" and "hate." What the white woman cannot grasp is that in wanting to have things "her own way," she has denied the very ground of being—the impersonal sympathetic and voluntary impulses that work through the whole cosmos. Her ideal consciousness cannot work impersonally, with a sense of the great realities that transcend the personal. The blood consciousness of the Indian is always aware of these realities; it is seeking to do the will of God—or of the Unknown. Such a consciousness "loves" and "hates" impersonally: that is, it acts, not from the egoistic will, but rather with a realization that man, as the embodiment of the great underlying realities, is never the author and controller of his own acts. In the last analysis, words like "love" and "hate" are empty, for they cannot convey the mystery of the great tides of creation and destruction, of attraction and repulsion, that sweep through one's being. The Indians "know" the male sun and the female moon in the sense that they submit to the great voluntary and sympathetic impulses that are "more deeply interfused" in them. They know that, as Cipriano says in *The Plumed Serpent*, " 'We are not created of ourselves. Of ourselves we are nothing.' " Neither is their sympathy or their hate "of themselves." As Lawrence said in a letter of 25 April 1926, "desire and anger are from God" (*CL*, 2:905). That is what the ideal consciousness cannot grasp.

Lawrence does not celebrate cruelty in "The Woman Who Rode Away." Although the Indians are "primitively male and cruel," the story is a parable that intends to show the need to relinquish the white consciousness and independence. Indirectly, it is an attack on egotism. Critics like Robert Langbaum, who see the story as an expression of a regressive death wish—another of Lawrence's efforts to escape the tensions and conflicts of life—are dismayed by the woman's acquiescence to Aztec cruelties. But Lawrence was defining the nature of a consciousness different from that which we take to be normal; Lawrence

needed violent material to shock the reader out of complacent precon-
ceptions about "normalcy"—just as Lawrence needed the four-letter
words in *Lady Chatterley's Lover* to shock the ideal consciousness into a
recognition of all that it excludes from life.

Of all the Southwest stories that dramatize the conflict between
ideal consciousness and blood consciousness, "St. Mawr" provides the
richest understanding of Lawrence's message. It enables the reader to
share the blood consciousness and to feel the dignity and beauty of it.
The story is a powerful antidote to sentimentality and cant, strongly
contrasting the ideal consciousness, exhibited especially in Lou Witt's
contemptible husband, Rico, with the blood consciousness, symbolized
in the red stallion St. Mawr and suggested in the two grooms, Lewis and
Phoenix. One begins to share Lawrence's sense of the vileness of an all-
too-human humanity and his sense of the reality which exists un-
distorted by the fictions of the ideal consciousness.

The keenness of Lawrence's depiction of phallic consciousness is
found in Lou Witt's first view of the stallion:

He was of such a lovely red-gold colour, and a dark, invisible fire
seemed to come out of him. But in his big black eyes there was a lurking
afterthought. Something told her that the horse was not quite happy:
that somewhere deep in his animal consciousness lived a dangerous,
half-revealed resentment, a diffused sense of hostility. (*SM*, 12)

The owner of the mews, Mr. Saintsbury, tells Lou that "if St. Mawr was
a human being, you'd say something had gone wrong in his life" (12).
Lawrence, as sensitive to the life flow in the animal as in human beings,
tells us that "St. Mawr seemed to look at her out of another world" (14).
In contrast with "the triviality and superficiality of Lou's human
relationships," the horse somehow "forbade her to be her ordinary,
common-place self" (15). She realizes that her husband, Rico, is "rather
like a horse," but in Rico the "full, dark, passionate blaze of power" has
been smothered by "anxious love" and an "anxious powerlessness"
(15). Rico is all "attitude," he is not "real." Unlike St. Mawr, Rico lives
entirely in the world of the "personal," with no sense of "another
world, an older, heavily potent world" in which the horse was "undominated and unsurpassed" (20).

But the two grooms do have a consciousness of a reality beyond
"the personal" and the purely human. Lewis, the Welshman, is—like
the Indians of the Southwest—"impersonal." He is subject to the
control of his employers, but, like St. Mawr, he remains "himself," his
male pride intact. Similarly, Phoenix, the son of a Mexican father and a
Navajo mother, is "unyielding" (*SM*, 20). When commanded or repri-
manded by Lou Witt or Rico, Phoenix shows a "gleam of malevolence or

contempt"; there is "an unyielding resistance and cruelty" beneath his outward submission (41). That same resistance is shown by Lewis, who must submit when Mrs. Witt insists on cutting his hair but who looks round "like a creature in a trap" and then refuses to let her clip his beard—that symbol, as Lawrence viewed it, of his "isolate manhood."

In contact with the greater realities, both Phoenix and Lewis see London as "a mirage" or a "prison." While the Londoners go about in their frantic pursuit of fun and in their incessant criticism and appraisal of other people, the grooms remain aloof. The personal, egoistical relationships of the Londoners are contrasted with the groom's "impersonal" relationship to the horse: "dark will devoid of emotion or personal feeling" (SM, 25). But as there is a constriction in the life flow of the stallion, so there is in that of the two men. For Phoenix, the existence of his employers "made his own existence negative. If he was to exist, positively, they would have to cease to exit" (41).

The nature of the blood consciousness in these two men is sharply defined in a conversation in which Lou Witt challenges her mother's belief that " 'real mind is all that matters in a man, and it's *that* we women love' " (SM, 49). Lou protests: " 'But what *is* real mind. The old woman [i.e., most of the men she has known] who knits the most complicated pattern? . . . As a matter of fact, mother, I believe Lewis has far more real mind than Dean Vyner or any of the clever ones. He has a good intuitive mind, he knows things without thinking them' " (49). Mrs. Witt replies that Lewis is a servant and " 'you could never be intimate with a man like Lewis.' " But Lou retorts:

> "I don't want intimacy, mother. I'm too tired of it all. I love St. Mawr because he isn't intimate. He stands where one can't get at him. And he burns with life. And where does his life come from, to him? That's the mystery. That great burning life in him, which never is dead. Most men have a deadness in them that frightens me so, because of my own deadness. Why can't men get their life straight, like St. Mawr, and then think? Why don't they think quick, mother: quick as a woman: only further than we do? Why isn't men's thinking quick like fire, mother?"
> (SM, 49)

She goes on to say, " 'Think, mother, if we could get our lives straight from the source, as the animals do, and still be ourselves' " (49–50). A "pure animal man," she said, would be "all the animals in turn, instead of one fixed, automatic thing"; but men have stopped thinking, she holds, because " 'men always do leave off really thinking, when the last bit of wild animal dies in them' " (50).

The characteristics that Lou singles out here are, in a marked degree, those of Lawrence himself, who seemed like an animal to Witter Bynner and like a chameleon to others. And Lawrence did think "quick," "quick as a woman"—that is, with the intuitive and sympathetic powers traditionally associated with women. Thinking "straight from the source" does not lead to the decisions and revisions of a Prufrock, because blood thinking registers feeling as well as thought—the instinctive-intuitive feeling that is really quick thought, like Lewis's. No one can sell *Lewis* on the idea that London and the trap of civilization are desirable or necessary; he knows (his blood knows, any healthy animal knows) that these traps are bad. They block the life flow. And if he must submit to the trap, he does not smother his resentment with "nervous love" for the humanity that accepts and submits cheerfuly to the trap.

In the second half of "St. Mawr," Lou and her mother take the stallion to America—to save it from gelding; and Lawrence recreates his own response to the beauty and mercilessness of the land. He is fully aware of the cruelty of nature—"the seething cauldron of lower life"; and he does not like the "rapacity" and the "half-sordid savagery." He realized, however, as he witnessed the "curious *tussle* of wild life," that it was nonsense to cling to "love" and to a god of love in the face of nature's "power." In the meditation of "the New England woman" who attempted to bring civilization to the ranch and who discovered the "animosity of the spirit of place," Lawrence duplicates his own relinquishment of the ideal consciousness and lingering Christianity. The woman's discovery

> had broken something in her. It had maimed her for ever in her hope, her belief in paradise on earth. Now, she hid from herself her own corpse, the corpse of her New England belief in a world ultimately all for love. . . . The gods of those inner mountains were grim and relentless, huger than man, and lower than man. Yet man could never master them. (*SM*, 153)

Her disillusionment reflects Lawrence's in 1916. But Lawrence, of course, did not lapse into fatalism. All savagery is "half sordid," he writes, "and man is only himself when he is fighting on and on, to overcome the sordidness" (153).

The blood consciousness does not accept sordidness because "that is nature's way." It is not blindly impulsive or unintelligent. On the contrary, the soul instinctively hates and recoils from sordidness, as it recoils from syphilis or leprosy (see *Studies in Classic American Literature*, 185). Nature is not "good." Yet neither is it "evil." Its destructive and voluntary powers are balanced by its creative, sympathetic powers. It is the "common sense" of the blood consciousness that proudly refuses to accept the blind sordid tussle of wild nature, as that same common sense refuses to divorce life from its animal origin in nature. The common sense of the blood consciousness insists on a balance of resistance to that which threatens one's pride and integrity, and on a sympathetic connection with that which commands wonder and admiration.

As Lawrence was writing his stories of the Southwest, he also revised Mollie Skinner's novel of the Australian frontier, which became *The Boy in the Bush*. Lawrence's major change in Skinner's novel was "to make a rather daring development, psychologically," in the hero, Jack Grant. In fact, Lawrence grafted his theory of the unconsciousness onto the hero: like Richard Lovat Somers of *Kangaroo*, Jack Grant oscillates between his deep sympathetic impulse and his voluntary reaction into independence. But Jack goes much further than Somers in his learning to act upon the promptings of his deeper consciousness. In the last chapters of the novel (written wholly by Lawrence, as Skinner admitted), one witnesses the blood consciousness in action.

The Australian sun has on Jack Grant the effect that the New Mexican sun had on Lawrence: Jack sees "the Great God in the roaring of the yellow sun, and the frightening vast smile in the gleaming full-moon"; and he acquires the courage to "have the fire of the Lord, and drink from the cup of the fierce glory of the Lord, the sun in one hand and the moon in the other" (*BB*, 185). He learns to live direct from the source: to act on his deep spontaneous desires—both his hatred of his rival, Easu, and his desire for *two* women, the sensual Monica and the spiritual, self-sacrificing Mary. Thus Jack seeks the fulfillment of his deep desires, much as, in "The Ladybird," Lady Daphne seeks her fulfillment in two husbands, one of the underworld and one of the spirit. Jack throws off all the conventional restraints and moral inhibitions of the middle class, determined to "fulfill his desires and satisfy his yearning" (239). He knows (rather like Richard Jefferies of *The Story of My Heart*) that life holds "strange unknown wells of secret life-source" which "had never stirred in the veins of man, to consciousness and effect. And if he could take Monica and set the dusky, secret, unknown sap flowing in himself and her, to some unopened life consciousness—that was what he wanted. Dimly, uneasily, painfully he realised it" (240).

The Australian bush, like New Mexico, demands a new consciousness, a new "answer" to its "call." Acting directly from the wild spirit within himself, or "the super consciousness of the whole soul" which Lawrence identifies as God (*BB*, 169), Jack kills Easu. Then, lost in the bush and perilously near death, Jack is changed for good: he becomes a "Lord of Death," one of those who undergo the death process (the death of all old allegiances and false associations) in order that a new life and a new consciousness may be born: "Only the wild, untamed souls walked on after death over the border into the porch of death, to be lords of death and masters of the next living" (324–25). So Jack's mission is to make room "for those who are not broken, those who are not tamed" (325).

The knowledge of death gives rise to faithfulness, tenderness, and intuitive care. When Jack is brought back from death by his friends, Lawrence writes: "Tom was there and Mary. He would leave himself to Tom's faithfulness and Mary's tenderness, and Lennie's watchful intuition. The mystery of death was in that bit of deathless faithfulness which was in Tom. And Mary's tenderness, and Lennie's intuitive care, both had a touch of the mystery and stillness of the death that surrounds us darkly all the time" (308–9). There is a solidarity, a kinship, of those who know the great mystery; they are bound together in a realization of their participation in the eternal rhythms of life and death (for "the Lord of Death is Lord of Life") and in a faithfulness to the "spark" of life between them. Perhaps Lawrence's own experiences of "death" had honed a life awareness that only those initiated into death's mysteries can grasp. Faithfulness, tenderness, and intuitive care are all manifestations of a consciousness that sees beyond immediate and temporal goals to the "stillness" of the eternal that lies behind the flux. In many ways, Jack Grant is like the Indians of "The Woman Who Rode Away": his consciousness is in harmony with the great cosmic realities of sun and moon; and as the "master of death," he is able to die to his old self as well as to kill the enemy of life, Easu, whose "fixed hard will" is comparable to that of the independent white woman. Jack is also like the grooms Lewis and Phoenix: he has an intuitive understanding of the stallion Stampede, "as if he were one blood with the horse" (124). Jack learns to act from the "super-consciousness of the whole soul" in which "man's divinity, and his ultimate power" reside (169).

Mollie Skinner wept when she saw what Lawrence had done to her hero; a number of critics have had similar feelings about another Lawrentian hero who declares, "The Lords of Life are the Masters of Death"—Cipriano of *The Plumed Serpent*, who executes the vile dogs who are his enemies. H. M. Daleski voiced the response of many critics when he said that Lawrence in this scene is "deliberately forcing himself to be demonic in the interests of making a grand male assertion" (232). But the "power" that Cipriano seizes in this revolution is not *personal*; it is "the old, twilit Pan-power," and Cipriano is "the Pan male." It is the divine will that such a male seeks to do—the will to destroy "false, inorganic connections" and "re-establish the living organic connections, with the cosmos, the sun and earth, with mankind and nation and family" (*A*, 125).

The Plumed Serpent is Lawrence's fullest attempt to depict the wholeness and balance that are both destructive *and* constructive. Americanism and Bolshevism have all but destroyed the pride and the manhood of the Mexicans; and Christianity, instead of strengthening them to achieve a greater manhood, has disintegrated their natural self-respect and the indomitable male spirit. There is no alternative but to create a new foundation for a new life.

In writing a novel that centers on the revival of an ancient god, Lawrence was working, I suspect, with a hint he had found in Leo Frobenius's *The Voice of Africa*. The German ethnologist impressed Lawrence by arguing that ancient African civilization was the lost Atlantis that had been destroyed when "Phoenicia and Grecia succeeded to the Empire of the Ocean held by the nations of the West" (*Voice of Africa*, 1:345). The ancient religion of Atlantis was "linked to the perfected system of a primeval age" (1:262) and prevailed also, Frobenius argued, in Etruria, a "high-toned philosophy which once girdled the world at its earliest dawn" (1:263). When he visited the South Nupé tribesmen on his expedition to the Sudan, Frobenius was eager to see the old god, which had been suppressed by the Muslim Fulbés and by Christian missionaries. The Nupés were afraid, and their chieftain, old Lilli, said apologetically: " 'We had the Dako-Boea [the Great Spirit of the tribe] here once, it is true; but the white folk came; they talked about Issa [Jesus] and then took our Dako-Boea away and burnt him. Since that happened we have no longer dared to speak to our Great Father' " (2:393). Frobenius, persisted, however, and the Nupés were elated, having made sure that "the white man" really "wished to revive the old customs, which the red and white people, Fulbes and missionaries, had destroyed and forbidden" (2:393–94). The great day came, and the Dako-Boea, a mask several yards high, danced in the square; whereupon Frobenius saw "profound emotion, a real stirring of the spectators' feelings": the Nupés "gave themselves up to jollity and gladness, once more inspired by the return of their ancient God" (2:395, 397). Frobenius's moving account of the restoration of the ancient god calls vividly to mind the joy felt by the Mexicans of *The Plumed Serpent* when Don Ramón resurrects the ancient god Quetzalcoatl. And as Frobenius stresses that a people debased and demoralized by the Europeanization of their tribes need to develop a vital culture of their own, so Lawrence emphasizes that the Mexicans need their own religion to give them a new manhood and a new pride.

In reviving the mysteries of Quetzalcoatl, Don Ramón interprets the plumed serpent as the symbol of the union of sky creature and earth creature, spirit and flesh, consciousness and unconsciousness, the lord of "the two ways." (One might recall, in passing, that Nietzsche's

Zarathustra kept an eagle and a serpent beside him.) It is the *pre-Aztec* mysteries that Don Ramón wishes to revive: not the religion that had degenerated into a cult of violence and human sacrifice, but the mysteries of the ancient Indian, who felt at one with the cosmos because he implicity accepted Cipriano's declaration: "We are not created of ourselves. Of ourselves we are nothing." A new spirit can arise only when strong men submit themselves to the divine will, accepting both the divine spirit of destruction and the divine spirit of creation. Joining together in submission to the authority of the greater man, the Mexicans can realize their greater manhood and greater womanhood by creating a society that is *theirs*, not imposed by white Americans or Bolsheviks. "A pair of blood brothers like Natty Bumppo and Chingachgook" would lead, as L. D. Clark observes, in the creation (362).

At the outset the heroine, Kate Leslie, is profoundly disillusioned by the degradation of life all about her. In the opening chapter, Kate's revulsion when she witnesses the bullfight mirrors Lawrence's own disgust with the hideous violation of life that was enthusiastically supported by debased Mexicans and by Americans seeking in "sensations" and "thrills" a cure for their inner emptiness. They are all "blood thirsty," as Lawrence angrily claimed when Witter Bynner and Spud Johnson decided to remain to see the bullfight (Nehls, 2:215): there is a violence that threatens always to erupt in the land where the will is dominant.

But there is also, Kate feels, in men like Cipriano and Ramón, a curious tenderness; they are not like the gringo puppets of the spiritual but are impelled by a deep religious desire that encompasses and transcends love and hate. They are not power seekers. Their power derives from the divine will, and as they begin slowly to create a new religion and a new society, they are driven, not by a spirit of revenge or by a spirit of love, but by a faith in the god who lies *beneath* the to-and-fro of strife and peace.

Like Ursula Brangwen, Kate is tempted again and again to resist the will of these men, who want her to be subjugated to their god. It is not until Kate realizes that the preservation of her independence is meaningless that she is able to surrender herself to their authority. For she finally realizes that her European individuality is an illusion: it is necessary that the old self die, in order that a new self—a soul—may be born. When she accepts Cipriano, it is not "love" that binds her to him but rather the knowledge that men and women must meet in "the abiding place"—in God, in an acceptance of a reality greater than the human ego and will. As Lawrence said in a letter to Dorothy Brett in 1925: "Love is chiefly bunk: an over-exaggeration of the spiritual and individualistic and analytic side." It is necessary to "leave aside some of that hateful *personal* insistence on imaginary perfect satisfaction, which is part of the inevitable bunk of love, and if they [a couple] meet as mere male and female, *kindly,* in their marriage, they will make roots, not weedy flowers of a love match'' (Huxley, 635).

It is hard for Kate to give herself up. Indeed, her white woman's conscious will reserves the right to *limit* her surrender—to hold onto the independence that is born of the Old World idealism. But she realizes that it is meaningless and horrible to continue unattached, independent, separate. Self-renewal and social renewal can occur only when men and women are capable of giving up their egotism and delivering themselves up to the authority of the life creator, the disciplined leader who *controls* the blind unconscious forces of nature even as he acts in harmony with the demands of those forces. Nature demands the death of the purely negative, divisive, voluntary spirit; it demands, too, the death of the bankrupt love ideal, which subverts all integrity and pride. The Holy Ghost, always seeking a new equilibrium, counsels a balance of male and female, voluntary and sympathetic, divisive and unitive impulses. In that balance a new life is born, an old way of life is allowed to die its natural and inevitable death.

Freudian critics have seen Lawrence's *Plumed Serpent* as regressive, an expression of Lawrence's unconscious death wish or his desire to return to the Nirvana of the womb. But Lawrence's point is one that the religious have always propounded: one must die in order to live. The old self must be discarded, and a new one must be born, living to do the will of God, not the petty human will. In *The Plumed Serpent* the divine will is realized in the death of Christianity, the religion of the one way, and in the creation of the religion of the two ways—a religion that does not renounce the flesh but that weds flesh and spirit in an acceptance of the deep impulses that urge man to achieve maximum of being

In *The Plumed Serpent,* in the unfinished tale ''The Flying Fish,'' and in his play *David,* written as he convalesced from the severe illness in 1925, Lawrence writes like a man who, aware of his slow dying, must hasten to record the articles of faith that reflect his deepest sense of mission and identification with the divine. What Cipriano and Don Ramón realize is echoed in ''The Flying Fish'' and in the beautiful prayer of Samuel in *David:*

> . . . like a fish I swim in the flood of God Himself. . . . I must . . . go down into the deeps of God. Speak, Lord, and I will obey. Tell me, and I will do it. I sink like a stone in the sea, and nothing of my own is left of me. I am gone away from myself, I disappear in the deeps of God. And the oracle of the Lord stirs me, as the fountains of the deep. Lo! I am not mine own. (*Plays,* 74–75)

When David is chosen to be the king, he knows, "Henceforth thou art not thine own. The Lord is upon thee, and thou art His" (81). And it is because he listens to God that he is able to create "a new song," the song of joy in the splendor of God and the creation (119–20). Without God, as the miserable Saul acknowledges,

> "Only men shall there be, like myriads, like locusts, clicking and grating upon one another, and crawling over one another. . . . Godless the world! Godless the men in myriads even like locusts. No God in the air! No God in the mountains! . . . So the world is empty of God, empty, empty, like a blown egg-shell bunged with wax and floating meaningless." (Plays, 117)

The horror of secularism, the wickedness of acquiescence to the human ego—these remain the great themes of David and of David Herbert Lawrence, who over a decade earlier, in 1913, had contrasted the passionate god-affirming David with the nihilistic artists who said, " 'We are God, all there is of him!' " (L, 2:101).

Reviewing the stories that Lawrence wrote during this period, one is impressed by the intensity and the persistence of his efforts to reveal what it means to think from the blood. However utopian his vision, these stories exhibit the blood consciousness in action, providing both directly and indirectly the praxis of Lawrence's religious alternative to Western civilization. These works are the product of a very concerted effort to unlearn—to repudiate entirely—"the whole trend of modern human life, the emotional, spiritual, ethical, and intellectual trend" (BB, 361). They are efforts to open consciousness to unexplored modes of life awareness.

In his personal life, Lawrence tried to act from the blood consciousness. In his writing, he sought to follow the rule formulated in Studies in Classic American Literature, "When genuine passion moves you, say what you've got to say, and say it hot" (23). Although he confessed to Aldous Huxley in 1927 that he was "in a state of despair about the Word either written or spoken seriously" (CL, 2:1020), he viewed his writing as action; and this Englishman who has been accused of flight from responsible social action took time in 1922 to write an influential attack on the Bursum bill, then before Congress, on the ground that the bill would destroy those "ancient centres of life," the Indian pueblos.

But Lawrence always wanted to do more than write and preach, and the splendor of New Mexico revived his old dream of a farm where, with horses and a cow, creative work might be carried on, a place in which people could be themselves and "form a nucleus. Then they would be able gradually to spread their influence and combat the other thing a little" (Nehls, 2:195). Less optimistic than in 1915, he added: "At least they would know they existed." In June 1923, writing to Knud Merrild, the Danish painter whose company he had enjoyed in New Mexico, he spoke of making "a life in common once more. . . . The 'world' has no life to offer. . . . We have to be a few men with honour and fearlessness, and make a life together. There is nothing else, believe me" (Huxley, 576). To Catherine Carswell he wrote: "I *could* start a little centre—a ranch—where we could have our little adobe houses and make a life, and you could come with Don and John Patrick. It is always what I work for. But it must come from the inside, not from the will" (Huxley, 589). Kai Gótzsche was also included in Lawrence's revised plan, but the painter was doubtful, and thought that "inside" Lawrence was "fighting himself," half wanting to build a new colony in Mexico, half wanting to return to England and culture.

Lawrence, earning now a bit more money, was indeed in a better position to begin his new colony than he had been in 1915. But his health was worsening, and his unchecked raging against the evils he saw in the modern world made him appear insane to Gótzsche. To Witter Bynner, Lawrence seemed insufferable, incapable of caring "for any human being" (Nehls, 2:245). Lawrence's "dreadful rage" in Mexico, when the minister of education postponed a luncheon to which he had invited Lawrence and Bynner, prompted Carleton Beals to observe that "everything sent him into convulsive loss of self-control" (Nehls, 2:228). Lawrence's violent denunciation of Frieda also appalled a number of observers. The intensity of his anger is revealed in a letter of November 1923 in which he renewed his old attack on the possessive woman who can only live for "love":

> I am no Jesus that lies on his mother's lap. I go my way through the world, and if Frieda finds it such hard work to love me, then, dear God, let her love rest, give it holidays . . . a man doesn't want, doesn't ask for love from his wife, but for strength, strength, strength. To fight, to fight, to fight, and to fight again. And one needs courage and strength and weapons. And the stupid woman keeps on saying love, love, love, and writes of love. To the devil with love! Give me strength, battle-strength, weapon-strength, fighting-strength, give me this, you woman!
>
> England is so quiet: writes Frieda. Shame on you that you ask for peace today. I don't want peace. I go around the world fighting. Pfui! Pfui! In the grave I find my peace. First let me fight and win through. (Nehls, 2:278–79)

The violence of the diatribe suggests that his illness was goading him into a new eruption of the volcanic rage that he had felt during the war. But his rejection of love was based, in part, on his conviction that human and racial differences are too great to overcome. He wrote to Rolf Gardiner in July 1924: "The great racial differences are insuperable. . . . The spirit of place ultimately always triumphs . . . don't talk to me of unison. No more unison among man than among the wild animals— coyotes and chipmunks and porcupines and deer and rattlesnakes. They all live in these hills—in the unison of avoiding one another" (Huxley, 612-13). To John Middleton Murry he wrote three months later: "All races have one root, once one gets there. Many stems from one root: the stems never to commingle or 'understand' one another" (Huxley, 623). Even more drastic is his letter to Dorothy Brett the next year: "A life in common is an illusion, when the instinct is always to divide, to separate individuals and set them one against the other. And this seems to be the ruling instinct, unacknowledged. Unite with the one against the other, and it's no good" (Huxley, 639). The voluntary or divisive instinct, not love, is supreme! In his detestation of this ruling instinct, Lawrence concluded that men could not be trusted. He did not want anybody's love or friendship, he told Dorothy Brett. " 'I just don't believe in it.' " People, unlike "horses or cats or any wild animal," were always "untrue to their pattern. . . . A tiger in the jungle is always a tiger, but men you can't trust—they always let you down and themselves" (Nehls, 2:346). He concluded too, in his bitterness, that "most people naturally dislike me—especially on second thoughts, they do. It's just part of the chemistry of life" (Huxley, 620-21). And to Murry he wrote in January 1925: "All I want to say is, don't think you can either love me or betray me. Learn that I am not lovable: hence not betrayable" (Huxley, 637).

This giving up on love and his acceptance of his role as a fighter had begun as early as *Aaron's Rod,* when Aaron realizes that there is the fight and only the fight: it is idle to suppose anything else. Anger is from God, and it is the part of the godly man, not to suppress anger in a mask of benevolence, but to release it. Cipriano declares: "We are men! We are fighters!" And so Lawrence declared in a letter of 4 July 1924 to Rolf Gardiner: "I am essentially a fighter—to wish me peace is bad luck— except the fighter's peace." There is no alternative, finally, to the fight against the obscenities of a perverted civilization. But in calling for the fight, Lawrence remained true to the premises of his Nietzschean psychology. The destructive impulse must be balanced by the creative desire; and men must be on guard against a hatred that sends them howling into the abyss: they must keep alive their warmth and tenderness, even though everything in the world provokes their anger.

9

PHALLIC CONSCIOUSNESS

1926: *The Plumed Serpent; Mornings in Mexico;* Italy: Spotorno, Villa Mirenda; painting oils: expressions of the phallic consciousness; interest in Kibbo Kift; **1927:** *Lady Chatterley's Lover* finished (first version); second version of *Lady Chatterley's Lover;* Etruscan trip; writes *Etruscan Places;* "The Escaped Cock"; **1928:** rewrites *Lady Chatterley's Lover,* privately published; *The Woman Who Rode Away and Other Stories;* to Switzerland in June, then to France; *Collected Poems; Sun; Lady Chatterley's Lover* attacked as obscene; **1929:** Scotland Yard seizes copies of *Lady Chatterley's Lover* and *Pansies;* paintings seized at the Warren Gallery; *The Escaped Cock;* completes *Apocalypse;* **1930:** dies on 2 March at Vence, France.

N*on ho la Voglia*—I've no will and no guts for anything: feel so unlike myself: *lo spettro di me stesso!"* (*CL,* 2:976). Thus Lawrence, "the shadow of himself," wrote to Earl Brewster on 13 May 1927. And there were days during the last three years of his life when he confessed that "something inside me weeps black tears" (*CL,* 2:1206). Yet there is little in his writing during these years to indicate that he was dying slowly of tuberculosis. The old themes are stated with the usual vigor and authority. It is necessary to maintain one's own integrity and individuality against the pressures of an evil world. At the same time, one must fight and, if one can, join with others who fight, for the construction of a new world. Health depends on a reverence for life itself, "creatively destroying as it goes," on an honesty in accepting both the creative and the destructive impulses within oneself, and on a return to an intuitive relatedness to others and to other kinds of being. But while these articles of faith are maintained as vehemently as ever, Lawrence's consciousness of death inevitably produced a slight shift in the tone and emphasis of his thought. Most striking is the emphasis on tenderness, which he had begun to stress in his depictions of Mexicans and dark-skinned men of the Southwest. And in *Lady Chatterley's Lover* there is a marked normalization of his mystic vision of unity—a recognition that there is, beyond the death of the self in the act of love, a warmth of heart that binds man and woman, and also man and man, together. "The phallic consciousness" is unitive (unlike the blood consciousness, which is both unitive and divisive). It is that instinctive sympathy which brings living creatures together; and because it grasps the realities of others' lives, it is "common sense" in its best sense. Yet such common sense is rare in a society dominated by rationalism and idealism.

His life during these last years followed the pattern already well established. He continued to remove himself from any contacts that threatened his inviolacy. From the Villa Mirenda near Florence he wrote to Dorothy Brett: "For me the human world becomes more and more unreal, more and more wearisome. I am really happiest when I don't see people and never go to town" (Huxley, 688). In May 1928 he repeated to Lady Ottoline the conviction he had reached during the war: "One ought to be tough and selfish: and one is never tough enough, and never selfish in the proper self-preserving way. Then one is laid low" (Huxley, 741). Microbes, he says, are "the pure incarnation of invisible selfishness"; illness is the body's inevitable reaction to the "chagrin" caused by defiling and disintegrative association with others; and the cause of his own illness was "primarily chagrin" (741). "The only thing to do in life," he wrote to Maria Huxley, "is to gather oneself together and keep oneself together in spite of everything and everybody." It is "disastrous" to "get far too much tangled up in other people's presences"—the cause of "the modern hysteria" (Huxley, 772). In October 1929 he again insisted (to Jehanne Moulaert): "Other people don't matter very much. The chief thing is to be one's own real self, and to be at peace with oneself. Then life comes easily again" (Huxley, 844). He was able at this time to speak with qualified admiration of people like his father and Norman Douglas, who "kept themselves unbroken, while the rest of us have cared too much and let ourselves be shattered by the depths of our affections. We must let things go, one after another, finally even love—only keeping oneself true to oneself, just that integrity. Nothing else matters in life or death" (Nehls, 3:245). To Brewster Ghiselin, the young American poet who visited Lawrence in 1928, Lawrence said that "'the uttermost mystery' for him . . . was how man, in the state of an animal moving in instinctive unconsciousness, in dynamic relation with his environment, 'came to say "I am I."'" (Nehls, 3:287). And in 1929, when it appeared that several of his paintings might be burned by the English High Court, Lawrence insisted that he could not risk their burning "for all the liberty of England": "I am an Englishman, and I do my bit for the liberty of England. But I am most of all a man, and my first creed is that my manhood and my sincere utterance shall be inviolate and beyond nationality or any other limitation" (Nehls, 3:358).

Yet the "crucifixion into isolate individuality"—a phrase he applied to Beethoven, who was "always in love with somebody when he wasn't really, and wanting contacts when he didn't really" (Huxley, 702)—was not, by the premises of his own psychology, healthy or endurable. As often as Lawrence insists on isolate individuality, he insists on the deep need for connection. In his impressive correspondence with Rolf Gardiner in 1926 and 1927, Lawrence revived his old dream of a passionate unison of purposive men under the banner of truth. Gardiner, who had read and understood Lawrence, had decided that the only way to resist the evils of industrialism and of "abstraction" in life was to join with others in the "Kibbo Kift, the Woodcraft Kindred," in a practical program to establish land reservations for camp training and nature craft, to encourage handicrafts and the foundation of craft guilds, and to build a new society based on the principles of economic justice and dedicated to world peace and brotherhood. Men were to feel a new pride—were to become "Men like Gods" (Nehls, 3:78). Gardiner first wrote to Lawrence in 1924, and Lawrence was skeptical about the idea of "unison," pointing out that there is no more unison among men than among the wild animals (Huxley, 613). But Lawrence was interested in John Hargrave's book *The Confessions of the Kibbo Kift*, and in July 1926 Lawrence said he would like to meet Gardiner, reaffirming his earlier hope for Rananim: "I should love to be connected with something, with some few people, in something. As far as anything *matters*, I have always been very much alone, and regretted it" (Huxley, 675). In October he wrote that he was "sympathetic, fundamentally," and told Gardiner of his idea to "take a place in the country, somewhere," where he and a few other men "might possibly slowly evolve a new rhythm of life: learn to make the creative pauses, and learn to dance and to sing together, without stunting, and perhaps also publish some little fighting periodical, keeping fully alert and alive to the world, living a different life in the midst of it, not merely apart" (Huxley, 679). It was necessary to establish "a fuller relationship between oneself and the universe, and between oneself and one's fellow man and fellow woman. It doesn't mean cutting out the 'brothers-in-Christ' business simply: it means expanding it into a full relationship, where there can be also physical and passional meeting, as there used to be in the old dances and rituals" (Huxley, 679). As in *The Plumed Serpent*, the meeting must occur on "the holy ground"—a center for those who accept the divine will. There must be "a holy centre: whole, heal, hale" (Huxley, 706). It has been argued that Lawrence's ideas were fascistic, but obviously Lawrence continued to think in almost purely religious terms, and although he was interested in the German Bünde, he feared that they would "drift into nationalistic, and ultimately, fighting bodies" (Huxley, 706). The core of any vital movement must be religious—the "religious sense of at-one-ness." But John Hargrave, Lawrence thought, was "too egoistic," "ambitious," "full of hate," and "cold": he lacked the qualities needed in a constructive leader: "tenderness as well as toughness" (Huxley, 708).

Lawrence was too ill to join in any active social movement, and he was certainly incapable of submitting to the authority of any leader who did not share his own vision of truth. Like Henry James, Lawrence was thus condemned to be a "monster of *Dis*sociation," not of association. But he felt that his illness was due, not only to the violation of his integrity by association with others, but also to "the absolute frustration of my primeval societal instinct" (Huxley, 693). When he read Dr. Trigant Burrow, the psychoanalyst who held that man's basic sympathetic and communal instinct had been frustated by the perpetration of the illusion of individuality, Lawrence agreed:

> The hero illusion starts with the individualist illusion, and all resistances [to unison] ensue. I think societal instinct much deeper than sex instinct—and societal repression much more devastating. There is no repression of the sexual individual comparable to the repression of the societal man in me, by the individual ego, my own and every body else's. I am weary even of my own individuality, and simply nauseated by other people's. (Huxley, 693)

Unlike those who preach a doctrine of egoistic individualism and self-fulfillment, Lawrence advocates an integrity and individualism that fight to carry out the divine will. In this statement, Lawrence endorses Burrow's phylogenetic conception of "instinct" as a mechanism devised by nature to ensure group cooperation and cohesion; and Lawrence anticipates the conclusions of human ethology, which traces cooperative, or sympathetic, behavior to a hereditary encoding designed for preservation of the species. At the same time, Lawrence anticipates the conclusion of existential psychologists, such as Erich Fromm and Irwin Strauss, who argue that "love," or a kind of symbiotic relatedness, is essential to the realization of one's deepest needs. "It is our being cut off that is our ailment, and out of this ailment everything bad arises," Lawrence wrote to Burrow in August 1927. He did not agree with Burrow that a "true societal flow" could occur if the individualist illusion were destroyed; Lawrence's psychology, postulating a frictional to-and-fro of sympathetic and voluntary impulses, ruled out any subscription to a "fully societal" behavior in men. But he believed that "the cut-offness"—the divorce from the "*principle* in the universe, towards which man turns religiously—a *life* of the universe itself" (Huxley, 696)—was the result, as Burrow maintained, of the individualist illusion perpetrated by a capitalistic society that emphasized possessions, egoistical exclusiveness, and the primacy of the individual.

There was still a need for leadership—for men who could lead mankind to a fulfillment of its deepest desires. But Lawrence's conception of leadership in his last years was no longer the fierce assertion of "power" that he had stressed in his essay "The Crown." His new conception of leadership is developed in a letter to Rolf Gardiner, dated 4 March 1928:

> I'm afraid the whole business of leaders and followers is somehow wrong, now. Like the demon-drive, even Leadership must die, and be born different, later on. I'm afraid part of what ails you is that you are struggling to enforce an obsolete form of leadership. It is White Fox's [John Hargrave's] calamity. When leadership has died—it is very nearly dead, save for Mussolini and you and White Fox and Annie Besant and Gandhi—then it will be born again, perhaps, new and changed, and based on reciprocity of tenderness. The reciprocity of power is obsolete. When you get down to the basis of life, to the depth of the warm, creative stir, there is no power. It is never: There *shall* be light!—only: Let there be light! (Huxley, 712–13)

The shift in Lawrence's thinking here is perhaps a reflection of his illness or his age—a growing reluctance to fight to assert his authority over others. But it may also reflect his recognition that he had been wrong to try to "enforce an obsolete form of leadership." His *own* calamity was that he had antagonized too many of his friends by the very assertion of his authority. And he appears to have recognized this fact when he warned Gardiner in a letter of 7 January 1928: "Don't forget, you are striving with yourself so hard, you hit other people in the eye fighting your own phantasm. And they resent it" (*CL*, 2:1031). His conclusion that "the reciprocity of power is obsolete" issued from experience, which demonstrated to him that modern men and women— separate, individual, cut off, their primal societal instincts weakened and all but dead—cannot submit, as primitive men did, to "the heroic soul in a greater man" unless they see in that heroic soul a warmth of heart that finally dispels egoistic suspicion and rivalry. At the end of his life, Lawrence seems to have concluded that tenderness must be stronger than the will to power in the religious leader.

He also realized that something greater than personal relationships must support any Rananim. If men and women were ever to come together "in ultimate trust," they had to share a religious sense of life and of relatedness to the cosmos. In Ceylon, in March 1922, in a letter to Robert Pratt Barlow, he had concluded that it was idle "to look to Buddha or the Hindu or to our own working men, for the impulse to carry through." The "most living clue of life," he wrote, was "in us Englishmen in England"; and he speculated that "the Roman Catholic Church, as an institution, granted of course some new adjustments to life, might once more be invaluable for saving Europe: but not as a mere political power" (*CL*, 2:698). By 1929, when he wrote his eloquent essay

"A Propos of *Lady Chatterley's Lover*," he had decided that in one way or another there must be a renewal of the ancient rituals that were still incorporated in Catholicism:

> . . . the greatest need of man is the renewal forever of the complete rhythm of life and death, the rhythm of the sun's year, the body's year of a lifetime, and the greater year of the stars, the soul's year of immortality. . . . It is no use asking for a Word to fulfil such a need. No Word, no Logos, no Utterance will ever do it. . . . It is the *Deed* of life we have now to learn. . . .
>
> It is a question, practically, of relationship. We *must* get back into relation, vivid and nourishing relation to the cosmos and the universe. The way is through daily ritual, and the re-awakening. We *must* once more practise the ritual of dawn and noon and sunset, the ritual of the kindling fire and pouring water, the ritual of the first breath, and the last. This is an affair of the individual and the household, a ritual of day. The ritual of the moon in her phases, of the morning star and the evening star is for men and women separate. Then the ritual of the seasons, with the Drama and the Passion of the soul embodied in procession and dance, this is for the community, an act of men and women, a whole community in togetherness. And the ritual of the great events in the years of stars is for nations and whole peoples. To these rituals we must return: or we must evolve them to suit our needs. For the truth is, we are perishing for lack of fulfilment of our greater needs, we are cut off from the great sources of our inward nourishment and renewal, sources which flow eternally in the universe. (*Phoenix II*, 510)

To create the ancient forms again, he goes on to say, "we have to go back, a long way, before the idealist conceptions began, before Plato" (510–11), back to the animistic world, to "Apollo, and Attis, Demeter, Persephone, and the halls of Dis" (511). But how?

Physical contact—the idea of a "civilisation of touch"—was the great clue. As he wrote to Rolf Gardiner on 18 December 1927, referring to the latter's efforts to build a new life, "I'd teach 'em, if I could, to dance and sing together. The togetherness is important. But they must first overthrow in themselves the money-fear and money-lust" (*CL*, 2:1027).

To the psychiatrist Trigant Burrow he wrote on 3 August 1927: "And I do think that the only way of true relationship between men is to meet in some common 'belief'—if the belief is but physical and not merely mental" (*CL*, 2:993).

A belief that is "but physical"! It sounds like a contradiction in terms. But Lawrence meant, of course, "the phallic consciousness," tenderness and warmth that can exist only through touch. As he wrote to Witter Bynner, "The new relationship will be some sort of tenderness," not that of "leader-cum-follower," but presumably a form of togetherness (CL, 2:1045). As keen as Freud to probe the roots of such a relationship, Lawrence recognized that the "physical flow," "the healing and sustaining flow to the height," is "sex, true sensual sex. But it has a thousand forms" (CL, 2:914). It was "the phallic consciousness" that united men and men, and men and women, in tenderness.

By "the phallic consciousness" he did not mean a male sexualized consciousness and certainly not a cerebral consciousness of sex. He describes the phallic consciousness as "the source of all real beauty, and all real gentleness" (Huxley, 716). It is "deeper" than "the cerebral sex-consciousness" and is "the root of poetry, lived or sung" (Huxley, 716). In another letter he calls it "the basic consciousness, and the thing we mean, in the best sense, by common sense" (Huxley, 724). It is manifested in living contact with others, nonegoistic, as an awareness of "the basic physical realities" (Huxley, 781). Perhaps it is best defined as a sympathetic awareness of the "life-flow" of another person or creature. In "St. Mawr," for example, Lawrence recognizes that the groom named Phoenix cannot exist "positively" because he must submit to his employers' control: "*Their* existence made his own existence negative. If he was to exist positively, they would have to cease to exist" (41). This same phallic awareness is directed toward the stallion St. Mawr, which lives in "another world, an older, heavily potent world" where the horse was "undominated and unsurpassed." Unable to accept the control of the unsympathetic white human world, the horse is "still himself" even in bondage (53) and is charged with latent hostility. It is Lawrence's phallic consciousness that accounts, to a great extent, for the power of his poems about animals. And it is often this consciousness, I think, that Lawrence's enthusiastic readers have in mind when they discover so much "reality" in his fiction.

When Lawrence spoke of the phallic consciousness as "common sense," he also had in mind the ability to respond directly "from the source." An ideal consciousness checks the immediate response. Confronted by the problems of contemporary civilization, the ideal consciousness seeks humanely, rationally, to solve these problems—by constructing more houses, more roads, more factories. Lawrence's immediate response was not mental but an intuitive recognition of the life damage caused by such "progress." Hence he said "Shit!" to the whole spectacle. And this ability to respond immediately and passionately was, he held, essential to sanity. As he said to Lady Ottoline in a letter of 28 December 1928, "I realise that one of the reasons why the common people often keep—or kept—the good *natural glow* of life, just warm life, longer than educated people, was because it was still possible for them to say fuck! or shit without either a shudder or a sensation. If a

man had been able to say to you when you were young and in love: an'
if tha shits, an' if tha pisses, I' glad, I shouldna want a woman who
couldna shit nor piss—surely it would have been a liberation to you, and
it would have helped to keep your heart warm" (CL, 2:1111). Earl H.
Brewster summarized Lawrence's view when he said that by writing
with "reverence for life," one purges the mind of "poison" when "the
hidden words and thoughts are brought into the clear daylight" (Nehls,
3:134). As the touching of others can dispel suspicion and bring people
closer together, with a warm glow of life, so the breaking down of
language taboos can restore a healthy awareness of the physical realities
that are suppressed by bourgeois proprieties and by the conventional
poses of the ego.

Lawrence's phallic consciousness, so closely related to his emphasis
on warmth and tenderness, is also a kind of feminine consciousness, of
the sort traditionally associated with the loving and caring mother. It is
thus the expression of the maternal attitude that Lawrence showed early
in life and continued to show in his last years. In 1926, at the Villa
Mirenda, he prepared a Christmas tree and invited the peasant children
with their mothers, "distributing sweets and presents to all." According
to Raul Mirenda, Lawrence also helped "the wives of peasants when
they had given birth to a child, providing a ration of milk for the mother
for a period of two months"; and Lawrence bore the expense of an
operation on a child "afflicted from birth with a double inguinal hernia"
(Nehls, 3:62). Walter Wilkerson was present when Lawrence, coming
upon a peasant child "sitting on a doorstep, howling his life out and
clutching his jaw," crouched "to the infant's level," asked " 'Che cosa
é?' and 'E il dento? E guasto? Fa noia?' [What's wrong? Is it your tooth?
Is it decayed? Does it bother you?] and then pulled a paper bag of boiled
sweets from his pocket with which he always seemed to be provided"
(Nehls, 3:67). On another occasion, according to Richard Aldington,
Lawrence, "ill as he was," went into his villa to get a piece of chocolate
and some sugar for a peasant boy who had offered Lawrence a bunch of
grapes (Nehls, 3:114). Earl H. Brewster said that Lawrence's compassion
"was of his *feelings* and ravaged him. . . . He felt keenly the suffering of
individuals and promptly sought to aid them: constantly, gifts of money
and thoughtfully chosen things were being made by him to people of all
sorts in various lands. He tried to help young writers. Injustice done to
others he felt so much as most of us do when it is meted out to
ourselves. It angered and wore on him" (Nehls, 3:407). Brewster opined
that compassion includes more than feeling—that it is "of the mind, not
suffering yet *understanding* and *forgiving*" (Nehls, 3:407). But Lawrence
rejected such mental understanding and forgiving as a forcing of life
against the deep sources of being. His view that "desire and anger are

from God" (Nehls, 3:58) reflected the basic principles of his "hormic" psychology, which derives tenderness or compassion, not from the moral teachings of civilization, but from instinct or impulse.

Lady Chatterley's Lover is an expression of both anger and tenderness—the tenderness becoming more precious as one sees it in relation to a hideous world of coercion, human debasement, and cold egotism. In attacking this world, Lawrence acted on the rule he recommended to Rolf Gardiner on 23 December 1928: "If one doesn't smash as one goes, it's no good. This silly White Fox [John Hargrave] blarney about pure constructive activity is all poppycock—nine-tenths at least must be smash-smash!—or else *all* your constructivity turns out feebly destructive" (Huxley, 777). *Lady Chatterley* is written on the premise, stated in a letter to Charles Wilson on 28 December 1928, that "the whole scheme of things is unjust and rotten, and money is just a disease upon humanity"; "you've got to smash money and this beastly *possessive* spirit. I get more revolutionary every minute, but for *life's* sake. The dead materialism of Marx socialism and soviets seems to me no better than what we've got. What we want is life and *trust*; men trusting men, and making living a free thing, not a thing to be *earned*. But if men trusted men, we could soon have a new world, and send this one to the devil" (Huxley, 779).

In many ways, Lawrence's last novel was anticipated by *The Virgin and the Gipsy*, written in 1925. The gamekeeper Mellors, in his green velveteens, is like the gipsy in his green jersey—an outcast, defiant, at odds with society, yet "too much master to himself, and too wary, to expose himself openly to the vast and gruesome clutch of our law. He had been through the war. He had been enslaved against his will, that time" (*VG*, 98). Again, the gipsy, like Mellors, is warm-hearted, with a natural phallic desire and consciousness. The rector, "somewhat distinguished as an essayist and a controversialist" (1), is a "conservative anarchist" (89), like Clifford Chatterley—a coward who believes in nothing yet maintains the dead form of convention out of fear. The rectory itself, with its "stagnant, sewerage sort of life" (42), is the counterpart of Clifford Chatterley's Wragsby, dark and unsavory in its closed-in oppressiveness. The hideous old Granny, with her cunning and her obscene will to power, anticipates Mrs. Bolton, though Granny is unique and one of the most memorable characters in all of Lawrence's fiction. As for Yvette, the virgin, she is in many ways like Connie Chatterley—honest, with a disarming penetration of the falsities that beset her and, like Connie, both attracted to the green man who is outside the pale and fearful of taking the great step that would cut her off from her respectable bourgeois society.

Yvette misses her chance. But Connie Chatterley summons up the courage to love. The tenderness that arises between Connie and Mellors is not easily established. They must overcome the distrust fostered by class, by social convention, and by "ideal consciousness." Connie, reared in the atmosphere of the Ideal, keeps her promise to marry the wounded Clifford Chatterley and discovers that persistence in the living death of her marriage has led her into a void. Clifford, paralyzed from the waist down, cannot love her physically; but it is not just a physical deprivation that wastes and nullifies Connie's life. Michaelis, the young ambitious playwright with whom she has a brief affair, is *physically* potent; but at bottom he is, like Clifford, cold and egoistic, and Connie's love-making with him becomes an egoistic struggle for satisfaction—for orgasm divorced from any warm relatedness. At the root of Connie's despair is her realization that the men she knows are all dead, all paralyzed, acquiescing passively to intolerable evils of advanced capitalism and industrialism, lacking the courage to challenge the dead form of their lives.

It is not until she meets Mellors that she comes into contact with a man who has managed to preserve his integrity against the bullying system and against the coldness of ideal consciousness. Grim, physically frail, forced to take orders from Clifford, the gamekeeper preserves his pride and self-respect, serving Clifford without groveling or capitulating to the way of life that has driven him into a subordinate position. In the woods, in touch with organic realities, he lives his solitary life. Nor does he *want* to connect with others. Like Lawrence, he cherishes his inviolacy as the one thing that he has to hold onto in a world gone mad in the worship of the bitch goddess of success. Even Connie, unable at first to throw off her conventional attitudes and assumptions, arouses his distrust and contempt.

It is only gradually that the two are able to meet "in ultimate trust" of each other. To meet as man and woman they must overcome their mutual suspicion; the cerebral tendency to stand apart or to withdraw in self-protective, defensive acts; their class consciousness; their fear of drastic change in an established way of life; the fear that sexual contact is a violation of self or a meaningless struggle for egoistic pleasure; the well-founded fear that society's retaliation for their trespass will be coldly brutal. When at last they do "let go" and give up their old consciousness, the new phallic consciousness binds them together in a tenderness whose preciousness can be measured only by contrast with the paralyzed and nullified state of the world in which they live.

As John Thomas and Lady Jane, the lovers are part of what Lawrence calls in ". . . Love was Once a Little Boy" "the true desire-stream." " 'Tha ma'es nowt o' me, John Thomas. Art boss? of me? Eh well, tha'rt more cocky than me, an' tha says less. John Thomas! Dost want *her?* Dost want my Lady Jane? Tha's dipped me in again, tha hast. Ay, an' tha comes up smilin' " (*LCL*, 428). Connie is desirable; Mellors is desirous. And "in the frail, subtle desirousness of the true male, towards everything female, and the equally frail, indescribable desirability of every female for every male, lies the real clue to the equating, or the *relating*, of things which otherwise are incommensurable" (*Phoenix II*, 452). Lawrence makes clear that "this subtle streaming of desire is beyond the control of the ego. . . . The individual has nothing, really, to do with love. That is, his individuality hasn't" (*Phoenix II*, 452). "Desire itself is a pure thing, like sunshine, or fire, or rain. It is desire that makes the whole world living to me, keeps me in the flow connected. It is my flow of desire that makes me move as the birds and animals move through the sunshine and the night, in a kind of accomplished innocence" (*Phoenix II*, 455). In this passage, Lawrence is calling for a new conception of man, far different from the egoistic version. A man is the center of energies that sweep through him and of energies that are resistant.

> Everything that exists, even a stone, has two sides to its nature. It fiercely maintains its own individuality, its own solidity. And it reaches forth from itself in the subtlest flow of desire. . . .
> So instead of the Greek: *Know thyself!* we shall have to say to every man: "*Be Thyself! Be desirous!*"—and to every woman: "*Be Thyself! Be Desirable!*"
> *Be Thyself* does not mean *Assert thy ego!* It means, be true to your own integrity, as man, as woman: let your heart stay open, to receive the mysterious inflow of power from the unknown: know that the power comes to you from beyond, it is not generated by your own will: therefore all the time, be watchful, and reverential towards the mysterious coming of power into you. . . .
> I am myself, and I remain myself only by the grace of the powers that enter me, from the unseen, and make me forever newly myself.
> And I am myself, also, by the grace of the desire that flows from me and consummates me with the other unknown, the invisible, tangible creation. (*Phoenix II*, 456–57)

Man is a conductor of energies, a vessel through which the divine energies flow: John Thomas and Lady Jane. With the utmost simplicity, Lawrence could see that desire is what makes the whole world living to a person; one is tied by sympathy, by fellow-feeling, to other forms of life and to the inorganic world as well. What stoics called "the sympathy of the whole" binds us to the world. Without it, the world is rubbish, indifferent matter at the disposal of the omnipotent ego; as it is to Clifford Chatterley and other "conservative anarchists."

Sexual fulfillment makes possible Mellors's new surge of opposition to "the electric thing"—the horror of industrialism and of cold willfulness seeking money and success. Gradually his old pride and defiance are charged with a new energy, and he seeks to create a new way of life on a farm, a free man, no longer subject to the humiliations of the blindly mechanical system. As Mellors grows in strength and pride, Clifford meanwhile goes soft inside, seeking in Mrs. Bolton's caresses the infantile bliss that is his final refuge from responsibility. Like Gerald Crich, he has reorganized and modernized the mines—has become "the God in the machine." But his cold power and will mask his inner collapse. Like Ernest Weekley, after Frieda had left him for Lawrence, Clifford is "decent" and vicious, yet his retaliation cannot touch the spirit of Mellors or Connie, who have found peace in their mutual trust and in their faith in a phallic reality that survives the assaults of life deniers. This positive conclusion to *Lady Chatterley's Lover* echoes what Lawrence had written to A. W. McLeod in October 1912:

> What does it matter if one is poor, and risks one's livelihood, and reputation. One *can* have the necessary things, life, and love, and clean warmth. Why is England so shabby?
>
> The Italians here sing. They are very poor. . . . But they are healthy and they lounge about in the little square . . . like kings. And they go by the window proudly, and they don't hurry or fret. And the women walk straight and look calm. And the men adore children—they are glad of their children even if they're poor. I think they haven't many ideas, but they look well, and they have strong blood. (Huxley, 67)

Writing in Italy fourteen years later, Lawrence continued to show some of the calm that he had admired in the *contadini*. He liked being older, he told John Middleton Murry in 1929, "if only my chest didn't scratch so much" (Huxley, 797). To Mark Gertler, Lawrence wrote that men when they pass forty "seem to undergo a sort of *spiritual* change of life, with really painful depression and loss of energy," but that "in the end, you come out of it with a new sort of rhythm, a new psychic rhythm: a sort of re-birth" (Huxley, 850). He accepted the new rhythm with the sort of equanimity that he accepted death—the equanimity shown in his last poems, in which he speaks confidently of returning to the source. And he "could still laugh, on occasion," Aldous Huxley observed, "with something of the old and exuberant gaiety" (Nehls, 3:173).

Yet Lawrence could never lapse into a passive equanimity. Huxley adds: "Often, alas, towards the end, the laughter was bitter, and the high spirits almost terrifyingly savage. . . . The secret consciousness of his dissolution filled the last years of his life with an overpowering sadness. . . . It was, however, in terms of anger that he chose to express this sadness. Emotional indecency always shocked him profoundly, and, since anger seemed to him less indecent as an emotion than a resigned or complaining melancholy, he preferred to be angry'' (Nehls, 3:173). Lawrence could never have subscribed to a "calm" unbroken by an active fight against the world.

The paintings he did during these last years were also intended to express the phallic consciousness. Indeed, Lawrence painted a phallus in every picture, and in the rich brown flesh tones that he had found in Etruscan paintings and in the vigor of strong sinuous lines, he sought to recover some of the Etruscan joy in vitality itself. In his essay "Introduction to These Paintings," he argues, with unusual liveliness and zest, that English painting is bankrupt because, since the Renaissance (and the terror and hatred of the body caused by syphilis) the " 'spiritual-mental' consciousness" has grown "at the expense of the instinctive-intuitive consciousness" (*Phoenix*, 552)—which is the phallic consciousness, although Lawrence does not use the phrase in this essay. What has been lost is "the flow of . . . intuition":

> A deep instinct of kinship joins men together, and the kinship of flesh-and-blood keeps the warm flow of intuitional awareness streaming between human beings. Our true awareness of one another is intuitional, not mental. Attraction between people is really instinctive and intuitional, not an affair of judgment.
>   . . . by intuition alone can man *really* be aware of man, or of the living, substantial world. By intuition alone can man live and know either woman or world, and by intuition alone can he bring forth again images of magic awareness which we call art. (*Phoenix*, 556)

In opposition to aesthetic theories that issue from mental consciousness—in particular, Frye's idea of Significant Form—Lawrence holds that "an artist *can* only create what he religiously *feels* is truth, religious truth really *felt*, in the blood and the bones" (562). But the English (save for Blake) could never think anything connected with the body religious, and it remained for Paul Cézanne to make the "first tiny step back to real substance" (567). Cézanne "wanted to live, really live in the body, to know the world through his instincts and his intuitions, and to be himself in his procreative blood, not in his mere mind and spirit" (568). "Far too inwardly proud and haughty to accept the ready-made clichés that came from his mental consciousness, stocked with memories" (576), Cézanne fought against an art that Samuel Taylor Coleridge would have called fanciful, and struggled to create a work of imagination, which Lawrence defines as "that form of complete consciousness in which predominates the intuitive awareness of forms, images, the *physical* awareness" (574). "Instinct, intuition, mind, intellect all fused into one complete consciousness, and grasping what we may call a complete truth, or a complete vision" (574)—this is the nature of the genuine creative act.

This remarkable art criticism is often slighted, but John Remsbury, in his essay " 'Real Thinking': Lawrence and Cézanne," argues persuasively that Lawrence's analysis of Cézanne's struggle against the cliché is an inspired example of "real thinking," which weds art criticism to a fine philosophical analysis of the relationships of "body" and "mind" in perception. Remsbury shows that Cézanne was indeed interested, as Lawrence claims, in true-to-life representation. Quoting Maurice Merleau-Ponty, as well as the philosopher Gilbert Ryles, on the phenomenology of perception, Remsbury shows that such representation is phenomenologically accurate. Lawrence admires Cézanne because the painter returns us to "the quick of experience," to the process of seeing, his pictures offering "a record of perception as it is lived by speaking to all the senses at once" (142). Remsbury stresses that, as Lawrence insisted, the so-called mental events cannot be separated from bodily events. As I interpret the implications of Remsbury's (and Lawrence's) remarks, "To be is to be perceived is to be imagined," where "imagination" refers to a kind of Coleridgean coalescence of subject and object in a unity such that the laws of nature are inseparable from the laws of intuition and intellect. And as Coleridge's secondary imagination "subordinates art to nature, the manner to matter," so Lawrence insists that the painter's imagination, as it struggles against the cliché or the photograph, is always governed by its respect for the stubborn physical realities that it seeks to see accurately, without sacrificing their reality to an idea—"the domination of the ready-made mental concept" (*Phoenix*, 582). The painter creates the world anew, the world's body which has been ignored by the abstractive mind in its preoccupation with power and control. The painter's vision is not "subjective"; it is an authentic record of reality as seen, felt, imagined.

The influence of Cézanne can be detected, I think, in Lawrence's painting, especially in the delicate, restrained coloring. Also there is a suggestion of Corot, whom Lawrence copied when he was young and in whom Lawrence found "The grey, plasm-limpid, pellucid advance / Of the luminous purpose of Life" (*CP*, 68). And there are strong suggestions of Blake, most notably of course in Lawrence's allegorical painting. Whatever the influences, Lawrence's paintings are religious in their effort to capture the felt truth that may be called reverence for life. He himself said that they were "almost holy" (*CL*, 2:1037). The energies of the body are presented, not with the intensity of a Van Gogh, whose response to nature Lawrence regarded as "subjective," but with an effort at the sort of objectivity that Lawrence admired in Cézanne. To use the language of *Women in Love*, it is the *otherness* of the body that Lawrence wishes his viewers to feel—the mystery of the living flesh and blood. Lawrence's painting *Contadini*, for example, depicts the wiry, "efficient" torso of a peasant as he sits with a sort of dynamic energy that is restive, ready for action even in its calm. There is a sharpness or hardness in some of the lines, particularly of the lean, trim, efficient head, which suggests a stubborn animal power, like a panther's; but the flesh is flesh, not an abstraction or an idealization. The lines of the collarbone are repeated in the modeling of the chest, the abdomen, and the pubic delta—repetitions that emphasize the sense of a coordinated power; but these W-shapes are not overemphasized. There is the reluctant repose, and the body's sinuous energy is intensified by the contrast with the cool architectural verticals of the background; but the strength is not caricatured or abstracted into the "idea" of strength. The *contadino* is solidly there as a man, not a Blakean allegorical figure, for though Lawrence introduced allegorical ideas into several of the paintings, he objected to Blake's overemphasis on allegory. Lawrence was best, I think, when he *began* with nature instead of with an idea—as his fiction is best when it resists "almost successfully" the ideas that drove him toward allegory.

The closing of the exhibition of his paintings at the Warren Gallery, the subsequent trial, the incredible attacks on him as a pornographer— all this has been recounted by Harry Moore and Edward Nehls. Most surprising is Lawrence's response to these attacks: ill as he was, he did not lapse into fatalism or resignation. His mission as well as his temperament demanded that he continue to fight. He said to Rhys Davis, in the course of an attack on the moneyed and the governing classes and on the young who tolerated these tyrants:

> "Kick," he said, "kick all the time, make them feel you know what they are. . . . The young know, they *know*, and yet they let be. Oh dear, it drives me to despair when I see them holding back, letting be. Because your chance is now; the world is all wobbling and wants a new direction."
> . . . Later he spoke of the way those elders had tried to curb him, how, indeed, they *had* curbed him. "I know I'm in a cage," he rapped out, "I know I'm like a monkey in a cage. But if anyone puts a finger in my cage, I bite—and bite hard." (Nehls, 3:273)

He did bite hard. In his last poems, which he collected under the titles *Pansies* (or *Pensées*) and *Nettles*, the crimes against life are recorded with a Juvenalian anger, a Swiftian *saeva indignatio*. Of the images he uses to depict the violation of life by capitalism and "the money-muck," the most frequent are those of prisons, iron hooks and cages; the most common inversion is that men have been turned into machines, the organic and spontaneous into the dead and the mechanical. The prison of the "Dark Satanic Mills" is "darker and more satanic" than in Blake's time, and "the iron has entered into the soul / and the machine has entangled the brain, and got it fast" (CP, 628, 629). As Henry James saw that all of life becomes a cage in which people are held for sale and exchange, so Lawrence saw everywhere the "prison house" (462). "All men are in captivity" (484); "we are all caged monkeys" (485); "The young to-day are born prisoners" (518), and "the work-prison covers / almost every scrap of the living earth" (521). The people have become "the robot-masses" with their "robot-feelings," their "robot jig-jig-jig," and "they move in a great grind of hate" (642, 645, 648); or they are "like lice" who "creep on the vast money-beast / and feed on it" (843).

Again and again he fulminates against the "beastly bourgeois" with his machinelike ego, which uses "all life only as power, as an engine uses steam or gas" (CP, 635). There are hordes of "the base," "the small-ones, ego-bound, little machines running in an enclosed circle of self" (637). There are the "rancid old men" who vent "The Grudge of the Old" (662, 502). Lawrence was appalled by his mother-in-law's determination to keep herself alive, one of the "terrible fungi, parasites of the younger life" (CL, 2:1206). And the rancid old are matched in baseness by the thrill-seeking young—"flat-chested, crop-headed, chemicalised women, of indeterminate sex, / and wimbly-wambly young men, of sex still more indeterminate" (CP, 531–32, 522). He looks for "Sun-Men" or "Sun-Women" (525); but everywhere, like Blake, he hears "the mind-forged manacles," he is witness to "the rape / of the itching mind and the mental self" (465). Men and women have lost "connection with the living cosmos" (617), and the catabolic process has begun: "Our epoch is over" (510). As his strength ebbed, Lawrence sometimes felt that he too was "nothing," "a blank," and that "desire has died in me" (507). "I am sick," he wrote: "because I have given myself away" (500); "I am ill because of wounds to the soul" (620); "I am worn out / with the effort of trying to love people / and not succeeding" (506). Despairingly, he concluded: "Now again and for ever breaks the great illusion / of human oneness" (635).

But now again, and as always, he counseled solitude and inviolacy. It is best if people will "leave me alone" (CP, 602); for "Always / at the core of me / burns the small flame of anger, gnawing / from trespassed contacts . . . / from hot, digging-in fingers of love" (601). "To be alone is one of life's greatest delights" (610); "what is lovelier than to be alone?" (646). In solitude he can "feel the living cosmos softly rocking / soothing and restoring and healing" (646)—as Wordsworth, in "Tintern Abbey," feels the "tranquil restoration" of the natural world. Lawrence searches for "centres here and there of silence and forgetting"—though he knows that "man has killed the silence of the earth / and ravished all the peaceful oblivious places / where the angels used to alight" (726, 725). With a stoic acceptance of the will of the gods and of his derivation from that will, he rejoices in his "Communion with the Godhead"—that is, his "direct contact with the source," with the "sun of suns": not the *human* version of life but life "unadulterated / with the human taint" (481). Here Lawrence celebrates the preverbal mystery of being, man as "substance itself, that flows in thick / flame of flesh forever travelling / like the flame of a candle . . ." (460). Man lives in the world of the four elements, the "Fire and the Wet, Earth and the wide Air" (706), and his experience of god-nature is not mystical but as direct as tasting in an apple "the summer and the snows, the wild welter of earth / and the insistence of the sun" (707).

His awareness of the gods is an awareness of the fundamental rhythms in the cosmos and in human life. Drawing on Empedocles, he stresses that "while we live / the kissing and communing cannot cease / nor yet the striving and the horrid strife" (*CP*, 710). Man is

> a rose tree bronzey with thorns
> a mixture of yea and nay
> a rainbow of love and hate
> a wind that blows back and forth
> a creature of beautiful peace, like a river
> and a creature of conflict, like a cataract: . . .
> (*CP*, 714)

In the processes of nature, "Back and forth goes the balance and the electric breath" (480). If an evil system has been perpetuated, it will die, for "All flows, and even the old are rapidly flowing away" (511). There will occur an "inward revolt of the native creatures of the soul" against "the triumph of the machine" (624, 625). There will be a return to the "Soft slow sympathy / of the blood" (471). "The future of religion lies in the mystery of touch" (611), and the "delirious / day of the mental welter" will pass away (471). Thus Lawrence reposes on his faith in the renewal of life—in the creative unknown from which he derives and for which he has "absolute reverence" (622).

Many of the poems are only half-written—mere jottings, materials for poetry rather than the achieved image of thought-passion. Richard Aldington said that "nearly all these Pansies and Nettles came out of Lawrence's nerves, and not out of his real self" (*CP*, 595). Although Vivian de Sola Pinto argues eloquently that Lawrence's satire is powerful, one can observe that with a little more effort, Lawrence could easily have reached the excellence of Blake's best poems. He shortened the labor, not to snatch the profit, but to hurry on to the next insight, the next bubbling proliferation of his vision. He was *discovering* as he wrote these poems, reaching always for preverbal experience to convey the joy of air, earth, fire, and water, of having a body, of tasting experience as one tastes an apple. When in "Kissing and Horrid Strife" he writes that "life is for delight / and for bliss / as now when the tiny wavelets of the sea / tip the morning light on edge, and spill it with delight / to show how inexhaustible it is," and when he adds, "And life is for dread, / for doom that darkens, and the Sunderers" (709), one thinks again of Wordsworth's line "And I grew up fostered alike by beauty and by fear." There is a kinship to Wordsworth in Lawrence's idea that the soul is built up by contact with the surrounding world, that it grows and unfolds by assimilating the energies of the world and finds at last its truest identity in recognition that it is part of "something far more deeply interfused."

What protected Lawrence from despair was always that he could take this long view, a stoical view that, as I noted earlier, Gilbert Murray summarized in his *Five Stages of Greek Religion:* " 'In the centre of your being groan not!' Accept the Cosmos. Will joyously that which God wills and make the eternal Purpose your own" (127). It is not surprising that Lawrence, in one of his last poems, "Stoic," quoted the line " 'in the centre of your being groan not!' " (*CP*, 703). In many ways Lawrence did accept this religion of "extraordinary nobleness." When Dorothy Brett was "wretched and glum," he advised her: " 'Cut it out, Brett. Cut it out. Think of the Beyond' " (Nehls, 3:50). And to Elsa Weekley, he talked one day in 1926 about "the stars, the millions of other universes, and the endlessness of space, saying, 'So you see our little lives aren't so very important after all' " (Nehls, 3:26). It was egotism that caused so much of human wretchedness—egoism and ego competition. Though he had as an artist the "pride and hauteur" he admired in Cézanne, he was remarkably free of the self-regard that breeds self-pity. Aldous Huxley observed in his introduction to Lawrence's *Letters:* "The self of most men is important enough to demand protection and various enhancements. For Lawrence, self seemed to have no interest. This detachment was the source of some of his freedom. It perhaps accounts for his enormous, uncalculated generosity of spirit. He never withheld himself. He was unreflectingly bounteous, in kindness and sometimes, very rarely, in anger" (Nehls, 3:294).

Lawrence's detachment stood by him to the end. When he wrote his last poems, it was not his own dying that absorbed his attention but the universal process—the return to the source and the renewal of life in the great rhythm of destruction and creation (*CP*, 719–20).

> And yet out of eternity, a thread
> separates itself on the blackness,

a horizontal thread
that fumes a little with pallor upon the dark.

Is it illusion? or does the pallor fume
A little higher?
Ah wait, wait, for there's the dawn,
the cruel dawn of coming back to life
out of oblivion.
. . . .
A flush of rose, and the whole thing starts again.

Selected Bibliography

Adams, John. *The Herbartian Psychology Applied to Education*. Boston: D. C. Heath & Co., 1898.

Aldington, Richard. *D. H. Lawrence: Portrait of a Genius But—*. London: William Heinemann, 1950.

Andrews, W. T., ed. *Critics on D. H. Lawrence*. Coral Gables, Fla.: University of Miami Press, 1971.

Arnold, Armin. *D. H. Lawrence and German Literature, with Two Hitherto Unknown Essays by D. H. Lawrence*. Montreal: Mansfield Book Mart, H. Heinemann, 1963.

Asquith, Lady Cynthia. *Diaries, 1915–1918*. Edited by E. M. Horsley, with a Foreword by L. P. Hartley. New York: Knopf, 1969.

Balbert, Peter. *D. H. Lawrence and the Psychology of Rhythm: The Meaning of Form in "The Rainbow."* The Hague and Paris: Mouton, 1974.

Beker, Miroslav. " 'The Crown,' 'The Reality of Peace,' and *Women in Love*." *DHLR* 2, no. 3 (Fall 1969): 254–64.

Ben-Ephraim, Gavriel. *The Moon's Dominion: Narrative Dichotomy and Female Dominance in Lawrence's Earlier Novels*. London and Toronto: Associated University Presses, 1981.

Blanchard, Lydia. "The 'Real Quartet' of *Women in Love*: Lawrence on Brothers and Sisters." In *D. H. Lawrence: The Man Who Lived*, edited by Robert B. Partlow, Jr., and Harry T. Moore. Carbondale: Southern Illinois University Press, 1980.

Blavatsky, Helene P. *The Secret Doctrine: The Synthesis of Science, Religion and Philosophy*. London: Theosophical Publishing Co., 1888.

Boadella, David. *The Spiral Flame: A Study of the Meaning of D. H. Lawrence*. Nottingham: Ritter Press, 1956.

Brunsdale, Mitzi M. *The German Effect on D. H. Lawrence and His Works, 1885–1912*. Berne: Peter Lang, 1978.

Burnet, John. *Early Greek Philosophy*. London: A. & C. Black, Ltd., 1930.

Burns, Aidan. *Nature and Culture in D. H. Lawrence*. Totowa, N.J.: Barnes & Noble Books, 1980.

Burrow, Trigant. *The Social Basis of Consciousness: A Study in Organic Psychology Based upon a Synthetic and Societal Concept of the Neuroses*. New York: Harcourt, Brace & Co., 1927.

Carpenter, Edward. *Civilisation, Its Cause and Cure, and Other Essays* (1889). London: Swan Sonnenschein, 1909.

———. *Love's Coming of Age* (1896). 6th ed. London: Swan Sonnenschein, 1909.

Carswell, Catherine. *The Savage Pilgrimage: A Narrative of D. H. Lawrence*. Cambridge: Cambridge University Press, 1981.

Cavitch, David. *D. H. Lawrence and the New World*. New York and London: Oxford University Press, 1969.

Chamberlain, Houston Stewart. *Foundations of the Nineteenth Century.* Introduction by George L. Mosse. Translated by John Lees. 2 vols. New York: Howard Fertig, 1968.

Chambers, Jessie (pseud., E. T.). *D. H. Lawrence: A Personal Record.* Edited by J. D. Chambers. 2d ed. London: Frank Cass & Co., 1965.

Clark, L. D. *Dark Night of the Body: D. H. Lawrence's "Plumed Serpent."* Austin: University of Texas Press, 1964.

———. "D. H. Lawrence and the American Indian." *DHLR* 9, no. 3 (Fall 1976): 305-72.

Clarke, Colin. *River of Dissolution: D. H. Lawrence & English Romanticism.* London: Routledge & Kegan Paul, 1969.

Corke, Helen. *D. H. Lawrence: The Croydon Years.* Austin: University of Texas Press, 1965.

Cowan, James C. *D. H. Lawrence's American Journey: A Study in Literature and Myth.* Cleveland and London: Press of Case Western Reserve University, 1970.

Daleski, Herman M. *The Forked Flame: A Study of D. H. Lawrence.* Evanston, Ill.: Northwestern University Press, 1965.

Dawson, Eugene W. "D. H. Lawrence and Trigant Burrow: Pollyanalytics and Phylobiology, An Interpretive Analysis." Ph.D. diss., University of Washington, 1963.

Delany, Paul. *D. H. Lawrence's Nightmare: The Writer and His Circle in the Years of the Great War.* New York: Basic Books, Inc., 1978.

Delavenay, Emile. *D. H. Lawrence: The Man and His Work: The Formative Years: 1885-1919.* Translated by Katharine M. Delavenay. Carbondale: Southern Illinois University Press, 1972.

———. *D. H. Lawrence and Edward Carpenter: A Study in Edwardian Transition.* New York: Taplinger Publishing Co., 1971.

Dervin, Daniel. *A "Strange Sapience": The Creative Imagination of D. H. Lawrence.* Amherst: University of Massachusetts Press, 1984.

Doolittle, Hilda (H. D.). *Bid Me to Live: A Madrigal by H.D.* New York: Grove Press, 1960.

Durham, John. "D. H. Lawrence: Outline for a Psychology of Being." Ph.D. diss., Occidental College, 1967.

Eisenstein, Samuel A. *Boarding the Ship of Death: D. H. Lawrence's Quester Heroes.* The Hague: Mouton & Co., 1974.

Ellis, Havelock. *Studies in the Psychology of Sex.* 4 vols. New York: Random House, 1936.

Engelberg, Edward. "Escape from the Circles of Experience: D. H. Lawrence's *The Rainbow* as a Modern *Bildungsroman.*" *PMLA* 78, no. 1 (March 1963): 103-13.

Erikson, Erik H. *Gandhi's Truth: On the Origins of Militant Nonviolence.* New York: W. W. Norton & Co., 1969.

Farr, Judith, ed. *Twentieth Century Interpretations of "Sons and Lovers": A Collection of Critical Essays.* Englewood Cliffs, N.J.: Prentice-Hall, 1970.

Ford, George H. *Double Measure: A Study of the Novels and Stories of D. H. Lawrence.* Reprint of 1965 edition. New York: W. W. Norton & Co., 1969.

Frazer, Sir James. *The Golden Bough: A Study in Magic and Religion.* New York: Macmillan Co., 1943; 1 volume abridged edition.

Freeman, Mary. *D. H. Lawrence: A Basic Study of His Ideas.* Gainesville: University of Florida Press, 1955.

Freud, Sigmund. *The Standard Edition of the Complete Psychological Works of Sigmund Freud.* Translated and edited by James Strachey. Vol. 12. London: Hogarth Press, 1958.

Friedenthal, Richard. *Luther: His Life and Times.* Translated by John Nowell. New York: Harcourt Brace Jovanovich, 1970.

Frobenius, Leo. *The Voice of Africa: Being an Account of the Travels of the German Inner African Exploration Expedition in the Years 1910–1912.* New York and London: Benjamin Blom, Inc., 1968.

Gatti, Hilary. "D. H. Lawrence and the Idea of Education." *English Miscellany* 21 (1970): 209–31.

Gilbert, Sandra M. "D. H. Lawrence's Uncommon Prayers." In *D. H. Lawrence: The Man Who Lived,* edited by Robert B. Partlow, Jr., and Harry T. Moore, pp. 73–93. Carbondale: Southern Illinois University Press, 1980.

Gomme, A. H., ed. *D. H. Lawrence: A Critical Study of the Major Novels and Other Writings.* Sussex, Eng.: Harvester Press; New York: Barnes & Noble, 1978.

Goodheart, Eugene. *The Utopian Vision of D. H. Lawrence.* Chicago: University of Chicago Press, 1963.

Green, Eleanor H. "Schopenhauer and D. H. Lawrence on Sex and Love." *DHLR* 8, no. 3 (Fall 1975): 329–45.

Gregory, Horace. *Pilgrim of the Apocalypse: A Critical Study of D. H. Lawrence.* New York: Viking Press, 1933.

Gutierrez, Donald. *Lapsing Out: Embodiments of Death and Rebirth in the Last Writings of D. H. Lawrence.* Rutherford, N.J.: Fairleigh Dickinson University Press, 1980.

Haeckel, Ernst. *The Riddle of the Universe at the Close of the Nineteenth Century.* Translated by Joseph McCabe. New York and London: Harper & Brothers, 1900.

Hamalian, Leo, comp. *D. H. Lawrence: A Collection of Criticism.* New York: McGraw-Hill Book Co., 1973.

Harper, Howard M., Jr. "*Fantasia* and the Psychodynamics of *Women in Love.*" In *The Classic British Novel,* edited by Howard M. Harper, Jr., and Charles Edge. Athens: University of Georgia Press, 1972.

Harrison, Jane Ellen. *Ancient Art and Ritual.* New York: Henry Holt & Co., 1913.

Herzinger, Kim A. *D. H. Lawrence in His Time: 1908–1915.* London and Toronto: Associated University Presses, 1982.

Hochman, Baruch. *Another Ego: The Changing View of Self and Society in the Work of D. H. Lawrence.* Columbia: University of South Carolina Press, 1970.

Hoffman, Frederick J. *Freudianism and the Literary Mind.* Reprint of 1945 edition. New York: Grove Press, 1959.

Hough, Graham. *The Dark Sun: A Study of D. H. Lawrence.* New York: Macmillan Co., 1957.

Howe, Marguerite Beede. *The Art of the Self in D. H. Lawrence.* Athens: Ohio University Press, 1977.

Humma, John B. "D. H. Lawrence as Friedrich Nietzsche." *Philological Quarterly* 53, no. 1 (January 1974): 110–20.

James, William. *The Principles of Psychology.* Cambridge, Mass., and London: Harvard University Press, 1981.

————. *Psychology.* Greenwich, Conn.: Fawcett Publications, Inc., 1963.

Jarrett-Kerr, Martin (Father William Tiverton, pseud.). *D. H. Lawrence and Human Existence.* London: Rockliff, 1951.

Jefferies, Richard. *The Story of My Heart: My Autobiography*. With an introduction by Elizabeth Jennings. London: Macmillan, and New York: St. Martin's Press, 1968.

Jenner, Katherine L. (Mrs. Henry). *Christian Symbolism*. Chicago: A. C. McClurg & Co., 1910.

Jung, Carl Gustav. *The Collected Works of C. G. Jung*. 2d ed., vols. 11 and 16. New York: Bollingen Foundation, 1966.

Kermode, Frank. *D. H. Lawrence*. New York: Viking Press, 1973.

Kuczkowski, Richard J. "Lawrence's 'Esoteric' Psychology: 'Psychoanalysis and the Unconscious' and 'Fantasia of the Unconscious.' " Ph.D. diss., Columbia University, 1973.

Langbaum, Robert. *The Mysteries of Identity: A Theme in Modern Literature*. New York: Oxford University Press, 1977.

Lawrence, Ada, and G. Stuart Gelder. *Young Lorenzo: Early Life of D. H. Lawrence*. New York: Russell & Russell, 1966.

Lawrence, D. H. *Aaron's Rod*. First published in 1922. Harmondsworth, Eng.: Penguin Books, 1950.

———. *Apocalypse*. Introduction by Richard Aldington. First published in 1931. New York: Viking Press, Compass Books, 1966.

———. *The Boy in the Bush*, with Mollie L. Skinner. Harmondsworth, Eng.: Penguin Books Ltd., 1981.

———. *The Collected Letters of D. H. Lawrence*. Edited by Harry T. Moore. 2 vols. New York: Viking Press, 1962.

———. *The Complete Plays*. New York: Viking Press, 1966.

———. *The Complete Poems of D. H. Lawrence*. Edited by Vivian de Sola Pinto and Warren Roberts. 2 vols. New York: Viking Press, 1964.

———. *The Complete Short Stories*. 3 vols. Harmondsworth, Eng.: Penguin Books Ltd., 1980.

———. *Etruscan Places*. First published in 1932. In *"Mornings in Mexico" and "Etruscan Places."* London: William Heinemann Ltd., 1956.

———. *Fantasia of the Unconscious*. First published in 1922. In *Fantasia of the Unconscious" and "Psychoanalysis and the Unconscious."* Introduction by Philip Rieff. Harmondsworth, Eng.: Penguin Books Ltd., 1977.

———. *The First Lady Chatterley*. First published in 1944. Harmondsworth, Eng.: Penguin Books, 1969.

———. *Kangaroo*. First published in 1923. New York: Viking Compass, 1976.

———. *Lady Chatterley's Lover*. First published in 1928. New York: Grove Press, Inc., 1957.

———. *The Letters of D. H. Lawrence*. Edited by James T. Bolton (vols. 1, 2, 3), George J. Zytaruk (vol. 2), and Andrew Robertson (vol. 3). 3 vols. to date. Cambridge: Cambridge University Press, 1979–84.

———. *The Letters of D. H. Lawrence*. Edited by Aldous Huxley. New York: Viking Press, 1932.

———. *The Lost Girl*. First published in 1920. Harmondsworth, Eng.: Penguin Books, 1950.

———. *Mornings in Mexico*. First published in 1927. In *"Mornings in Mexico" and "Etruscan Places."* London: William Heinemann Ltd., 1956.

———. *Movements in European History*. First published in 1921. Oxford: Oxford University Press, 1925.

———. *Phoenix: The Posthumous Papers of D. H. Lawrence*. Edited by Edward D. McDonald. First published in 1936. New York: Viking Press, 1968.

―――. *Phoenix II: Uncollected, Unpublished, and Other Prose Works by D. H. Lawrence.* Edited by Warren Roberts and Harry T. Moore. London: William Heinemann, 1968.

―――. *The Plumed Serpent.* First published in 1926. New York: Vintage Books, Inc., 1951.

―――. *Psychoanalysis and the Unconscious.* First published in 1921. In *"Fantasia of the Unconscious" and "Psychoanalysis and the Unconscious."* Introduction by Philip Rieff. Harmondsworth, Eng.: Penguin Books Ltd., 1977.

―――. *The Rainbow.* First published in 1915. Harmondsworth, Eng.: Penguin Books, 1976.

―――. *Sea and Sardinia.* First published in 1921. Harmondsworth, Eng.: Penguin Books, 1944.

―――. *Sons and Lovers.* First published in 1913. Harmondsworth, Eng.: Penguin Books, 1979.

―――. *Studies in Classic American Literature.* First published in 1923. Harmondsworth, Eng.: Penguin Books, 1977.

―――. *The Symbolic Meaning: The Uncollected Versions of "Studies in Classic American Literature."* Edited by Armin Arnold. New York: Viking Press, 1961.

―――. *The Trespasser.* First published in 1912. London: William Heinemann, 1955.

―――. *Twilight in Italy.* First published in 1916. In *D. H. Lawrence and Italy: "Twilight in Italy," "Sea and Sardinia," "Etruscan Places."* New York: Viking Press, 1972.

―――. *The White Peacock.* First published in 1911. London: William Heinemann Ltd., 1955.

―――. *Women in Love.* First published in 1912. New York: Random House, Modern Library, 1950.

Lawrence, Frieda. *The Memoirs and Correspondence.* Edited by E. W. Tedlock, Jr. London: William Heinemann, 1961.

―――. *"Not I, But the Wind . . . ."* New York: Viking Press, 1934.

Leavis, F. R. *D. H. Lawrence: Novelist.* New York: Simon & Schuster, 1955.

MacDonald, Robert H. " 'The Two Principles': A Theory of the Sexual and Psychological Symbolism of D. H. Lawrence's Later Fiction." *DHLR* 11 (Summer 1978): 132–55.

Miko, Stephen J. *Toward "Women in Love": The Emergence of a Lawrentian Aesthetic.* New Haven, Conn., and London: Yale University Press, 1971.

―――, ed. *Twentieth Century Interpretations of "Women in Love": A Collection of Critical Essays.* Englewood Cliffs, N.J.: Prentice-Hall, Spectrum, 1969.

Moore, Harry T., ed. *A D. H. Lawrence Miscellany.* Carbondale: Southern Illinois University Press, 1959.

―――. *The Intelligent Heart: The Story of D. H. Lawrence.* New York: Farrar, Straus & Young, 1954.

Moynahan, Julian. *The Deed of Life: The Novels and Tales of D. H. Lawrence.* Princeton, N.J.: Princeton University Press, 1963.

Murray, Gilbert. *Five Stages of Greek Religion.* New York: Columbia University Press, 1930.

Murry, J. M. *D. H. Lawrence: Son of Woman.* First published in 1931. London: Jonathan Cape, 1954.

Nahal, Chaman. *D. H. Lawrence: An Eastern View.* New York: A. S. Barnes & Co., 1971.

Nehls, Edward, ed. *D. H. Lawrence: A Composite Biography.* 3 vols. Madison: University of Wisconsin Press, 1957–59.

Neville, George. *A Memoir of D. H. Lawrence (The Betrayal)*, ed. Carl Baron. Cambridge: Cambridge University Press, 1981.

Nietzsche, Friedrich. *A Nietzsche Reader*. Selected and translated by R. J. Hollingdale. Middlesex: Penguin Books, Ltd., 1983.

———. *The Portable Nietzsche*. Edited and translated by Walter Kaufmann. New York: Viking Press, 1954.

Niven, Alastair. *D. H. Lawrence: The Novels*. London: Cambridge University Press, 1978.

Page, Norman, ed. *D. H. Lawrence: Interviews and Recollections*. 2 vols. Totowa, N.J.: Barnes & Noble, 1981.

Panichas, George A. *Adventure in Consciousness: The Meaning of D. H. Lawrence's Religious Quest*. The Hague: Mouton, 1964.

———. *The Reverent Discipline: Essays in Literary Criticism and Culture*. With a Foreword by G. Wilson Knight. Knoxville: University of Tennessee Press, 1974.

Petrie, M. W. Flinders. *The Religion of Ancient Egypt*. London: Archibald Constable & Co. Ltd., 1908.

Pinto, Vivian de Sola. *Crisis in English Poetry, 1880–1940*. New York: Harper Torchbooks, 1958.

Pritchard, R. E. *D. H. Lawrence: Body of Darkness*. Pittsburgh: University of Pittsburgh Press, 1971.

Remsbury, John. " 'Real Thinking': Lawrence and Cézanne." *Cambridge Quarterly* 2 (Spring 1967): 117–47.

Rieff, Philip. *The Triumph of the Therapeutic: Uses of Faith after Freud*. New York: Harper & Row, 1966.

Ross, Charles L. "Homoerotic Feeling in *Women in Love*: Lawrence's 'Struggle for Verbal Consciousness' in the Manuscripts." In *D. H. Lawrence: The Man Who Lived*, edited by Robert B. Partlow, Jr., and Harry T. Moore, pp. 168–82. Carbondale: Southern Illinois University Press, 1980.

Ruderman, Judith. *D. H. Lawrence and the Devouring Mother: The Search for a Patriarchal Ideal of Leadership*. Durham, N.C.: Duke University Press, 1984.

Russell, Bertrand. *The Autobiography of Bertrand Russell: 1914–1944*. Boston: Little, Brown & Co., 1968.

Sagar, Keith M. *The Art of D. H. Lawrence*. Cambridge: Cambridge University Press, 1966.

———, ed. *D. H. Lawrence and New Mexico*. Salt Lake City, Utah: Gibbs M. Smith, Inc., 1982

Sanders, Scott. *D. H. Lawrence: The World of the Five Major Novels*. New York: Viking Press, 1973.

Schneider, Daniel J. *D. H. Lawrence: The Artist as Psychologist*. Lawrence: University Press of Kansas, 1984.

———. " 'Strange Wisdom': Leo Frobenius and D. H. Lawrence." *DHLR* 16, no. 2 (Summer 1983): 183–93.

———. "The Symbolism of the Soul: D. H. Lawrence and Some Others." *DHLR* 7, no. 2 (Summer 1974): 107–26.

Schopenhauer, Arthur. *The Will to Live: Selected Writings of Arthur Schopenhauer*. Edited by Richard Taylor. New York: Frederick Ungar Publishing Co., 1967.

———. *The World as Will and Idea*. Translated by R. B. Haldane and J. Kemp. 3 vols. London: Trübner, 1883–86.

Spencer, Herbert. *First Principles*. New York: De Witt Revolving Fund, 1958.

———. *The Principles of Psychology*. New York: D. Appleton & Co., 1877.

Spilka, Mark. "Lawrence's Quarrel with Tenderness." *Critical Quarterly* 9 no. 4 (Winter 1967): 363–77.

———. *The Love Ethic of D. H. Lawrence.* Bloomington: Indiana University Press, 1955.

Stoll, John E. *The Novels of D. H. Lawrence: A Search for Integration.* Columbia: University of Missouri Press, 1971.

Swigg, Richard. *Lawrence, Hardy, and American Literature.* New York and London: Oxford University Press, 1972.

Tedlock, Ernest W., Jr. *D. H. Lawrence, Artist and Rebel: A Study of Lawrence's Fiction.* Albuquerque: University of New Mexico Press, 1963.

———, ed. *D. H. Lawrence and "Sons and Lovers": Sources and Criticism.* New York: New York University Press, 1965.

Tenenbaum, Elizabeth Brody. *The Problematic Self: Approaches to Identity in Stendhal, D. H. Lawrence and Malraux.* Cambridge, Mass., and London: Harvard University Press, 1977.

Tindall, William York. *D. H. Lawrence & Susan His Cow.* New York: Columbia University Press, 1939.

Tylor, Edward B. *Primitive Culture: Researches into the Development of Mythology, Philosophy, Religion, Language, Art and Custom.* 2 vols. New York: Henry Holt & Co., 1889.

Vivas, Eliseo. *D. H. Lawrence: The Failure and the Triumph of Art.* Bloomington: Indiana University Press, 1961.

Waters, Frank. "Quetzalcoatl versus D. H. Lawrence's *Plumed Serpent.*" *Western American Literature* 3, no. 2 (Summer 1968): 103–13.

Weininger, Otto. *Sex and Character.* Translated from the 6th German edition. London: William Heinemann, 1907.

Weiss, Daniel A. *Oedipus in Nottingham: D. H. Lawrence.* Seattle: University of Washington Press, 1962.

West, Anthony. *D. H. Lawrence.* Denver, Colo.: Swallow Press, 1950.

Widmer, Kingsley. *The Art of Perversity: D. H. Lawrence's Shorter Fictions.* Seattle: University of Washington Press, 1962.

Williams, Raymond. "Introduction." In *D. H. Lawrence on Education,* edited by Joy Williams and Raymond Williams. Harmondsworth, Eng.: Penguin Books, 1973.

Worthen, John. *D. H. Lawrence and the Idea of the Novel.* London: Macmillan Press Ltd., 1979.

Yudhishtar. *Conflict in the Novels of D. H. Lawrence.* Edinburgh: Oliver & Boyd, 1969.

Zoll, Alan R. "Vitalism and the Metaphysics of Love: D. H. Lawrence and Schopenhauer." *DHLR* 11, no. 1 (Spring 1978): 1–20.

Zytaruk, George J., ed., *The Quest for Rananim: D. H. Lawrence's Letters to S. S. Koteliansky, 1914 to 1930.* Montreal and London: McGill-Queen's University Press, 1970.

INDEX

Aldington, Richard, ix, 95, 183, 192
Andrews, Esther, 107
Asquith, Lady Cynthia, 2–3, 68, 100, 105, 114, 115, 121
Asquith, Herbert, 105

Balzac, Honoré de, 64, 98
Barlow, Robert Pratt, 180
Baron, Carl, 17
Baudelaire, Charles Pierre, 75
Beals, Carleton, 174
Beethoven, Ludwig von, 177
Beker, Miroslav, 119
Ben-Ephraim, Gavriel, 86
Bennett, Arnold, 69
Bergson, Henri, 58
Besant, Annie, 53, 180
Birrell, Frank, 20, 94, 95
Blake, William, 104, 156, 188, 189, 190, 191
Blanc, Louis, 53
Blanchard, Lydia, 107
Blavatsky, Helena, 141, 142. See also Lawrence, D. H.: influences on
Brett, Dorothy, 137, 171, 175, 177, 193
Brewster, Achsah, 25, 90, 139, 143
Brewster, Earl H., 64, 90, 138, 143, 147, 176, 183
Brooke, Rupert, 115
Brown, Hilda, 127, 143
Browning, Robert, 15, 111
Burnet, John, 101–2, 154. See also Lawrence, D. H.: influences on: Greek philosophers
Burns, Aidan, 143
Burrow, Trigant, 179, 181. See also Lawrence, D. H.: influences on
Burrows, Louie, 28, 30, 31, 35, 36, 38, 40, 41, 42, 44, 59, 70, 109
Bynner, Witter, 7, 133, 166, 171, 174, 181

Campbell, Gordon, 65, 73, 81, 86, 89, 90
Carpenter, Edward, 53–56, 59, 82, 93. See also Lawrence, D. H.: influences on

Carswell, Catherine, 1, 2, 13, 23, 42, 90, 92, 95, 98, 99, 104, 113, 118, 124, 127, 135, 138, 139, 174
Cézanne, Paul, 188, 189, 193
Chamberlain, Houston Stewart, xi, 76–79, 93, 140, 145. See also Lawrence, D. H.: influences on
Chambers, David, 5, 6, 7
Chambers, J. D., 11
Chambers, Jessie, 6, 7, 15, 20, 22, 27, 28, 29, 31, 35, 39, 48, 53, 59, 62, 70, 104
Chambers, May, 2, 3, 6, 7, 9, 18, 21, 22, 23, 24, 94, 109
Clark, L. D., 171
Clarke, Colin, 119
Coleridge, Samuel Taylor, 188, 189
Collings, Ernest, 74
Collishaw, Mabel Thurlby, 3, 4, 5, 12, 13
Conrad, Joseph, 134, 147
Cooper, James Fenimore, 144–45
Corke, Helen, 27, 28, 29, 31, 35, 38, 39, 41, 61, 62, 63, 65, 107
Corot, Jean Baptiste Camille, 189
Cowan, James C., 124
Crèvecoeur, Michel, 144

Daleski, H. M., 169
Dana, Charles, 146
Darwin, Charles, 50, 98
Davey, J. G., 57
Davies, Rhys, 25, 190
Dax, Alice, 20, 36, 53, 61, 85
De la Mare, Walter, 45
Delany, Paul, 87, 95
Delavenay, Emile, ix, x, xi, 13, 47, 53, 55, 59, 70, 76, 77, 106, 107
Dervin, Daniel, 118
De Sola Pinto, Vivian, 98, 192
Doolittle, Hilda, 7, 107
Dostoevsky, Fyodor, 72, 75, 85, 117, 141. See also Lawrence, D. H.: influences on
Douglas, Norman, 2, 25, 137–38, 177
Dowden, Edward, 15

Ellis, Havelock, 54
Emerson, Ralph Waldo, 79
Empedocles, 101, 102, 140, 192. *See also*
    Lawrence, D. H.: influences on
Erikson, Erik H., x, 8, 18, 26

Flaubert, Gustave, 69, 75, 95
Ford, Ford Madox, 59, 66
Forman, Henry James, 138
Forster, E. M., 96
Frank, Waldo, 142
Frankl, Viktor, 142
Franklin, Benjamin, 144
Frazer, Sir James, 75, 90, 122, 153
Freud, Sigmund, 141, 142, 182
Frobenius, Leo, 147, 170. *See also* Law-
    rence, D. H.: influences on
Fromm, Erich, 142, 179
Frye, Roger, 188

Gandhi, Mahatma, 22, 23, 26, 42, 87, 99,
    108, 131, 180
Gardiner, Rolf, 175, 178, 180, 181, 184
Garnett, David, 42, 94, 95
Garnett, Edward, 72, 79
Gatti, Hilary, 32
George, David Lloyd, 105
Gertler, Mark, 91, 114, 121, 126, 187
Ghiselin, Brewster, 177
Gibbon, Edward, 77, 140
Goldring, Douglas, 127
Goodheart, Eugene, 143
Gótzsche, Kai, 174
Grant, Duncan, 8, 95
Gray, Cecil, 106, 112

Haeckel, Ernst, 49, 50, 101, 142
Haller, William, 15
Hardie, Kier, 53
Hardy, Thomas, 76
Hargrave, John, 178, 180, 184
Harrison, Jane, 75, 76, 122. *See also*
    Lawrence, D. H.: influences on
Hawthorne, Nathaniel, 145
Heinemann, William, 72
Heraclitus, 101, 102. *See also* Lawrence, D.
    H.: influences on: Greek philoso-
    phers
Herzinger, Kim A., 87, 90
Heseltine, Philip, 94, 95
Hochman, Baruch, 162
Hoggart, Richard, 15
Hopkin, Sally, 30, 36, 53, 127
Hopkin, William E., 2, 4, 12, 13, 24, 28,
    53, 127
Hough, Graham, 162
Howe, Marguerite Beede, 131

Hunt, Viola, 59, 66
Huxley, Aldous, 1, 2–3, 90, 124, 173, 187,
    193
Huxley, Maria, 177
Huxley, Thomas H., 50

Ibsen, Henrik, 55

James, Henry, 179, 191
James, William, xi, 49, 50, 51. *See also*
    Lawrence, D. H.: influences on
Jefferies, Richard, 126, 168
Jenner, Katherine L., 65, 91
Jennings, Blanche, 17, 27, 34, 43, 48
Jesus, 104
Johnson, Spud, 171
Jung, C. G., 66

Keynes, John Maynard, 20, 94, 95, 113
Koteliansky, S. S., 13, 90, 95, 126, 129,
    133
Kuzkowski, Richard J., 142

Langbaum, Robert, 164
Lawrence, Ada, 2, 4, 5, 11, 24, 30, 32, 40,
    41, 48, 50
Lawrence, Emily, 2, 11, 13
Lawrence, D. H.
—ideas of
  —on the individual: rare individuals
    who are responsible, 52, 53, 63;
    celebration of higher man, 58; rejec-
    tion of evolution, 78–79; uniqueness
    of the individual, 78–79
  —on psychology: priority of impulse,
    50; belatedness of consciousness, 51;
    selfhood a oneness with the infinite,
    52, 171–72; infantile men, 55; sup-
    pression of desire breeds illness and
    cruelty, 72, 73, 91; divine will is Law
    and Love, power and love, 74, 101,
    139, 141, 148; belief in the blood, 74;
    impulse to unite and to separate,
    Jews and Christians, south and
    north, 77, 140–41; need for "death"
    before life, 90–91, 115, 123; desire for
    maximum of being, 92; need to heed
    the Holy Ghost, 92, 140, 144, 145,
    146, 172; passion for unanimity,
    96–97; systole/diastole, or balance of
    creation and destruction, 102, 121;
    evil of the absolute conscious ego,
    103, 120; disbelief in oneness of
    mankind, 114, 175, 191; introjection
    of external world, 155; blood con-
    sciousness, 155–56; duality of blood
    consciousness, 158–59; phallic con-

sciousness, 176–77, 182, 188; individuality submerged in desire-stream, 185–86. *See also* Lawrence, D. H.: ideas of, on religion
—on religion: love connected with religious feeling, 43; rejection of Christianity, 47; acceptance of a cosmic God, religious materialism, 48–49; God known in desire, 50, 98; artist as spokesman of divine will, 73–74; *tat tvam asi*, 79; "the eternal stillness" in art, 80, 86; need for faith in what one ultimately is, 89; desire for new Jerusalem, Rananim, 93, 178; death preferable to violation of soul, 115; acceptance of unity of life and death, 122; God made man is the goal, 143; animism, 153; pantheism, 154; pride arising from a religion of one's own, 170; horror of secularism, 173; need for rituals, 181; communion with the Godhead, 192. *See also* Lawrence, D. H.: ideas of, on psychology
—on sexuality and love: threat of the famale, 26, 46, 61–62, 134–37; sexuality a manifestation of cosmic energies, 54; attack on "Joy-Hogs," 55; proper relation of man and woman, 55–56; *égoisme à deux* of married couples, 56; most people are slaves of the life force, 61–64; a new self through love, 71, 72; creation is the product of female and male together, 81–82, 143; denunciation of homosexuals, 95–96; tenderness, 180, 182. *See also* Lawrence, D. H.: ideas of, on psychology
—on society: education—sacred mission of the teacher, 33; opposition to "ideal" education, 33; utterance of racial consciousness, 86; need to destroy the machine and the system, 87, 184, 191; need for a leader, for aristocracy, 98, 99, 147, 180; need for purification, 99; Blutbrüderschaft, 106–7, 118; to work is not to live, 126; fear of collective will, democracy, 132–33; dominance of the spiritual will, 140; limitations of Israel, Ceylon, Australia, America, 147–48, 150; liberation in New Mexico from materialism and idealism, 150, 167; societal instinct, 179; civilization of touch, 181, 182; intuition or instinct of kinship, 188. *See also* Lawrence, D. H.: ideas of, on psychology and on religion

—influences on, by: his mother—intolerance and realism, 9, pride, 11; his father—generosity, independence, 10, Lawrence's hatred of the respect for, 23–24, 25–26, 177; Congregational Church, 14, 15; Schopenhauer, 49–51; William James, 49–51; Edward Carpenter, 53–56; Nietzsche, 57–60; Jane Harrison, 75–76, 122; Houston Chamberlain, 76–79; Greek philosophers, 101–3; Dostoevsky, 103; Madame Blavatsky, 142; American Indian religion, 154; Frobenius, 170; Trigant Burrow, 179
—personal characteristics and attitudes of: naturally blithe disposition, 2; maternal sympathy and sense of responsibility for others, 2, 4–7, 21, 32, 183; responsiveness to nature and sense of wonder, 2–3, 16; sense of connection with other forms of being, 3, 156–57; tendency to withdraw, 3, 12, 106, 177; authority of *homo religiosus*, feeling of superiority, 7, 13–14; inviolacy of spirit, 8, 12, 13; hatred of confinement, 11; Puritanism, 15, 18; hatred of uncleanness, 18, 99–100; idealized love of men, 19–20; ambivalence of feelings toward mother, 21–22; resentment of her bourgeois assumptions, 22–23; view of illness as punishment, 26, 191; desire for freedom, 27, 69–70; fear that love will destroy his integrity, 27; exaggeration of his love for mother, 29; impersonality as artist, 31; resentment against teaching, 32, 34–35; shyness before women, 35–36; blames women for cowardice, 38–40; artificial manner, 60; unworldliness, 67; devastation and rage during the war, 90, 105, 113, 114; disgust with homosexuals, 95; self-preservation, 107; self-doubt, 112; self-castigation, 130–31; equanimity, 138–39; rage at Frieda, modern world, 174, 188
—works cited:
—*Aaron's Rod*, 107, 108, 109, 112, 113, 128, 130, 131, 132, 133, 138, 147, 148, 149, 175
—*Apocalypse*, 154, 161
—"A Propos of *Lady Chatterley's Lover*," 181
—*Birds, Beasts and Flowers*, 130
—*The Boy in the Bush*, 144, 159, 168–69
—"The Captain's Doll," 136
—"The Christening," 23

—"Communion with the Godhead,"
192
—*The Crown*, 100–101, 102, 103, 123,
143, 180
—"Daughters of the Vicar," 35, 36
—*David*, 172–73
—"Education of the People," 32, 33
—*Etruscan Places*, 153, 154, 157–59
—"Fanny and Annie," 136
—*Fantasia of the Unconscious*, 11, 141
—"The Flying Fish," 125, 146, 172
—"The Fox," 135, 136
—"Introduction to *Mastro-don Gesualdo*
by Giovanni Verga," 158
—"Introduction to Pictures," 159, 160
—"Introduction to These Paintings,"
188
—*Kangaroo*, 105, 132, 147, 148–49, 168
—"Kissing and Horrid Strife," 193
—"The Ladybird," 124, 168
—*Lady Chatterley's Lover*, 10, 26, 124,
165, 184–87
—*Look, We Have Come Through!* 45
—*The Lost Girl*, 130, 137
—". . . Love Was Once a Little Boy,"
185
—"The Man Who Is Not Loved," 45
—"Men in New Mexico," 152
—"A Modern Lover," 35, 36, 38, 39–40
—"Monkey Nuts," 135
—*Mornings in Mexico*, 16, 153, 159, 160
—*Movements in European History*, 78,
103, 129, 139, 140
—*Nettles*, 190
—"New Eve and Old Adam," 110–12
—"New Heaven and Earth," 99
—"Odour of Chrysanthemums," 80
—"The Old Adam," 35, 37
—"Pan in America," 155
—*Pansies*, 190
—*The Plumed Serpent*, 124, 159, 164,
169–72, 178
—"The Princess," 161–62
—*Psychoanalysis and the Unconscious*, 139,
141, 148, 158–59
—"The Punisher," 33
—*The Rainbow*, 32, 42, 43, 51, 56, 78, 80,
83–87, 102, 106, 110, 111, 123, 129
—"The Reality of Peace," 115, 120,
121–22
—"A Rise in the World," 67–68
—"Samson and Delilah," 135
—*Sea and Sardinia*, 130
—*The Sisters*, 75, 79
—*Sons and Lovers*, 11, 20, 21, 22, 23, 24,
25, 26, 29, 44–45, 47, 62–63, 69–70, 77,
80, 133

—"St. Mawr," 165–67, 182
—"Stoic," 193
—*Studies in Classic American Literature*,
122, 143–46, 167, 173
—*Study of Thomas Hardy*, 43, 70, 78,
91–93, 103, 141
—"Sun-Men," 191
—"Sun-Women," 191
—"The Thorn in the Flesh," 71–72
—"Tickets, Please," 134
—*Touch and Go*, 125
—*The Trespasser*, 20, 28, 45, 63–64, 65,
69, 77, 102
—*Twilight in Italy*, 78, 103, 141
—*The Virgin and the Gypsy*, 124, 184
—*The White Peacock*, 19, 20, 30, 35, 39,
41, 54, 55, 60, 61, 62–63, 65, 66, 77,
134
—"The Witch à la Mode," 35, 36,
38–39, 44
—"The Woman Who Rode Away,"
163–64, 169
—*Women in Love*, 20, 31, 32, 55, 56, 78,
110, 115–20, 123, 124–25, 129, 132,
160, 190
—"You Touched Me," 135, 136
Lawrence, Frieda, 20, 27, 34, 42, 43, 44,
45, 46, 68, 70, 71, 72, 80, 81, 84, 89,
97, 106, 107, 108, 109–13, 123, 132,
134, 135, 137, 174, 187
Leavis, F. R., 131
Lesemann, Maurice, 150
Lewis, Wyndham, 59
Low, Dr. Barbara, 73
Low, Ivy, 89
Luhan, Mabel Dodge, 10, 137, 149, 152,
161
Luther, Martin, 87, 93, 108

McCarthy, John Russell, 95
MacDonald, Ramsay, 53
Mackenzie, Compton, 146
McLeod, A. W., 81, 187
Magnus, Maurice, 143
Mann, Thomas, 49, 65
Mansfield, Katherine, 91, 106, 112, 115,
119, 127
March, Edward, 89, 91, 114
Maupassant, Guy de, 69
May, Rollo, 142
Melville, Herman, 146
Merleau-Ponty, Maurice, 189
Merrild, Knud, 174
Meyer, Bernard C., 134
Meyers, Jeffrey, 117
Meynell, Viola, 105
Minchin, Cecily Lambert, 127–28

Moore, George, 69
Moore, Harry T., ix, 190
Morrel, Lady Ottoline, 1, 91, 93, 94, 95, 97, 99, 101, 104, 133, 150, 177, 182
Morris, William, 53
Moulaert, Jehanne, 177
Mountsier, Robert, 130
Murray, Gilbert, 122, 138, 153, 193
Murry, John Middleton, 7, 88, 89, 94, 100, 104, 105, 106, 110, 119, 133, 175, 187
Mussolini, Benito, 180

Nehls, Edward, 190
Neville, George, 5, 9, 10, 12, 18, 19, 20, 25, 28
Nichols, Robert, 126
Nietzsche, Friedrich, 40, 51, 52, 54, 57–61, 65, 75, 76, 82, 99, 109, 136, 141, 147, 160, 171, 175
Noyes, John Humphrey, 106

Panichas, George A., 15, 105
Parmenides, 101
Pater, Walter, 40
Petrie, W. M. F., 122
Plato, 96, 181
Poe, Edgar Allen, 145
Popham, Rosalind Thornycroft, 143
Pound, Ezra, 59
Pritchard, R. E., 162
Pryse, James M., 141

Radford, Dollie, 138
Remsbury, John, 189
Rieff, Philip, 143
Ross, Charles L., 117
Ruderman, Judith, 118
Ruskin, John, 53
Russell, Bertrand, 8, 66, 94, 95, 96–97, 98, 101, 107
Ryles, Gilbert, 189
Sanders, Scott, 117
Sartre, Jean Paul, 70, 142
Savage, Henry, 72, 88, 94

Schopenhauer, Arthur, 41, 43, 49, 50, 51, 54, 58, 61, 65, 66, 81, 82, 101, 102, 115, 134, 141
Shaw, George Bernard, xi, 14, 53, 61, 134
Skinner, Mollie, 168, 169
Snowden, Philip, 53
Spencer, Herbert, xi, 49, 50, 65, 66, 74, 98, 101, 102, 140, 142
Spilka, Mark, 86
Stone, Ida Purnell, 27
Straus, Irwin, 179
Strindberg, August, 61, 82, 134
Swinburne, Algernon Charles, 49, 50

Taine, Hippolyte, 77, 140
Taylor, Rachel Annand, 21
Teilhard de Chardin, Pierre, ix
Tenenbaum, Elizabeth Brody, 143
Thoreau, Henry David, 126
Tolstoy, Leo, 75–76
Tylor, E. B., 122, 153, 159

Van Gogh, Vincent, 189
Verga, Giovanni, 158
Verlaine, Paul, 75

Webb, Beatrice, 53
Webb, Sidney, 53
Weekley, Elsa, 193
Weekley, Ernest, 71, 137, 187
Weininger, Otto, xi, 82, 83
Wells, H. G., 64
West, Rebecca, 59, 131, 143, 147
Whitman, Walt, 56, 146
Wilkerson, Walter, 183
Williams, Raymond, 34
Wilson, Charles, 184
Woolf, Leonard, 90
Wordsworth, William, 43, 47, 48, 191, 193

Yorke, Dorothy, 107
Young, Francis Brett, 130

Zytaruk, George J., 95

DATE DUE

GAYLORD			PRINTED IN U.S.A.